PERGAMON INTERNATIO
of Science, Technology, Engineering
The 1000-volume original paperback libra
industrial training and the enjoym
Publisher: Robert Maxwell,

PLANNING THEORY

_____ **Publisher's Notice to Educators** _____

THE PERGAMON TEXTBOOK
INSPECTION COPY SERVICE

An inspection copy of any book published in the Pergamon International Library
will gladly be sent without obligation for consideration for course adoption or
recommendation. Copies may be retained for a period of 60 days from receipt and
returned if not suitable. When a particular title is adopted or recommended for
adoption for class use and the recommendation results in a sale of 12 or more
copies, the inspection copy may be retained with our compliments. If after examination the lecturer decides that the book is not suitable for adoption but would like to
retain it for his personal library, then our Educators' Discount of 10% is allowed on
the invoiced price. The Publishers will be pleased to receive suggestions for revised
editions and new titles to be published in this important International Library.

PLANNING THEORY

by

ANDREAS FALUDI Dipl-Ing, Dr techn
Professor of Planning Theory, Delft University of Technology

PERGAMON PRESS

OXFORD · NEW YORK · TORONTO
SYDNEY · PARIS · FRANKFURT

U. K.	Pergamon Press Ltd., Headington Hill Hall, Oxford OX3 0BW, England
U.S.A.	Pergamon Press Inc., Maxwell House, Fairview Park, Elmsford, New York 10523, U.S.A.
CANADA	Pergamon of Canada Ltd., P.O. Box 9600, Don Mills M3C 2T9, Ontario, Canada
AUSTRALIA	Pergamon Press (Aust.) Pty. Ltd., 19a Boundary Street, Rushcutters Bay, N.S.W. 2011, Australia
FRANCE	Pergamon Press SARL, 24 rue des Ecoles, 75240 Paris, Cedex 05, France
WEST GERMANY	Pergamon Press GmbH, 6242 Kronberg-Taunus, Pferdstrasse 1, Frankfurt-am-Main, West Germany

First edition 1973

Reprinted 1975

Reprinted 1976

Library of Congress Cataloging in Publication Data
Faludi, Andreas.
  Planning theory.

(Urban and regional planning series, v. 7.)
1.   Regional planning.   2. Cities and towns—
Planning—1945-   3. Planning.   I.   Title.
II. Series.
HT391.F26   1973   309.2'12   73-11236
ISBN   0-08-017741-7
ISBN   0-08-017756-5 (flexicover)

Urban and Regional Planning Series
Volume 7

Printed in Great Britain by A. Wheaton & Co., Exeter

To Raya

Contents

Part IV. The Politics of Rational Planning

Foreword

THIS book is a venture in establishing planning theory as an intellectual endeavour aimed at solving some of a whole range of problems which planners face. It is academic in the twofold sense of building on my own efforts, for better or for worse, to give students an understanding of planning, and also of its aiming to induce more academic discussion concerning planning theory. This is based on my firm belief in the positive rôle of the academic in the development even of such practical fields as planning, despite the conflicts which this may create and to which I shall turn later in Chapter 1.

Having said this, I hasten to disclaim one academic pretence, which is at the same time an issue which is very relevant to the understanding of planning. Very often, in answering questions raised in planning education, one must first unravel what planning means to oneself as a human being. I happen to hold firm views on the question of the purpose of planning. Therefore I do not even pretend to present a dispassionate view of what, ultimately, planning is about. Where the planning theorist refuses to deal with the question of the purpose of planning *qua theorist*, the planning practitioner or the planning student fills the gap with his own, possibly home-made, philosophy. I therefore believe that the effort of building planning theory also includes the search for what planning is about. My own answer to this question (which is that of planning promoting human growth) has given a perspective to my own thinking and will provide what I shall call the rationale of the type of planning theory proposed in this book.

Having always stated this as my view, albeit one which I think is supported by reason, I still do not see myself as imposing it on students. They are (as indeed my readers will be) perfectly capable of identifying those elements in my argument which they can agree with and those points where they diverge, drawing on other sources than this book. No doubt they will consider what my critics will have to say, thus improving the quality of our discussions and the depth of their own thinking. My experience is that if I take a stand on an issue about which they feel deeply, this helps them to clarify their own position.

A second reason why I make no attempt to take up a neutral position *vis-à-vis* the question of what planning is striving to achieve is the egotistic but straightforward one that I hope to benefit more from being criticized for the position which I see myself taking than from any attempt to argue the case with myself. Discussion in this field of planning theory is inadequate (and what there is is often clouded by issues which are not directly relevant to planning). It is to generate fruitful discussion that I put my views forward, inviting my critics to pour scorn on the flaws in my argument and wishing that my presentation is clear enough to facilitate their task; and in the hope that I may achieve the academic requirement of impartiality when reviewing their counter-arguments.

The structure of the book is designed to render my views of planning theory as explicit as possible. To this end the first part deals with the question of what planning theory is, identifying it by the kinds of problems which it seeks to solve, and the methodological status which it claims. The sequence of Parts II–IV arises out of considerations made in Part I and in ways explained in the last section of Chapter 2, "The plan for the book". Briefly, Part II provides *A Conceptual Framework for Planning Thought*; Part III shows how one would work *Towards a Positive Theory of Planning* based on this; Part IV extracts from the previous two whatever may be given in terms of immediate advice on *The Politics of Rational Planning*, that is politics concerned with creating the preconditions of planning becoming more rational. In the Epilogue, I speculate on the nature of a future planning society, in which the effort of planning rationally becomes a general preoccupation, thus turning planning theory into an area of the greatest concern.

Since I think that planning will become much more widespread than at present, I refuse to let present professional boundaries constrain my area of concern. That my examples are mainly (though not exclusively) drawn from physical planning is coincidental, a mere reflection of the fact that this is the field where I come from and in which I teach. However, the intention is broad: to provide a general theory of planning ranging over all organized human efforts to render decisions and actions more rational.

Acknowledgements

I SHALL always remember the years during which my ideas for this book crystallized as one of the significant turning points in my life. The development of my thoughts during this period has given me satisfaction not so much for their achievements (which I hesitate to describe as anything but modest) but for their direction, their tortuous, twisting path, moments of doubt and despair, and the chores involved notwithstanding. Because the point in my life when this development began coincided with my coming to Britain, and because I think it meaningful to credit a community or a nation with some standing of its own, it seems apposite to begin with acknowledging the great influence which British life and culture have had on me.

My, albeit incomplete, induction to the subtleties of the British way of life is a by-product of numerous encounters and friendships. The influences to which I have been exposed are indeed too numerous to be accounted for entirely, but outstanding amongst them were two: those coming from Professor Maurice Broady who made my first year at Southampton as a British Council Scholar into one of substantial reorientation; and those coming from the Department of Town Planning at Oxford Polytechnic which, as a body under the imaginative but unobtrusive leadership of H. D. Thomas, has experienced such an amazing development during these years.

More specifically about this book, my thanks are due to Professor Ray Pahl of the University of Kent at Canterbury for planting the idea of turning my lecture material into a book. I am further indebted to the Pergamon Urban and Regional Planning Advisory Committee for giving me their support, and to its Chairman, Professor George Chadwick of the University of Newcastle upon Tyne, and to John Friend of the Institute for Operational Research for their searching comments and questions raised at various stages of writing. Of others who have made suggestions on various parts of the book Steve Chait, Professor Yehezkel Dror, Professor John Friedmann, Mrs. Myra Frank, John Minett, Eric Reade

xi

and Mike Silvester are those whom I can remember—with apologies to those whom I have left out! A group of final-year students read Part I and asked relevant questions and reassured me on the interest which the material holds for planning students. I have also been stimulated by working in a teaching team with Geoff Crispin, Mike Cuddy, Bob Ross and Keith Steventon of Oxford Polytechnic.

Mrs. Peggy Ducker, Senior Editor of Pergamon Press, had to spend an inordinate amount of time turning my manuscript into readable English, an unenviable task which she discharged with enormous care, sensitivity and tact for which I owe her my thanks. Mrs. Heather Jones coped admirably with my foreign accent on tape and with my handwriting on paper. Her witty comments on what I had written, and her unfailing support, were a great help.

As to my wife, the turning point in my life leading to this book coincided with our marriage—in itself a turning point! Without her, neither my life nor this book would be what they are. Indeed, it is doubtful whether the latter would have materialized but for her support. My thanks are therefore due to her for her great share in both.

PART I

WHAT IS PLANNING THEORY?

THEORIES provide explanations. Explanations are responses to states of tension resulting from observing unexpected events (Toulmin, 1960). They represent efforts to reduce surprise caused by such events by giving plausible accounts of how they have come about, accounts which must not contradict anything that the subject knows. The moving force behind the desire to reduce surprise is that there are always challenges and opportunities arising in our environment for which we wish to be prepared.

Plausible accounts may be used, not only for explaining events in the past and present, but also as a basis for controlling the future. Thus, human beings are capable, not only of explaining what is, but (within limits) also of making things happen to suit themselves. For instance, they are able to forestall the occurrence of some future event which they think will cause them tension. In the language of this book, equating a state of tension with a *problem*, human beings can solve, anticipate and forestall problems by invoking cogent accounts of why events occur and then deriving ideas from these accounts of how to prevent problems from arising.

The first part of this book is concerned with the kinds of tension which planning theory can resolve, and the kinds of narratives which it gives. To identify the sources of tension which planning theory helps to resolve means to define what I shall term *The Problem of Planning Theory*. Describing the kinds of accounts which planning theory invokes in solving its problems requires us to delve into the field of methodology to find which are admissible as providing explanations. From this exploration, I shall specify *The Underlying Theory Models* of this book. This will then provide

1

the vantage point for presenting the next part concerned with *A Conceptual Framework for Planning Theory*.

REFERENCES

TOULMIN, S. E. (1960) Quoted by HARVEY, D. (1969) *Explanation in Geography*, Arnold, London.

CHAPTER 1

The Problem of Planning Theory

In ADDRESSING oneself to planners on the subject of planning theory, it is safe to assume that their anticipations vary. No consensus exists on the subject of, and the potential benefits to be derived from, planning theory. It is therefore apposite to devote the first chapter to this question. Raising it will lead me to identify two types of theory which currently come under planning theory: *procedural* and *substantive* theory. The latter helps planners to understand whatever their area of concern may be. The former can be seen as planners understanding themselves and the ways in which they operate which, at present, are less clearly seen as problematic. I shall argue that planning theory should be concerned with this rather than with substantive theory.

The problem of planning theory has various facets which planners experience simply as the problem of understanding planning, or as the practical one of making comparisons and transferring experiences, or finally as that of systematically designing planning agencies and their procedures (meta-planning).

Being concerned with organizations, planning theory draws on the social sciences. If we identify the basis of planning theory in the social sciences, this draws attention to a problem which the planning profession faces in its search for identity: the social sciences are an alien intellectual tradition. I shall suggest, nevertheless, that the planning profession should welcome the fact that academics concerned with planning theory take cognizance of the social sciences.

LACK OF CONSENSUS ON THE AREA OF CONCERN OF PLANNING THEORY

As I have commented in the companion volume to this book (Faludi, 1973), where the question of planning theory is raised in the literature what one tends to find is a selection of items drawn from different disciplines and addressing themselves to a variety of problems. The bibliography compiled to Berkman (1967) which, as far as I know, is the only attempt to survey the literature in so-called planning theory systematically, is a case in point.[1] It represents a mélange of categories such as "Basic works", "Nature of planning", "Methodology and techniques", "Goal formulation and objectives" and five sub-sections on the use of specific types of models. The selection contains both works concerning the activity of planning *per se*, and others dealing with specific fields of planning such as city planning, traffic planning and so forth. Under these headings, it includes papers relating to some of planning's substantive areas of concern.

A similar eclecticism becomes evident in the most authoritative statement that we have about the British planning profession's concept of planning theory. This is given in the now Royal Town Planning Institute's revised examination syllabus on "Theory of Planning". The objectives of this paper are those of testing ". . . the candidate's understanding of the nature and objectives of physical planning, its rôle in society, fields of action, and relevant theories concerning Land Use, Settlement and Urban Change" (Town Planning Institute, 1969).

The paper neatly divides into two parts which have been described as *procedural*, and as *substantive* theories (Faludi, 1972a), and which, in the companion volume to this book, I identify as theory *of* planning and theory *in* planning respectively, thus paraphrasing Britton Harris (1967): "We have great need of a science *of* planning in order to determine what is science *in* planning."

Such a distinction is made in most of the small number of papers concerned with the subject of planning theory, though few make it as explicitly as Hightower does in his review of the content of American courses. His finding is that though ". . . there is no consensus evident on one or a number of rival definitions of the field . . .", one can still distinguish between "theories of the planning process" and "theories concerning phenomena with which planning is concerned" (Hightower, 1969).

I myself investigated concepts of planning theory held by planning students in their final year. The same distinction between subject-matter

---

[1]Since this was written, a very useful review by Friedmann and Hudson (1973) came to my attention. Also there is some discussion in the German planning literature which I am not taking account of. See, for instance, Fehl *et al.* (1972).

and process-oriented theory was evident. This obviously reflected their course and, to the extent that they had practical experience, their first-hand impressions of planning practice. Indeed, the distinction between procedural versus substantive theory not only pervades current thinking on the subject, it also reflects two fundamentally different types of problems faced by planners. I shall now identify these and argue that procedural rather than substantive theory should be regarded as planning theory proper.

TWO TYPES OF PROBLEMS FACED BY PLANNERS

Planners face a wide range of problems in their day-to-day work. Many of these have to do with understanding whatever planners believe to be their concern, be it the "land use system", or people. Naturally, they wish to know what motivates the objects of their planning, what forces bring about change and so on. Increased understanding, it is thought, will lead to an identification of the particular "levers" one needs to pull to produce a certain effect. Any concept or technique which holds out the promise of identifying such levers is taken up enthusiastically. This was the case with the "neighbourhood community idea" (Dennis, 1958) and currently seems to be happening with methods like factor analysis and with devices like computers and models.

As planning is concerned with the best way of producing results, it is understandable that this type of analysis leading to greater knowledge of their area of concern looms large in the planners' minds. The assumption is simply that the right course of action would emerge from such understanding. McLoughlin (1969), in his book on *Urban and Regional Planning —A System Approach*, builds on this assumption arguing for *location theory* as a foundation for planning. Indeed, a diagram of traffic flows representing the object of his planning is so characteristic of his approach that it appears on the dust cover of his book. I certainly do not wish to argue that understanding the forces operating in the planners' area of concern is irrelevant, or that efforts directed towards the deepening of this understanding may not lead to improvements in planning. It is only that a second range of problems exists which planners face. These are different in kind from those of understanding their area of concern. They relate to the planner himself, the agencies in which he operates, and the procedures which he adopts.

To illustrate this point, the areas of health, social policy and economic development, where this has also been argued, can be cited. Morris (1971) claims that the decline of deaths from cholera epidemics in mid-nineteenth-century Britain preceded advances in medical knowledge and attributes this to improvements to "the ability to manage resources for social ends". Townsend (1970) argues that the shortcomings of the Labour Government's implementation of its social policies in the sixties "make the case for changes in government machinery, information and research services". Discussing the establishment of the Central Policy Review Staff in the Cabinet Office, he outlines the form which it should take including membership, activities, and access to the Prime Minister. Seers (1972) says similarly about planning for economic development:

> . . . the fundamental question is: Who meets whom—and why do they bother to? Are there personal conversations between the chief planner, and the President or Prime Minister? Does the cabinet committee discuss development strategy? If so, how often? Who attends? Who proposes the agenda? And who prepares the papers?

These issues are more basic, and at the same time more general, than those of understanding whatever it is that planners are concerned with. They are basic because unless these issues are to some extent resolved, even the most refined substantive theory will not result in effective planning. They are more general because they apply to whichever form of planning one cares to think about. One can therefore observe that planners in many areas are dealing with the same issues.[2] That town planners argue about them is evident from a perusal of topics covered in their journals and a range of such papers has been included in the companion volume. There, attention has also been drawn to a very similar interest in organizational and procedural issues by social workers and operational researchers. Because what I termed procedural theory contributes to understanding these basic and general issues, I wish to reserve the designation of *planning theory* for this in preference to substantive theory.

---

[2]For this reason, Glass (1959) suggested already many years ago, that "it would be preferable to use the term 'planning' in the purist sense, on the assumption that all aspects—economic, social, physical, national, regional and local planning—have to be regarded jointly as parts of the same enterprise." Design theorists are thinking along similar lines conceiving of "the logical act of designing" as "largely independent of the thing considered" (Archer, 1969).

POINTS OF CONTACT BETWEEN PROCEDURAL AND SUBSTANTIVE THEORY

The distinction between theory *in* planning and theory *of* planning (planning theory) should not result in an entirely separate development of the two. Clearly, both types of theory are needed for effective planning. Indeed, there are signs that both sides are drawing closer together. Evidence for contacts between the two exists where aspects of procedural and substantive theory enter each other's explanatory schemes. But even here, as I shall argue below, planners should view procedural theory as forming an envelope to substantive theory rather than vice versa (Fig. 1.1).

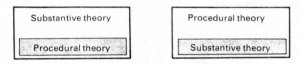

Fig. 1.1. Procedural and substantive theory

Recent views of urban and regional systems picture them as socio-technical complexes with their institutional part embracing planning agencies of various kinds. Thus procedural theory is seen as part of substantive theory. This is evident in urban sociology where a move away from a consideration purely of the phenomena of agglomeration and the internal differentiation of urban populations towards that of the underlying institutional change has come naturally. It is also true for approaches which have originally been much more exclusively interested in spatial phenomena, like regional science. Here, Isard and his associates (1969) are now offering a "general theory" which explicitly includes the institutional and thus non-spatial dimension of urban and regional systems.

On the side of planning theory in the sense in which this term is used in this book, there is also concern for incorporating certain aspects of substantive into procedural theory. Bolan (1969) calls these "issue attributes". I shall refer to them as features of the image underlying planning, that is the sum total of knowledge concerning relevant aspects of the environment. These features describe the state of theory *in* planning, for example whether it allows reliable predictions to be made or whether the element of uncertainty is great. The argument will be that these features affect the mode of planning in which a planning agency engages. The type of planning theory which I propose thus incorporates considerations of the state of substantive theory.

Of course there is no way of saying that to view procedural theory as forming an envelope to substantive theory is always preferable to the reverse view described above of seeing substantive theory as the envelope. It is only that planners still neglect planning theory in the procedural sense, seeing it as ephemeral, more vague, and more easily replaceable by sheer common sense than the complex and currently very respectable operations based on substantive theory, such as building models of urban and regional systems. They thereby deprive themselves of the sound intellectual basis for their activity of planning which would distinguish them from their geographical colleagues, a deficiency which this book will try to remedy.[3]

FACETS OF THE PROBLEM OF PLANNING THEORY

What are these problems which planning theory can help to solve? In the way in which they present themselves to planners at various stages of their career, one may describe them under the three headings of *understanding* planning, its agencies and procedures; *comparing* their different forms and transferring experiences from one to the other; *designing* planning agencies and their procedures. I shall give account of each of these facets, and of ways in which planning theory approaches them.

Understanding Planning

At some stage of their career, all planners face the question of how a reasonable person would engage in planning. Man's understanding of

[3]Davidoff and Reiner (1962) argue similarly that "urban planning education has been excessively directed to substantive areas and has failed to focus on any unique skills and responsibilities of the planner". Ten years later, Robinson (1972) voices the same complaint. However, planners are not alone in depriving themselves of an intellectual basis of their activities. Simon (1969) argues that departments of engineering, business studies and so on, devote too much attention to basic disciplines and too little to design, what he calls the science of the artificial.

this world, and his ability to act in it, depends on his constructing an imagery in his own mind. This applies equally well to the planner's understanding of himself and his operations. Thus "understanding planning" as a problem really means that the planner faces the challenge of constructing an image of himself in his rôle as a planner; the agencies in which he operates; their procedures; the environment as it is affected by, and is affecting, the operations of these agencies. To aid planners in constructing such self-images, this book proposes a model of planning agencies forming part of the proposed conceptual framework for planning thought.

The problem of understanding planning is obviously most acute for the planner in the formative stages of his career. With the growth of full-time planning education, an increasing number of planners spend these years in planning schools. Since one of the aims of planning education is that of conveying precisely this understanding of planning, the problem of understanding planning is an immediate one for a growing number of academics in planning. They are compelled to create sets of concepts which help them in giving answers—however tentative—to questions raised by their students such as: Why does planning proceed in this or that manner? Why has this or that change taken place in the realm of planning agencies? Is this particular response to that planning problem an adequate one and what are the implications of taking alternative approaches? How do current trends and existing policies affect planning?

As suggested in the companion volume, it is therefore from academics that the main impetus for devising frameworks for the study of planning has come in the past. These frameworks must incorporate reasoned views about what planning is trying to achieve. This book presents one particular way of doing this by building on a view of planning as promoting human growth, and by providing a model of planning agencies based on this rationale.

Comparisons and the Transfer of Experiences

Later in his career, a planner will seek to compare his experiences with those of colleagues. Curiosity apart, he obviously believes he will *learn* from them: an urban planner might wish to study the approaches adopted by planners working in other authorities; he might equally well turn to his colleagues working on a regional scale, or even seek information from abroad. Alternatively, our planner could look into other fields where planning is practised. No matter what the particular field, on a certain level approaches to problems tend to be similar. There is, therefore, much to be gained from transferring experiences from, say, urban planning to social planning, or from economic planning to educational planning, and of course *vice versa*.

This comparison of planning in different, what will be termed, planning environments (see Chapter 10), and in different areas of concern, may coincide with problems experienced by the practitioner or student who simply wishes to understand planning. More frequently, though, the interest of the planner comparing his own approach with that of colleagues is practical. To help him, a whole range of provisions exist for obtaining information, ranging from professional journals to conferences and courses of various kinds. But to derive benefits from any comparison, the planner is driven to constructing frameworks into which both his activity and that with which he compares it fit. This involves searching for what activities have in common, including whatever their purpose may be, for it is only in the light of knowledge concerning their common purpose that one can formulate preferences one way or the other. Thus, comparisons lead the planner to act in the same way as does his quest for understanding; that is to construct frameworks for thinking about planning. It is only against such frameworks that any comparison becomes meaningful.

Not only practitioners feel the need to engage in comparison. The theorist himself also resorts to comparative studies to test the usefulness of his framework. This combination of the construction of theoretical frameworks and their application advances thinking. Planning theory and the practical interests of planners are thus complementary to each other, despite the occasional tension which exists between practitioners and theorists. By providing conceptual tools which can be brought into focus on planning problems, planning theory assists the planning practitioner in transferring experiences from one context to the other. It thus identifies what constitutes data for comparative purposes, and what may be disregarded as particular to one situation. During the process, the planning theorist sharpens his tools and benefits from the experiences of the practitioner.

Meta-planning

The third problem which planners face, and which planning theory may help to solve, is that of systematically improving planning agencies and their procedures. As in the two previous cases, to tackle it they need a framework.

Sometimes, the problem dealt with under this heading is very pronounced, for instance when new institutions are created with their own planning powers. In intermediate cases, the problem is that of devising and implementing major reforms in existing institutions. Using a short-hand form, the problem may be described as *meta-planning* (Wilson, 1969). Examples are: local government reform now under way in Great Britain; the setting up of the Development Corporation of a new town; the drafting of legislation introducing major changes such as the 1968 Town and Country Planning Act in Great Britain following recommendations of the Planning Advisory Group (Ministry of Housing and Local Government, 1965). On a lower level, the same problem occurs where departmental responsibilities are rearranged. Indeed, even the day-to-day problems of planners usually require some degree of meta-planning to the extent that procedures must be chosen and links to other sections forged so as to facilitate planning.

Not all planners face these problems to the same extent. Though professional circles discuss them widely, it is usually the senior practitioner who feels their challenge most acutely. His responsibility is to direct operations and to liaise with other administrators, politicians and the community at large. These contacts give him ample opportunity for reflecting on the effectiveness of planning. Any of his actions designed to effect change in organizations reflects his image of what a planning agency and its procedures should be like, an image which he builds and modifies as a result of such reflection.[4]

The interest of any practitioner engaged in meta-planning is obviously a practical one. But on this level it is increasingly recognized that the accumulated experience of working in middle-management does not

---

[4]Power (1971, 1972) has introduced a new term for the planner creating, servicing and manipulating decision networks describing him as a "reticulist". Perhaps "practising planning theorist" would be more to the point.

suffice in today's world of rapid change, and in particular in the realm of organizational skills. Current answers to this situation are the management consultant brought in from outside, and the mid-career course varying in length from several weeks to one or two years on secondment to institutions of higher education.

Drawing on the services of a consultant has its special problems for both parties. In order to make an impact, consultants often have to educate their clients, that is give them a better understanding of their own problems and instil new attitudes in them. This is why mid-career courses designed explicitly to convey this understanding and to change old attitudes are becoming increasingly prominent corollaries of change, not only in planning, but in organizations generally. For these mid-career courses, the top-flyers amongst practitioners are whisked away from their desks, cloistered in the ivory towers of *academe* (which practitioners otherwise frown upon) and turned into "senior management material". Their curricula are, quite rightly, far less concerned with the understanding of substantive areas of concern than with organizational problems. Here, planning theory again helps by providing frameworks against which to compare actual organizations and their approaches. These are the same frameworks as are used for conveying an understanding of planning, and for comparative studies. The problems experienced by planners during various stages of their careers therefore require responses which build on the same basis. In the form of one summary statement, the problem of planning theory is: *In any given situation, which type of planning agency, and which procedure, will serve the end of planning best?*

PLANNING THEORY, METHODOLOGY, AND THE SOCIAL SCIENCES

In making pronouncements concerning his subject matter, the scientist invokes the authority of the methodologist, presenting his findings as useful knowledge because of the research methods by which he has arrived at them, methods which the methodologist has declared as valid. Research methods, or what is commonly called scientific method, are simply procedural standards (Ackoff, 1962). Similarly, the planner invokes the authority of the planning theorist, claiming that his is a valid solution because he has observed certain procedural requirements in obtaining it,[5] requirements which the planning theorist formulates for him, much as the methodologist does for the scientist.[6]

As regards the contribution of the social sciences to planning, any review of the growing literature, in particular concerning sociology and planning, will reveal that most authors see the "sociology *of* planning" as an important part, if not the basis of, any collaboration between the two disciplines (for instance: Reade, 1971; Schmidt-Relenberg, 1968). This sociology of planning forms an important element of planning theory: planning agencies are organizations firmly embedded in a network of institutions. Their interaction with other agencies requires establishing social relations, much as their internal operations do. Since planning agencies also operate in the political realm, the same may be said, *mutatis mutandis*, of politics. Planning theory therefore tries to take cognizance of social science findings.

PLANNING THEORY AND THE PLANNING PROFESSION

The existing town planning profession shows concern for planning theory. Through its partial control over planning education it may also exercise some influence over its development: a good reason for discussing the ambiguous relationship between planning theory and the town planning profession.[7]

One of the component elements of the definition of a profession is that its skills are based on theory (Millerson, 1964). The application of this theory and its development give the members of the profession status and also their livelihood. Town planning is no exception. It developed out of architecture, engineering and surveying, its area of concern being that of the "system of land use and settlement", to use a modern term. The

[5]On the view of planning as a *method* of making decisions and therefore applicable in many fields, see amongst others Banfield (1959), Glass (1959), Davidoff and Reiner (1962) and Robinson (1972).

[6]One must only add the *caveat* that the rôles of planner and planning theorist are as yet much less clearly differentiated than are those of the methodologist of science and the scientific researcher.

[7]There is sometimes talk about "social" and "economic" planners as if there were such professions on *a par* with town planning. But, only town planning enjoys something approximating professional status.

modus operandi which was advocated until recently, for instance by Kantorowich (1967), may be characterized as architecture writ large. Its central feature is the concept of the planner as a designer of the artistic genre. Planning theory is reduced to a kit-bag of "how to do it" prescriptions and somewhat elusive notions of the creative mind. But to base its distinctiveness from architecture merely on the difference of the scale of operations lends an uneasy feeling. This unease provides a partial explanation for the enthusiastic reception of the "systems approach" at a time when it appeared vital to planners to emphasize the distinction between planning and architecture (Faludi, 1972b): here is an approach with very respectable family connections of which one of its proponents has said:

> We put this framework forward simply because it is our belief that it solves far more problems than it creates and it is at the same time an elegant and beautiful means of understanding the man/environmental relationship, and a potentially powerful means for its control and guidance (McLoughlin, 1969).

But the problem is that, as with "design",[8] the planning profession cannot claim any exclusive rights to the systems concept either, even when it is applied to land use. For this application is also claimed by geographers, and indeed, there appears nowadays to be a predominance of geographers, in any case, on the research side of planning.

Of course, physical planning goes beyond the mere *explanation* of spatial phenomena. In identifying what distinguishes it from geography, the planner may say that planning has not to do with analysis, but with *synthesis*, that planning is concerned with manipulating things, not only with understanding them (Minett, 1972). Implicitly, Minett makes a distinction as I have between theory *in* planning and theory *of* planning because what distinguishes manipulation from explanation is the introduction of an actor and his purposes (which is what planning theory is about). The implications are still the same: planning theory is applicable in a much wider field than just physical planning; it deals with the activity of planning, and it must take cognizance of the social sciences.

For the town planning profession, these implications are perhaps even more uncomfortable than operating side by side with geographers. The

---

[8] I am distinguishing "design" from more recent developments in design theory. The latter overlaps with planning theory; advocates of the former concept tend to deny the value of theory altogether.

record of collaboration between town planners and social scientists is not good nor, one must add, does their education necessarily equip social scientists with the skills and attitudes required in planning. As regards expanding the scope of planning to include all those fields where planning theory of the kind proposed might be applied, the case is being argued under various headings both inside and outside the planning profession (Amos, 1971; Royal Town Planning Institute, 1971). The main problem is that any such expansion erodes the rank and file's feeling of security based on the specificity of the town planner's current area of concern as defined by existing planning legislation.

This tangle is complicated still further by the existence of planning schools which have developed mainly in the sphere of town planning. Here, I think it is the introduction of undergraduate courses in particular which poses most sharply the question of what planning theory is. Under-graduate programmes have been introduced because their very existence appears to connote recognition of planning's claim to independent status which has been the issue in Britain in the mid-sixties (Faludi, 1971, 1972b). But if courses are to consist of more than a collection of academic disciplines clustered around a rather nebulous concept of planning (one which, furthermore, the teachers of those disciplines frown upon because of its low intellectual status) then there must be a core of planning theory in any such course.[9]

The need for the development of planning theory is therefore felt most urgently by planning teachers, and in particular by those who teach under-graduates, of which there is a growing number. Of course, this develop-ment will not be without pain: by advancing planning theory in this general sense, academics are becoming critical of the inadequacy of the foundations of the profession's activities which are aimed exclusively at one field. They thereby appear to threaten the membership of the profes-sion. This development could all too easily lead to the demand for even more control over the planning schools than is currently exercised. The indications are therefore that the schools wish to disengage from the planning profession in order to preserve and extend their academic freedom

---

[9]Probably the earliest proposal for a planning curriculum devised around a core of amongst others, planning theory comes from Perloff (1957).

(Education for Planning Association, 1972; Holliday *et al.*, 1972; Kitchen, 1973; Adamson, 1973[10]).

As somebody who is teaching planning theory, I can only welcome such a move, because it complements my own view of the theory *of* planning as having an applicability far beyond town planning, and that, in Fagin's words, to "limit the scope of planning to land-use arrangements is a harmful effort to limit the common word planning for exclusive use of a narrow segment of the planners' role in government" (Fagin, 1959). But I also think that there are reasons why the town planning profession should welcome rather than resent the growth in their midst of a body of teachers vigorously asserting the independence of academic pursuits whilst at the same time trying to derive conclusions from the social sciences. To start with, there is the point of principle that the critical stance and independence which the academic traditionally claims as his prerogative are simply of the essence of theoretical work. A body of academic thinking subservient to the needs and aspirations of any profession is a contradiction in terms. Since the planning profession wanted the prestige attached to undergraduate planning education, it should also accept the implications which flow from having it. Beyond this, there are also positive advantages to the existence of academic theorists. As Kaplan (1964) says, theorizing has novel responses as its behavioural correlate. The academic study of planning may therefore provide stimuli for innovations in planning practice. Finally, there may also be tremendous potential in the planning education sector to influence many educational fields outside town planning in ways which might be beneficial to the profession: with some justification, outside observers sometimes frown upon an element of delusion which is introduced when town planners discuss their profession's broadening of its area of concern, and utter warnings against the "broad-minded town planner" (Cockburn, 1971). The argument does not apply, I think, to planning education, where the most exciting educational developments are now taking place. My belief is therefore that in current planning education we have the nucleus of a future type of education for people intending to have an impact in all sorts of fields. If the profession promotes

---

[10]This disengagement is not at all unique to planning. Hughes (1958) notes that professional education usually involves the replacement of stereotype images by more subtle, complex, and even ambiguous perceptions of professional rôles.

rather than hinders this development, it will result in an influx into other institutions of people who are capable of engaging in a dialogue with town planners. This should remedy a deficiency which appears at present to hinder their work greatly—quite apart from the *kudos* attached to having fathered a new type of education.

There can be no disadvantage to the town planning profession in having its academics engaged in theorizing, not even where that takes them into the social sciences. Indeed, what Foley (1960) said some time ago is still valid: "... if ever there were a challenge, it is precisely in bringing the intimate sense of the problems and the direct knowledge of the practice as provided by the professional together with the conceptualizing and theory-testing experience of the social scientist".

Nobody therefore argues seriously that there should not be physical planning. Land is one of the scarce resources to be allocated to competing uses. All that one argues is that physical planning should be carried out more meaningfully, that is, side by side with planning in other fields. Developing the type of planning theory proposed does therefore *not* decrease the importance of physical planning. It does argue for what I shall term multiplanning agencies in which physical planning can be performed sensibly. It neither supports nor negates any claim for "professional leadership" in planning, but simply outlines proposals for the integration of various types of planning in ways which would erode the question of professional boundaries altogether for the level of strategic planning in any case.

The prospects of planning theory are exciting. Its advancement has been tremendously stimulated by developments in physical planning in the past. Even though the ultimate pretension of planning theory is for wider applicability, this, what is called town and country planning in Great Britain, is an area in which ideas about the workings of planning can use-fully be tested, because it is one where the philosophy and the methods of planning are relatively more advanced than in most other spheres: there is a relatively well-developed and still expanding set of institutions admini-stering the powers under the planning acts, and there is much experi-mentation with new ways of linking these institutions together and of making their planning more meaningful and more responsive. Witness the introduction of public participation as a statutory requirement into the process of plan preparation, the delegation of powers of control from central to local government as reflected in the differentiation between structure and local plans, and the delegation of certain decisions from council committees to officers. All these may be seen as experiments with new approaches to planning with significance far beyond physical planning.

The town planning profession and planning theory have little to fear and much to gain from each other. Planning theory is now asserting itself as part of the development of self-consciousness in the planning education sector. Like sensible parents, the planning profession should nurture the growing feeling of independence—and be assured that it will be remembered for that!

REFERENCES

ACKOFF, R. *et al.* (1962) *Scientific Method: Optimizing Applied Research Decisions*, John Wiley, New York.

ADAMSON, S. (1973) The RTPI's new clothes, *Journal of the Royal Town Planning Institute*, Vol. 59, pp. 23–4.

AMOS, F. J. C. (1971) The development of the planning process, *Journal of the Royal Town Planning Institute*, Vol. 57, pp. 304–8.

ARCHER, B. (1969) The structure of the design process, in *Design Methods in Architecture*, edited by Ward, A. and Broadbent, G. Lund Humphries, London.

*BANFIELD, E. C. (1959) Ends and means in planning, *International Social Science Journal*, Vol. 11, pp. 361–8.

BERKMAN, H. J. (1967) *An Introductory Bibliography in Planning Theory*, Exchange Bibliography No. 33, Council of Planning Librarians, Monticello, Illinois.

*BOLAN, R. (1969) Community decision behavior: the culture of planning, *Journal of the American Institute of Planners*, Vol. 35, pp. 301–10.

COCKBURN, C. (1971) Lecture given at a conference on "Planning Education—Challenge and Response" held at Oxford Polytechnic.

*DAVIDOFF, P. and REINER, T. A. (1962) A choice theory of planning, *Journal of the American Institute of Planners*, Vol. 28, pp. 103–15.

DENNIS, N. (1958) The popularity of the neighbourhood community idea, *Sociological Review*, Vol. 6, pp. 191–206.

EDUCATION FOR PLANNING ASSOCIATION (1972) The approach to the RTPI, *Education for Planning*, Vol. 2, pp. 21–2, 49–50.

FAGIN, H. (1959) Organizing and carrying out planning activities within urban government, *Journal of the American Institute of Planners*, Vol. 25, pp. 109–14.

FALUDI, A. (1971) The experiences of sociologists in their collaboration with planners, *Uses of Social Sciences in Urban Planning*, Seminar Proceedings, Planning & Transport Research & Computation Co. Ltd., London.

FALUDI, A. (1972a) The teaching of planning theory—Conference at Oxford Polytechnic, *Journal of the Royal Town Planning Institute*, Vol. 58, pp. 228–9.

FALUDI, A. (1972b) The specialist versus generalist conflict, *Oxford Working Papers in Planning Education and Research*, No. 12, Department of Town Planning, Oxford Polytechnic, Oxford.

FALUDI, A. (1973) *A Reader in Planning Theory*, Pergamon, Oxford.

FEHL, G. *et al.* (Editor) (1972) *Planung und Information—Materialien zur Planungs-forschung*, Bertelsmann Fachverlag, Gütersloh.

*FOLEY, D. L. (1960) British town planning: one ideology or three? *British Journal of Sociology*, Vol. 11, pp. 211–31.

FRIEDMANN, J. and HUDSON, B. (1973) *Knowledge and Action: A Guide to Planning Theory*, School of Architecture and Urban Planning, University of California, Los Angeles.

*GLASS, R. (1959) The evaluation of planning: some sociological considerations, *International Social Science Journal*, Vol. 11, pp. 393–409.

HARRIS, B. (1967) The limits of science and humanism in planning, *Journal of the American Institute of Planners*, Vol. 33, pp. 324–35.

HIGHTOWER, H. C. (1969) Planning theory in contemporary professional education, *Journal of the American Institute of Planners*, Vol. 35, pp. 326–9.

HOLLIDAY, J. C. *et al.* (1972) Education for practice 1990, *Journal of the Royal Town Planning Institute*, Vol. 58, pp. 106–8.

*HUGHES, E. C. (1958) Quoted by DYCKMAN, J. W. (1961) What makes planners plan? *Journal of the American Institute of Planners*, Vol. 27, pp. 164–7.

ISARD, W. *et al.* (1969) *General Theory: Social, Political, Economic and Regional*, MIT Press, Cambridge, Mass.

KANTOROWICH, R. H. (1967) Education for planning, *Journal of the Town Planning Institute*, Vol. 53, pp. 175–84.

KAPLAN, A. (1964) *The Conduct of Inquiry: Methodology for Behavioral Science*, Chandler, Scranton, Penn.

KITCHEN, T. (1973) Planning education in Britain, *Journal of the Royal Town Planning Institute*, Vol. 59, pp. 20–3.

MCLOUGHLIN, J. B. (1969) *Urban and Regional Planning—A Systems Approach*, Faber & Faber, London.

MILLERSON, G. (1964) *The Qualifying Associations—A Study in Professionalization*, Routledge & Kegan Paul, London.

MINETT, M. J. (1972) Contribution to discussions held at a conference on "The Teaching of Planning Theory" at Oxford Polytechnic.

MINISTRY OF HOUSING AND LOCAL GOVERNMENT (1965) *The Future of Development Plans: A Report by the Planning Advisory Group*, HMSO, London.

MORRIS, R. J. (1971) Cholera: the social disease, *New Society*, 8 July, pp. 52–6.

PERLOFF, H. S. (1957) *Education for Planning: City, State, and Regional*, Johns Hopkins Press, Baltimore.

POWER, J. M. (1971) Planning: magic and technique, *Beyond Local Government Reform*, Institute for Operational Research, Tavistock Institute, London.

POWER, J. M. (1972) The reticulist function in government: manipulating networks of communication and influence, Paper presented to the Canberra Seminar on Administrative Studies.

READE, E. (1971) Sociology in planning education, *Official Architecture and Planning*, Vol. 34, pp. 783–4.

ROBINSON, I. M. (1972) Introduction, *Decision-Making in Urban Planning* (edited by ROBINSON, I. M.), Sage Publications, Beverly-Hills-London.

ROYAL TOWN PLANNING INSTITUTE (1971) *Town Planners and their Future* (Discussion paper), London.

SCHMIDT-RELENBERG, N. (1968) *Soziologie und Städtebau*, Karl Kämer, Stuttgart.

SEERS, D. (1972) The prevalence of pseudo-planning, *New Society*, 18 May, pp. 352–4.

SIMON, H. A. (1969) *The Sciences of the Artificial*, MIT Press, Cambridge, Mass.

TOWN PLANNING INSTITUTE (1969) Revised Final Examination of the Town Planning Institute.

TOWNSEND, P. (1970) The reorganisation of social policy, *New Society*, 22 October, pp. 722–4.

WILSON, A. G. (1969) *Forecasting "Planning"*, Centre for Environmental Studies, London.

*Included in FALUDI, A. (1973) *A Reader in Planning Theory*, Pergamon, Oxford.

CHAPTER 2

The Underlying Theory Models

THE previous chapter has identified the problem of planning theory, and what we shall now discuss is a methodological issue: the meaning of *theory* in the context of this book (with the understanding that planning theory from now on means theory *of*, rather than theory *in* planning).

Theory is sometimes equated with a framework for thinking. Providing such a framework, that is an account which puts experiences into a context, is clearly one thing which theorists do. But there are further claims made on behalf of theory. The following definition says that a theory must be logically consistent and also give an account which allows predictions to be made:

> It may refer to an abstract conceptual scheme which in itself may be little more than a number of definitions, or it may have a systematic reference so that each abstract term is systematically related to the others, rendering the categories exclusive of each other, but pointing to their articulation. If, from such a categorical system, laws may be derived possessing predictive value, then we may say that a *theoretical* system has been evolved. Strictly speaking only this last kind of system is a system of theory . . . (Mitchell, 1968).

This chapter distinguishes between concepts of theory as between different types of accounts given in efforts to remove tension caused by surprising experiences. From this discussion of issues which themselves have by no means been resolved conclusively (Ryan, 1970), I shall attempt to clarify the theory models underlying this book. The argument will be that what this book provides is not an empirically established theory of planning (what I shall call a *positive theory of planning*), but rather a model as a tool which might, in due course, help in building such a theory. Until this somewhat elusive aim is reached, this model, and its derivatives, have to serve as makeshift theories in lieu of any theories of the more respectable kind, a situation which is not at all uncommon in many fields of action.

21

THE MEANINGS OF EXPLANATION

Theory is a form of human thought invoked in answering to questions of why particular events occur. Methodologists call this answer an *explanation*. Explanations are narratives which remove the element of surprise when observing a phenomenon.

The *pattern* and the *deductive model of explanation* and what they mean in terms of planning theory must first be identified. In distinguishing between them I draw on Kaplan (1964). The pattern model refers to an account which makes sense of an observed event by presenting it as part of a larger whole. The deductive model demonstrates that, given some general propositions or laws, and initial conditions, the event was what one should have expected. In terms of planning theory, the conceptual framework for planning thought referred to above is an example of the pattern model of explanation setting out to explain planning phenomena by showing how they constitute parts of a unified and organized whole (in the way that evaluation may be explained as forming part of a planning agency's efforts to plan rationally). If laws of planning existed, then explanations following the deductive model could also be given simply by subsuming planning phenomena under them. *Alas*, nothing of this kind exists, as I shall argue later.

Conceptual frameworks providing an explanation according to the pattern model are sometimes called a "general theory" by their proponents. Talking about political theory, Easton (1965) identifies three objectives of general theory, emphasizing the coherence which it gives to our views of a whole field of intellectual endeavour:

> ... to establish criteria for identifying the important variables requiring investigation in all political systems; to specify the relationships among these variables; and to achieve these goals through a set of generalization that hang together with greater rather than lesser logical coherence and inter-dependence.

Opponents of such an approach denounce frameworks as "grand theory". They consider that an explanation following the deductive model is the only legitimate way of showing why a particular event has occurred. This means to subsume a phenomenon under a more general class of phenomena:

> To say that particular instances are 'referred' to general principles means thus that they are deducible from those principles together with something which serves to mark out whatever particular is in question. To explain something is to exhibit it as a special case of what is known in general (Kaplan, 1964).

Proponents of the exclusive use of this deductive model of explanation emphasize the great stringency of the requirements which an explanation of this kind must meet, and the advantages which this has for our knowledge of reality. The deductive approach commits one to empirical observations based on hypotheses. Only where the observations corroborate the hypotheses may they pass as laws to be invoked in explaining events. This discipline is in contradistinction to the looseness of the requirements imposed by explanations under the pattern model: "But the most hopeful feature of theories that really try to explain phenomena is that they have a built-in pressure toward, and possibility of, correction, whereas nothing forces one to change conceptual schemes . . ." (Barry, 1970).

Beyond this difficulty of relating whole frameworks to empirical facts, there is the added one of controlling the way in which values influence their construction. The *cause célèbre* is Parsons' framework for sociological thought called "structural functionalism" being allegedly conservative in its emphasis on "systems maintenance" over change (Barry, 1970). Fortunately, the mere fact that it is possible to demonstrate underlying values such as in the case of structural functionalism tends to obviate this very problem. Also, before explanations following the deductive model may be given, one must have laws. These derive from testing hypotheses which themselves require the prior formulation of a framework. Formulating any framework means to select one possible framework in preference to others and thus to take one's stand. Therefore social theory, which is concerned with people, *has* to take a stand on normative issues. Any criticisms of frameworks such as Parsons' can only legitimately be directed against his particular stand, and not against the fact that a stand has been taken.

The only real implication that flows from criticisms of the pattern model of explanation is therefore that such assumptions ought to be made explicit so as to facilitate criticism. Beyond this, the difference between a position accepting both models of explanation, and that of preferring the deductive to the exclusion of the pattern model, is smaller than appears at first glance. This is because there are points of convergence. The first is that both models play their part in the *process* of obtaining explanations. The second is that the pattern and the deductive model belong to different stages in the development of an area of intellectual pursuit. The third is that, where it can be applied at all, the deductive model distinguishes a more mature stage. Providing a deductive type of explanation therefore stands as the ultimate aim of theory with pattern models being developed, amongst others, with this end in view, despite the fact that it is rather remote (for planning theory anyway) simply because of the great rigour which it induces into theory and research.

THE ROUTE FOR PLANNING THEORY

For planning theory, this means that one of its aims is the establishment of a range of laws under which particular phenomena of planning may be subsumed and thus explained. The model of planning agencies forming part of the conceptual framework for planning thought is a tool for the establishment of such laws.

The route for developing planning theory (Fig. 2.1) begins with raw data on planning. These are the experiences and the actions of planners. However, the world is so complex that it is beyond the capacity of human beings to grasp it. It is therefore impossible to describe any of these experi-

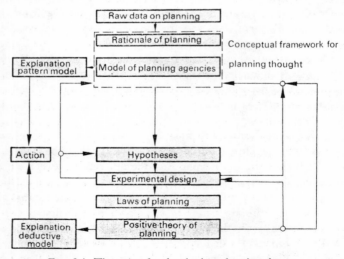

FIG. 2.1. The route for developing planning theory

ences without introducing some *a priori* assumptions. One is consequently compelled to select certain aspects which one wishes to describe to the exclusion of an infinite variety of others.[1]

This process of sieving information and focusing on particular aspects of reality is an essential part of all human thought and nothing specific to theory. However, one should expect of the theorist that he would be explicit about the principle on which he has based his selection of aspects to be included. The principle is called a rationale, that is "... the basic idea, the point of view behind the formation and structure of the concept of a model" (Willer, 1967). In planning theory this "explanation of the nature of the included phenomena" is the view of *planning as a rational process of thought and action which ultimately aims (as science does) at promoting human growth* (see Chapter 3).

The notion of a rationale is closely linked to that of a model, the construction of models being the next phase in the development of theory. A model "... is a conceptualization of a group of phenomena constructed by means of a rationale where the ultimate purpose is to furnish the terms and relations, in propositions, of a formal system which, if validated, becomes theory" (Willer, 1967).

The model to be constructed is a model of planning agencies. After this, the next step on the route to explanation is that of deriving a theory from that model. For this end, hypotheses are formed.[2] Following set procedures, one compares these with observations made in experiments. Laws are hypotheses which have passed this test. Where such laws form a system of interconnected propositions, there they add up to a positive theory with the pretence of describing some part of the world as it is.

This description of how theories are developed is one to which both methodological schools might agree. Disagreement, if any, will be about the way one describes the stages and also about the uses to which each of them put it. This results in different strategies for developing planning theory.

If the proponents of the deductive model could have their way, only such laws and theories which have been established beyond reasonable doubt

[1] This, incidentally, implies that any account of the experiences of planners is also filtered in this way. There are simply no "raw" data as such, but only data which are more or less refined.
[2] For examples see Chapters 7–9.

would be used in providing explanations. They could then concentrate on increasing the fund of laws to be invoked. For planning theory, this would mean that, firstly, the rationale of planning theory must be identified explaining the nature of what is meant by planning. On this basis, a model is constructed. But its sole purpose is the formation of hypotheses based on it. If these pass the test, then they become laws of planning which would allow one in future to explain the phenomena covered by them. Any of the problems described in the previous chapter, the strategy suggests, should be solved by reference to a body of such laws which are interrelated and thus form a positive theory of planning.

The other school would disagree that all efforts should be concentrated on developing a theory of this kind. In such uncharted fields as planning this would entail abstention from practical advice until empirical hypotheses have been established well enough to be invoked as laws. Opponents would argue that models, even before hypotheses have received empirical backing, may themselves provide explanations following the pattern model. They accept the lower degree of reliability of such explanations as a cost to be borne when better explanations are impossible to obtain.

AN INSTRUMENTALIST VIEW OF PLANNING THEORY

The acceptance of models as providing explanations, albeit less reliable ones, is based on the maxim that "... the actual conduct of inquiry ... concerns itself, not with ultimates, but with the next step to be taken" (Kaplan, 1964). There is more to this maxim than the desire to avoid airy-fairy arguments about what could be achieved in an ideal world. The underlying issue is the divergence between a "realist" and "instrumentalist" view of what theories are.[3]

The issue is this: realists hold that a good theory provides a map of the world as it is and therefore prefer a deductive model of explanation based on laws. The instrumentalist view is that good theories are guides to successful action, no matter whether they represent the world accurately or not. But, of course, the more they do this, the better they guide action. Instrumentalism therefore gives no licence for disregarding empirical

---

[3]"Realist" and "instrumentalist" are technical terms used in the literature on methodology. The difference between them has nothing to do with the distinction between a "realist" and "idealist".

findings. It is only more sympathetic to man as an actor wishing to orient himself here and now than realism is.[4]

There are a number of reasons why I accept the instrumentalist position in preference to the purist attitude towards the way theory may inform practice. Two are negative: the deductive model, firstly, fails to deliver the goods, at least as and when they are needed. The time which it takes for results of research to become available is often considerable. This is a run-away world in which action is taken all the time, either with or without adequate intelligence. Research findings therefore may all too easily address themselves to yesterday's problems. For instance, Berelson (1970), writing about the application of research to the way in which family planning might be spread, turns against the academic *cliché* that

> ... you need *full* understanding based on a long run programme of 'basic' research before you can successfully deal with a social problem of this sort ... we regularly take action successfully on all sorts of social problems without having full knowledge of 'how it works'.
> ... basic research, as it would be defined by many sociologists or psychologists or anthropologists is not warranted, because it will not yield enough results to be helpful in the short run.

Proponents of the purist view agree with this observation that research is time-consuming. For instance, Lipsey (1966) discusses the requirements of testing the hypotheses: "Government control reduces (increases) efficiency, changes (does not change) the distribution of income, leads (does not lead) to an increase of state control in other spheres." His estimate is that the task could keep a research team occupied for between ten and twenty years. Clearly, it is unlikely that any decision-taker interested in this question would be willing to wait for their advice![5]

In view of the scale of effort required to develop theories of this kind, it is hardly surprising that not too many of them exist. Social scientists, though tending to pay much regard to the importance of theory, admit that the social sciences have not been too successful in building them, and this is the second reason for prefering the instrumentalist view. The social

---

[4]Technically, the disagreement is about the status of correspondence statements linking theoretical terms to observable variables. Realists claim that they are synthetic statements, instrumentalists that they are analytical. See Ryan (1970) and Kaplan (1964).

[5]On the efforts which would be needed for the development of a positive theory of planning see my editorial comments to Part V in Faludi (1973).

sciences are fraught with questions of values, of the complexity and relative inconsistency of the phenomena with which they are concerned,
and the difficulty of obtaining reliable data concerning human beings who
soon become conscious of being observed. Of the social sciences, economics
and experimental psychology are therefore the only ones which consistently
lay claim to developing theories which meet the stringent requirements
outlined above. Sociologists and political scientists are much more likely
to express scepticism concerning the status of whatever theories exist in
their fields. Olsen's summary judgement on sociology is for instance that
it "... is still far from being a mature science, although it is certainly
striving in this direction" (Olsen, 1968). Barry is similarly cautious
concerning political theory (which, only in the past fifteen years "has shown
signs of starting to become a theoretical subject") by emphasizing "... the
distance still to go to the goal of verified theoretical and general propositions" (Barry, 1970).

It is therefore difficult to base practical advice on positive social-science
theory. Furthermore, not only are there points on the debit side of positive
theory due to its sheer absence, but there are also points for accepting
the less rigorous notion of theory as providing explanations following the
pattern model.

Firstly, the pattern model of explanation very much complements the
way in which human beings operate. Where the methodologically tough-
minded scientist refrains from practical advice unless he can draw on some
well-established theory and subsume the case on which advice is needed
under its propositions, the man of action cannot help but use the pattern
model. The need to make sense out of this world, to construct coherent and
extensive maps of it, is inherent to all of us. If there are established laws
and theories, then so much the better. The conceptual framework which
our man of action constructs from necessity shall include them. But where
there are not (as is the case every so often), coherent models based on an
explicit rationale are better than no guidance at all. Without such guidance,
the framework on which action is based remains vague, implicit, very
much a private affair and thus not open to improvement through criticism.

Secondly, and this flows directly from what I have said in the previous
paragraph, conceptual frameworks providing an explanation following the
pattern model need not be devoid of empirical backing. To provide a
framework in a recognized area of practical concern shared by many

people means to create a vehicle for them to communicate with each other. Like a language, frameworks may contain many elements of truth. Thus a conceptual framework receives empirical backing through the extent to which it creates a language in which practitioners may converse (as well as, in the long run, by leading to testable hypotheses). If adequate, it will be filled in and extended during the process, thus fulfilling the criterion of an explanation under the pattern model: "A sound explanation is one that grows on us as our knowledge grows" (Kaplan, 1964).

I am therefore arguing for accepting *both* models of explanation, the pattern and the deductive model, as useful in practice. Models based on a rationale and forming a conceptual framework belong to the earlier periods in the development of theory. Their immediate practical use is to create a language for comparing experiences. While being used in practice, frameworks at the same time undergo a fair amount of informal testing and adaptation. Working towards the deductive model of explanation, and introducing all the refinements to the conceptual framework which formulating testable hypotheses entails, further improves their quality.

But testing hypotheses is only the last step in a long process of refining conceptual frameworks. Presently, and in the foreseeable future, no advice based on reasonably well-established laws of planning can therefore be given. However, the thinking which goes into constructing a conceptual framework can still inform decisions taken. To aid this process, I shall spell out the implications of the view of planning underlying my particular framework. This will amount to an extension of this framework. Even though, clearly, even an extended framework is less reliable as a basis for action than more respectable theories are, it is more readily available to the point where it provides the *only* guidance. But to underline the difference from an empirically established type of theory still further, and to signify my awareness of the extent to which it is a theory influenced by my values, I describe it as a *normative theory of planning*.

As shown in the companion volume to this book, the distinction between normative and positive theory in this field of planning has been made variously. Like others have done before, in the part outlining my normative theory of planning I describe how the conceptual framework may be used to develop ideas about how planning ought to proceed. The value against which it should be measured is the promotion of human growth in the sense in which I shall define this concept in the next chapter. The propositions in that part incorporate whatever relevant generalizations and illustrative examples have come to my attention (and to this extent the theory is not purely normative), but mainly they are based on the framework itself. They are not statements about how planning is. Rather, they purport to be useful to planners accepting my view of planning in solving their problems of understanding planning, of transferring experiences, and in particular those of designing and modifying their agencies and procedures. It is in the acceptance of a normative theory of planning as useful in solving these problems that its criterion of success or failure must be sought.

THE PLAN FOR THE BOOK

The plan for the rest of this book flows from these considerations concerning the route for developing planning theory and the giving of advice based on it. Whether the aim is solely that of developing a positive theory of planning or not, the first step must be that of constructing a model based on a rationale. Rationale and model form *A Conceptual Framework for Planning Theory* (Part II) outlining the account which planning theory ought to be able to give, that is an account of how planning agencies promote human growth.

Part III describes how I propose to move *Towards a Positive Theory of Planning*. This part includes one chapter on the planning environment as a refinement of the framework developed in Part II. This refinement results from the greater precision with which I have had to formulate the terms of my model to turn them into tools for research, thus demonstrating the fact that the continuous refinement of a framework is one of the important by-products even of preparing, let alone doing, research.

Part IV develops the framework further providing the basis for *The Politics of Rational Planning* aimed at creating the conditions under which planning may fulfil its rationale. Here I shall give my views on multi-planning agencies, on the way decisions ought to be taken in planning, on the structure of planning organizations and their procedures, and on how planning comes to fruition, always relating these to Part II.

REFERENCES

BARRY, B. M. (1970) *Sociologists, Economists and Democracy*, Macmillan, London.

BERELSON, B. (1970) On family planning communication, *Understanding Society* (edited by Social Science Foundation Course Team, The Open University) Macmillan, London.

EASTON, D. (1965) *A Systems Analysis of Political Life*, John Wiley, New York.

FALUDI, A. (1973) *A Reader in Planning Theory*, Pergamon, Oxford.

KAPLAN, A. (1964) *The Conduct of Inquiry: Methodology for Behavioral Science*, Chandler, Scranton, Penn.

LIPSEY, R. G. (1966) *Positive Economics*, Weidenfeld & Nicolson, London.

MITCHELL, G. D. (1968) *A Dictionary of Sociology*, Routledge & Kegan Paul, London.

OLSEN, M. E. (1968) *The Process of Social Organization*, Holt, Rinehart & Winston, London–New York.

RYAN, A. (1970) *The Philosophy of the Social Sciences*, Macmillan, London.

WILLER, D. F. (1967) *Scientific Sociology*, Prentice-Hall, Englewood Cliffs, N.J.

PART II

A CONCEPTUAL FRAMEWORK
FOR PLANNING THOUGHT

THIS part develops the conceptual framework for planning thought consisting of the rationale of planning theory and the model of planning agencies. The chapter on the rationale of planning theory is based on an argument for regarding the concept of rational planning as superior to any other concept of planning. The reason suggested for engaging in rational planning is that it promotes human growth both as a product and as a process.

The model of planning agencies consequently builds on one basic assumption which also underlies the final two chapters of Part II: that they may be understood as analogous to the human mind engaging in purposive thought and action. Drawing this analogy allows one to utilize the results of a great amount of thinking having gone into both the understanding of human thought, and into the formulation of rules for describing the results of thought processes as valid. Thus, Chapter 4 draws on attempts to build models of the human mind. Chapter 5 describes the operations of planning agencies in terms of the model, thereby drawing an analogy between the deductive model of explanation and the formulation of programmes for action (which is what planning means).

The analogy between planning agencies and the human mind inspires further thoughts about rational planning. It is evident that all subjects, be they individuals or organizations, suffer from limitations of their ability to meet its requirements. Chapter 6 identifies reasons for these limitations and describes how individuals cope with them by employing certain approaches. It is argued that planning agencies can use approaches analogous to these, that is employ planning strategies or engage in creative planning. Even the notion of will-power may be applied to planning agencies, much in the same way as the view that commitment required to generate will-power must be balanced against that sceptical attitude which is conducive to perpetual criticism of planning proposals. To propose the basic features of organizations and procedures which would meet these delicate require-ments will be the main issue in Part IV.

CHAPTER 3

The Rationale of Planning Theory

In THIS chapter, I shall try to specify the rationale of planning theory as that of planning promoting *human growth* by the use of rational procedures of thought and action. This requires prior discussion of the concept of human growth itself, and the reasons for putting it forward as a worthwhile ideal. We shall examine human growth both as a *product*, and as a *process*. But not even as a product may we see human growth as co-terminous with numerical growth and an increase in economic wealth. It stands rather for a continuing enrichment of human life, and the widening of the range of goals which human beings are capable of pursuing.

Planning promotes human growth as a product in two ways. Firstly, it identifies the best way of attaining ends. Secondly, it contributes to learning, and hence to future growth. Lastly, as regards human growth as a process, planning may be identified as a vehicle for controlling and accelerating that process. In all this, I perceive planning as analogous to that other activity which has resulted in unparalleled human growth: science. Planning and science can be seen as twin sisters born from the same desire of man to free himself from the strictures of ignorance and fear. Planning and science propel this process of man becoming master over his world and himself along a path towards further human growth. Planning theory improves upon the process by providing guidelines for meta-planning.

PLANNING AS RATIONAL ACTION

Planning has always meant taking intelligent, rational action. However, what constitutes intelligent action is the subject of much argument. Often, people identify it with responding to problems in specific and, to their proponents, obvious ways. Thus, it might be argued that: the environment ought to be protected; scarce resources should be preserved; help should be given to underprivileged groups; public transport ought to be given priority over private transport; certain patterns of urban growth should underlie the future development of a region. What I wish to argue is that, in presenting proposals such as these, the proponents of substantive policies imply that they have gone through a rational thought process. The planning literature calls this the *rational planning process* of going through generation of alternatives, evaluation, and choice based on that evaluation.[1]

Proponents of policies invoke this rational planning process because presenting an argument means to reconstruct and communicate a conclusion in such a way that somebody else is led to draw the same inferences. Rationality in this context is ". . . a shorthand way of pointing out . . . the . . . standards which I and others appeal to when we try, individually or collectively, to give our 'reasons' in a clear and demonstrable form" (Gould, 1971). To achieve this we present our proposals as superior to the alternatives. An environmentalist may therefore support a demand for controls on industrial effluents discharged into rivers by painting a picture of their state if such measures are not taken; the advocate of better welfare benefits may describe the consequences of not giving these benefits. More sophisticated advocates consider many alternatives. But they still claim that their proposals are demonstrably superior to other conceivable courses of action, "demonstrably" referring to a, if only crude, process of rational thought which they claim to have followed.

Of course, very often proposals do not originate from a truly rational thought process at all, and the arguments advanced are as has been described above: reconstructions for the purpose of communicating ideas in a way which will gain their acceptance. The moving force behind a proposal may be different from what is said explicitly. For instance, it may be a feeling of threat against which a proposal appears to provide a remedy.[2] In other cases, there may be hidden motives behind the painting of bleak pictures which the advocate of a certain policy may not even be aware of. Some such motive is occasionally imputed to the environmental lobby, namely that by decrying the effects of economic growth, they

---

[1]For an early statement of what rational planning involves, see the "Note on conceptual scheme" in Meyerson and Banfield (1955). See also Banfield (1959).

[2]In the case of the neighbourhood community idea, it has been argued by Dennis (1958) and Glass (1959) that to break urban settlements up into small neighbourhoods seemed to alleviate fears of an uprising of the urban proletariat.

implicitly wish to preserve their own privileged positions. In other cases, it may simply be that the members of a skilled group wish to underline the importance of the means which they have to offer, means which promise solutions to allegedly serious problems. This is common amongst professionals, and the case has been argued extensively in relation to town planners and their "physical determinism" (Broady, 1968).

Uncovering and analysing motives as they underlie practical proposals is very interesting. The sociology of knowledge provides concepts for doing so which say, basically, that men think the way they do because of their relative positions in society. In the field of planning, this line has been taken recently by a number of writers (Dennis, 1970; Davies, 1972). Young planners are prone to reduce their findings to the formula of planning being "middle class". This verdict combines with slightly romantic notions concerning "the people", thus strangely implying that somehow or other the middle class are not people.

Undoubtedly, such an ideological critique of planning proposals enriches intellectual discussion. But ideological critique has relatively little to contribute to the essential rôle of planning as making decisions. A decision-taker presented with a multitude of arguments made by the advocates of particular courses of action is faced with the problem of judging which course of action to accept as worth implementing. He must resolve, if only tentatively, to accept some reasons put before him as valid grounds for adopting one line in preference to others. For him, the information provided by ideological criticisms is a useful signpost to what may underlie a proposal, but it must not paralyse him lest he should become defunct as a decision-taker. He is more likely, therefore, to evaluate the arguments as they are manifestly made (meaning in their reconstructed form), judging premises for their acceptability and conclusions for whether proper inferences have been drawn. Furthermore, the decision-taker will combine these premises of individual courses of action into more holistic conceptions, balancing demands on the use of scarce resources against each other and thus coming to conclusions which may be judged intelligent in terms of his total situation. In short, he will combine particular demands and proposals into one overall rational choice.

The form which I have suggested advocates of particular courses of action would use in presenting their argument, and the procedure used by an intelligent decision-taker in determining the practical desirability of any one of a number of proposals is thus the same, namely that of the rational planning process. Since, in making the intelligence of a course of action plausible one always has to take recourse to this standard, the definition of an intelligent proposal as one that can be reconstructed as having resulted from a rational planning process is primary to any other one. This argument has particular relevance to public decision-making where choices, and the reasons leading up to them, must be communicated to allow for public discussion and democratic control.

Planning may therefore be defined as deciding on a course of action by satisfying oneself that it is possible to present one's choice in a form which could have resulted from a rational planning process, even if this has not actually been the case. Much as in science, where the form of presenting findings does not necessarily correspond to the process of their discovery (Medawar, 1967), the effort of presenting a course of action in this way has the advantage of facilitating criticism and of establishing an unambiguous basis for agreement or conflict.[3]

This notion of planning is identical to what, in different contexts, has been termed *systems analysis* and *operational research*. Thus, Quade (1968) defines systems analysis as

> . . . a systematic approach to helping a decision-maker choose a course of action by investigating his full problem, searching out objectives and alternatives, and comparing them in the light of their consequences, using an appropriate framework—in so far as is possible analytic—to bring expert judgement and intuition to bear on the problem.

Similarly, Beer (1966) describes operational research as follows:

> Operational research is the attack of modern science on complex problems arising in the direction and management of large systems of men, machines, materials and money in industry, business, government and defence. Its distinctive approach is to develop a scientific model of the system, incorporating measures of factors such as chance and risk, with which to predict and compare the outcome of alternative decisions, strategies and controls. The purpose is to help management determine the policy and actions scientifically.

[3]It is rare for practising planners to forego the appeal which advocating particular solutions has with the public and to emphasize the central obligation of the planner to the process by which decisions are made. Amos (1971) is surely an exception when he says that rather than to pronounce official views on "residential density, public participation, land ownership, or any other topic . . . " the Royal Town Planning Institute "could seek to ensure that the processes of critical analysis are as exhaustive and unbiased as possible".

During the sixties, therefore, what could be observed was a confluence between systems analysis, operational research and planning (Robinson, 1972). For instance, in Britain a distinct school of thought emerged which took a "systems view" of planning (McLoughlin, 1969; Chadwick, 1971) thereby drawing on the literature in these related fields. This was challenged recently for its attempt to arrogate to planning an area that had hitherto been considered a prerogative of the polity: the formulation of goals against which to evaluate alternatives (Dimitriou, 1972). With this goes a deep distrust of the very attempt to take rational, "scientific", approaches, so that Kahn (1969) even talks of a "political science challenge" to planning. Certainly, formulations like Friedmann's (1969) describing planning as the application of "scientific-technical intelligence" to the solution of practical problems are therefore liable to be criticized, much as my, basically identical, view of planning as a rational form of decision-making outlined above. However, it will become obvious throughout this book that I see politics and rational planning as complementary, and not as conflicting: as with "scientific method", by facilitating criticism, the requirements of presenting decisions as following from certain presuppositions improves the quality of debates and ultimately also that of the choices made in planning matters.[4]

HUMAN GROWTH

Having shown that planning means to present choices as if one had made them going through a rational planning process, we now turn to the central question of this chapter: why should one plan? The answer is that the aim of planning is human growth. At the same time, this is also the rationale of planning theory, that is the point of view taken in building a conceptual framework for planning thought.

In this section I shall describe what I mean by human growth (leaving aside for the moment the establishment of the link between rational planning and human growth). In giving reasons for seeing it as an ideal worth pursuing I shall draw on a number of authors, most of whom have been influenced by cybernetics. Since this discipline promises to offer explanations of processes of growth, this influence is not surprising. Indeed, the

---

[4]Dyckman (1961) draws the analogy between planning and science, extending it even to their morality.

very existence of models of growth which, as their proponents claim, fit the growth even of social systems is itself a supportive argument for accepting human growth as an ideal.

Defining Human Growth

Human growth is not a simple concept. It has two aspects: growth as a *product*, and as the *process* leading to the same product. Of these, one may feel inclined to emphasize one or the other. But the continuing process of growth utilizes the products of previous growth. Also, the aim of a growth process may sometimes not be that of obtaining material products, but the ability to achieve still further growth. For instance, Diesing (1962) describes growth as an "... increase of integrative power, or mastery, or creativeness, as well as increased complexity of the problems and materials to be mastered". Deutsch (1966) also links his concept of growth to learning capacity. Growth for him refers to: the application of learning capacity to increase a system's openness; the increase of a system's ability to make effective responses to the environment; the increase in the range and diversity of goals which we are capable of following.

The last point is particularly relevant in our present climate of *pluralism*. Opponents of rational planning will probably find my concept of planning as leading to human growth questionable because of its connotation of "mankind", of "the social system", or some other reified collective entity, growing without adequate attention being paid to the individual or to sub-groups in society. But my concept of growth, like that of Deutsch, means the fulfilment of an increasingly diverse range of goals.[5] Similarly, Etzioni's normative model, *The Active Society* (1968), includes the notion of widening the area of choice, and in particular of increasing the range of goals pursued. The active society is hence *responsive*, aiming at "... the

---

[5]Deutsch spells this out in the last chapter of his book discussing the "politics of growth". There he says that growth not only refers to the system growing, but also to the growth of sub-groups. Thus, the "dimensions of growth" include growth in sheer man-power; economic growth; growth in operational resources ("uncommitted resources" which are essential for growth); growth in self-determination; growth in the ability to change patterns of communication and organization; *and* the growth of goal-seeking ability, including the facility of selecting *new* goals.

uninhibited, authentic, educated expression of an unbounded membership".

It is therefore plain that, as a product, growth cannot solely be measured in numerical terms such as population increase, GNP, and standard of living indices. It also refers to increase in the variety of goals attained, as well as to capacity for future goal attainment. Therefore the recent arguments concerning the *Limits to Growth* (Meadows *et al.*, 1972), directed as they are against continuing expansion, do not apply to the concept of growth which is advanced here. If one were to conclude that such limits threatened the future of mankind, then it would be possible within the concept of growth proposed to justify limiting numerical growth in the name of future goal-seeking ability. Likewise, it seems plausible that, since this would enable more people to attain their ends, one could argue for a more equal distribution of economic assets within the same concept, even if this was to the detriment of overall growth.

The production of material goods apart, growth as a *process* refers mainly to learning and creativity, defined as the gaining of insights into the existing order of things, and the transformation of that order into a new one (Diesing, 1962). It is that process by which man creates himself which brings us to reasons for putting forward human growth as the rationale of planning theory.

Reasons for Regarding Human Growth as an Ideal

The reasons for my regarding human growth as the end of planning, and thus as a suitable rationale of planning theory, are: my view of man as guiding his own development; the interpretation which human growth gives to past developments; the availability of models of growth.

Views of man. Such views of man and of the development of mankind have been advocated in the past. But the bane of concepts like growth, and of similar ones like progress, has been their lack of empirical relevance. Without this, whether growth takes place or not remains very much a question of faith. With the availability of models of growth, this has changed. Hence, an exciting range of books like Deutsch's *The Nerves of Government* (1966), Buckley's *Sociology and Modern Systems Theory* (1967), and Etzioni's *The Active Society* (1968) has appeared which try to synthesize cybernetic thinking with social and political theory. These authors present growth as an empirically verifiable concept, and the conditions of growth as open to analysis and manipulation. Therefore, the argument will be that the very availability of models of growth, though in itself not an adequate reason for viewing it as an ideal worth pursuing, makes growth as a concept more meaningful than it has been up until now.

Human growth is inextricably linked with the notion of man perpetually shaping this world, including the guidance of his own development. I personally find this view an appealing one because it seems to me that to guide one's own development consciously is a value in itself and justification for regarding human growth as a worthwhile ideal. I shall therefore demonstrate the link which I think exists between human growth and self-guidance. However, both aspects of this Promethean view of man presuppose something else: consciousness, or the awareness of knowledge (Etzioni, 1968). Being aware of knowledge, including the process by which it is created, and by which it results in action, adds an entirely new dimension to human growth: "When reason becomes self-conscious it changes into something it never was before. It becomes capable of studying its own working . . . and of improving this working by changing the structure" (Diesing, 1962).

Broadly speaking, the argument concerning human growth and self-guidance as based in consciousness which these authors advance is this: many of the existing barriers to further human growth (for instance in the sense of a more equitable distribution of resources) must be sought in our ways of doing things. If these could be changed, human growth could continue. Such change often involves changing habits and even whole world outlooks. Therefore, to remove some of the barriers to human growth means to change ourselves. But only by being aware of our own habits, our ways of looking at this world, including how they affect our actions, may we deliberately guide our own development towards the removal of barriers to human growth. Such self-awareness one calls one's consciousness. Since research designs have been based on it, consciousness is a respectable concept even in experimental psychology (Young, 1971). This book assumes that processes analogous to individual consciousness exist in society. They result in societal self-awareness which, much as individual consciousness, can be inferred from observations.

The three authors quoted have a common emphasis on consciousness. Deutsch (1966) discusses it as a kind of feedback. Feedback, in turn, is the central notion of cybernetics, that is the science of communication and control. In feedback, "... some of the out-put energy of an apparatus or machine is returned as in-put ...". This input then controls the future output of the machine or process so that, in cybernetics "... we now have an array of self-controlling machines that react to their environment, as well as to the result of their own behavior; that store, process and apply information; and that have, in some cases, a limited capacity to learn".

Because human beings possess consciousness, their capacity to learn is infinitely greater than that of even the most sophisticated machine. But this consciousness need not be regarded as something completely beyond our understanding. Deutsch presents consciousness as the *highest level of feedback* and hence as a process of information resulting in action. He thereby links consciousness to other types of (lower-order) information processes. There is the simplest one (the thermostat is often quoted as an example) whereby a variable (such as temperature) is kept constant. There is the second type whereby the "behaving object" (be it a more complex mechanism or a living being) finds that it cannot achieve its ends and therefore adapts them. This is called goal-changing feedback or learning. There is, finally, the third type of feedback which Deutsch emphasizes as central to the social and political processes which he is interested in, that is the scanning of internal data, or consciousness. Consciousness is important to Deutsch because it relates to self-determination:

> A society or community that is to steer itself must continue to receive a full flow of three kinds of information: first information about the world outside; second, information from the past, with a wide range of recall and re-combination; and third, information about itself and its own parts ... ..

The test of functioning on all these levels would be the capacity to learn, that is to produce internal rearrangements so as to bring about changes in the system's behaviour. This is linked to Deutsch's concept of growth as presented earlier, and he refers to a "theory of growth" going with his "theory of self-determination".

Similarly with Buckley (1967) who builds on Deutsch, and who first of all emphasizes the importance of the social over the physical environment:

> As we progress from lower to higher biological adaptive systems we note, as a general rule, the gradually increasing role of other biological units .. as part of the significant environment. The variety and the constraints represented

by the behavior of these units must be mapped, as well as that of the physical environment. With the transition from the higher primate social organization to the full-blown human, symbolically mediated, socio-cultural system, the mapping of the subtle behaviors, gestures and intentions of the individuals making up the effective social organization becomes increasingly central, and eventually overshadows the mapping of the physical environment.

But to operate in a social environment not only requires developing images of the behaviour of others, it also depends on the development of an awareness of which images one projects oneself. Such a reflective quality leads to self-awareness. It enables actors ". . . to map, store, and selectively or normatively act towards not only the external variety and constraints of the social and physical environment but also to their internal states". This again means that an actor possessing consciousness is able to change himself in a deliberate manner, thereby to improve his chances of attaining his ends, and hence to grow.

Finally, in his book on *The Active Society*, Etzioni (1968) also links the concept of self-guidance with those of consciousness and growth. Firstly, he describes his active society clearly as one which is growing: "The study of the active society is the study of a society realizing *its* values and an exploration of the barriers which deter society from realizing these values and investigating ways to accelerate their fulfilment." Many of these barriers to continuing growth in society lie in society itself. For realizing his values, and thereby guiding his future development, man must therefore turn his attention to society:

> Man is *not* unless he is social; what he is depends on his social being, and what he makes of his social being is irrevocably bound to what he makes of himself. He has the ability to master his internal being, *and the main way to self-mastery leads to his joining with others like himself in social acts.*

Etzioni's book thus has as its sub-title "A theory of societal and political processes". These processes are subject to social laws, laws which penetrate the individual's mind by way of socialization. But social laws, as opposed to the laws of the natural sciences, may be *changed* collectively. Society is "malleable"; as Diesing (1962) says, it is the prime object of the creative exercise of reason.

Societal malleability implies a danger. Change may result in more freedom for members of society but may also transform it so that man's domination over man is increased. The active society is one which has opted for the first alternative, drawing on its consciousness, the commitment of its members, and on power that "allows resetting of the social code". However, the resetting of the social code in an active society means that it exercises collective self-guidance in the pursuit of its own growth. Hence, the active society is one that is master of itself.

Like these authors I am proposing to regard human growth as an ideal in the sense of man firstly transforming his physical environment and utilizing its resources; and secondly shaping human institutions, thus including the social environment into the orbit of his control. Because growth in the latter sense also means self-guidance, this concept incorporates a view of man as gaining mastery over himself by power of his faculty of reason.

Growth as an evolutionary principle. Growth, in the sense of an increase in the variety of goals which living organisms can achieve, is a principle underlying the process of evolution. Human growth provides an interpretation to the historical development of mankind, explaining secular trends such as technological and economic progress, the expansion of the human habitat, institutional differentiation, urbanization and scientific progress, as forming part of an overall process. Combining the evolution of life with that of mankind, it is even possible to interpret the progression of life-forms from the most primitive organisms to the most complex socio-cultural systems as one overall process of growth. Buckley (1967) argues this way, unifying the evolution of life and of mankind by identifying in them a common thread of continuing growth in terms of an increase in learning capacity. Equating this with intelligence, one is reminded of Diesing's interpretation of what growth and historical development may mean: "If history does move toward a goal, that goal can only be intelligence . . . because intelligence (which makes all other values achievable— AF) is the only unconditional value" (Diesing, 1962).

Learning, Buckley says, is achieved by natural selection in the case of biological adaptive systems; by behavioural change in the case of animals; and by people or social organizations anticipating future possibilities and exercising conscious choice. In this ascending scale, complexity increases along three dimensions: the time-span for the results of learning to take effect becomes shorter; the fidelity of the information becomes greater;

the methods of storage are refined until, eventually, what one finds are the "entirely extrasomatic socio-cultural depositories" of libraries and data banks.

So one could construct indices of growth which relate to the capacity of exercising control over the environment, and ultimately also to that of exercising self-guidance. Growth thus becomes a measurable concept: we can apply it to interpret past developments. For instance, Buckley's dimensions of growth may be related to indicators like the reduction of the time taken for information retrieval and the greater precision of data. These signal growth because they increase learning capacity. Their development can be measured over time, giving a clear idea of the historical process of growth.

Intuitively, one might expect that such observations would confirm the view of life progressing, and of man developing from lower to higher cultural forms. Thus, the existence of measurable concepts of growth could amplify the many philosophical views of history as embodying the principle of human growth (and, incidentally, of developing towards democracy as a form of political organization enabling still further growth, such as Buckley suggests). Therefore, empirically relevant concepts make growth as a principle underlying evolution, and human growth as the end towards which history has striven, intellectually more palatable than they have been thus far. This brings me to the third, supportive, reason for regarding human growth as the rationale of planning theory.

Models of growth. Models of growth belong to the family of cybernetic models. Cybernetic models are capable of explaining goal-seeking behaviour. Hitherto, the explanation of such behaviour has caused problems, especially as regards social organizations. In the past, one has sought to explain such behaviour by reference to the goals pursued. However, this means invoking the end of a process or activity to explain its existence, which is methodologically unsound. Cybernetic models turn this explanation on its head by inferring *the existence of ends from manifest behaviour* such as feedback processes. The end of such a process is simply that condition under which the mechanism or being stops receiving feedback because it is on course (Deutsch, 1966). Even where this is never actually the case, this state may be deduced from the pattern of information flows.

One may not only discern lower-order feedback processes and their effects (as with a domestic thermostat), but also higher-order ones, like Deutsch's learning. This is because learning means changing the end of action. But with ends being related to patterns of information flows, changing them must involve changes to the channels forming these patterns. To invoke a simple example, when a learner driver develops the habit of glancing at the rear mirror, we take this as evidence for his having adopted the end of avoiding danger from the rear as one worth entertaining simultaneously with others. In its own way, even this small example of learning contributes to growth of the chances of survival, and one may therefore say that one has observed a process of growth.

Similarly with consciousness which one can observe much as one observes learning simply by looking at patterns of information flows. For instance, when a management consultant is called in to assist a firm in making its own "corporate appraisal" (Hussey, 1971), and when this appraisal results in changes to the procedures by which decisions are made, one can observe a highest-order feedback, or consciousness, in action leading to further growth.

Models of growth do not only provide leads in observing growth, they also indicate concrete steps to be taken for the promotion of growth. Buckley (1967) provides one such model. He distinguishes between two processes building on two different types of feedback: morphostasis and morphogenesis. Morphostasis is the process whereby a system preserves its given form. The type of feedback associated with this is called *negative* feedback whereby information concerning the system going "off course" results in counter-action. As against this, morphogenesis refers to those processes which tend to elaborate a system, that is which lead to growth. It relies on *positive* feedback whereby information concerning the system going "off course" results in more action of the same type, thus amplifying the original movement. An example which Buckley quotes and which is a familiar one to urban planners is that of urbanization: the more land-use activities are concentrated in one locality, the greater its attraction as a location of further activities.

The problem of guiding growth is then that of identifying the deviation-amplifying mechanisms which propel it along. This is what Maruyama (1970) describes as the "second cybernetics" of growth. In identifying concrete steps to be taken in the pursuit of further growth one can draw on this second cybernetics. One does not depend on those "Inexorable Laws of Historical Destiny" which Popper (1961) claims are often inherent to the idea of planning.[6]

THE CHOICE TO BE MADE

Having outlined my reasons for seeing human growth as an ideal worth pursuing let me add that I do not claim that one *has* to pursue it. In addition to having reasons what is needed is the optimism required to face up to the perpetual challenge which human growth poses: the challenge to pursue growth relentlessly, and to fight the obstacles of growth, wherever they may be; the challenge to abandon or check certain types of growth where they develop pathological aspects, however dear they may be to one's heart; the challenge of facing up to the anxieties involved in making decisions in the pursuit of growth; the challenge of sharing responsibility for mankind's future. It also requires having faith in man's ability, and in particular in his faculty of reason.

Therefore, as Etzioni (1968) says, there is this very real choice to be made between accepting a challenge and letting mankind drift into the future. New powers are becoming available for self-destruction, and subtle and persuasive means of opinion moulding may further extend the control of man over man. This arises out of fear, of man's unwillingness to face up to the challenges of growth, of his efforts to close himself to the possibilities lying ahead of him. Grauhan and Strudelt (1971) elaborate on this choice drawing on most of the authors quoted above. They consider the question of whether a purely procedural definition of rationality is adequate or not, and come down very strongly on the side of a substantive definition: the goals of rational choice must themselves be rational. These must contribute to "self-enhancement" (in my terms: to growth), that is: ". . . the principle of on-going enrichment of the life of the individual in society and of on-going reduction of its destructive elements". But

---

[6]For instance, it is perfectly conceivable to accept the emerging concern for the human environment, and the ensuing elaboration of institutions and procedures to protect it (including their self-justification, and their struggle for a clientele) as yet another incidence of the widening of the range of goals that we are capable of pursuing, without in any way having to accept the doomsday philosophy that often seems to accompany it.

whether the individual, or society, opt for self-enhancement as a goal is, in principle, an open question:

> The fact that an individual can deliberately commit suicide shows that the more conscious he is about his own choices, the more clearly he has to choose existence first in order to choose any other goal. It is not by chance that even the proponents of a procedural concept of rationality give as the only material standard of appraisal, the survival quality (Grauhan and Strudelt, 1971).

If we apply this to society, there are, as with individuals, pathological aspects of societal choices made in furtherance of self-enhancement. This, for instance, is the case when élites attain high levels of self-enhancement at the expense of others. Also Grauhan and Strudelt give the concept of self-enhancement a further, historical dimension. They recognize it as a dynamic concept to be measured in terms of "the potentialities realizable at any given time in history".

This turns the choice for or against self-enhancement, for human growth or, in the last consequence, death, into the perpetual challenge which I have earlier described. It is a challenge which is exacerbated by the un- certainty which characterizes any choice, uncertainty that concerns, amongst others, the possibility of choices having counterproductive implica- tions. Even given the best of intentions, choices may lead to unintended consequences, and to the closure of future opportunities. Therefore, choices carry elements of risk. This, incidentally, is an important reason why choices must ultimately be made in a political arena (Grauhan, 1973). But to shy away from choices means to shy away from that responsibility which a secular view of man squarely places upon him: the responsibility for his own fate.

THE RATIONAL PLANNING PROCESS AND HUMAN GROWTH

Having argued for human growth as an ideal, I must now link it with planning. More precisely, I shall demonstrate that (distinguishing be- tween human growth as a *product* and as a *process*) rational planning results in growth as a product, and that the rational planning process may itself be viewed as a vehicle for the very process of growth.

As regards growth as a product, one may take both a narrow and a wide view. The narrow view is that the goals in the planning process represent an operational definition of what human growth means in concrete situations. As argued earlier, there is no better way for any decision-taker to satisfy himself that he will attain his ends then to present his choices as if he had arrived at them by a rational planning process. As Davidoff and Reiner (1963) put it: ". . . intuition or experiences unsupported by reason are weak reeds on which to rest".

So, the rational planning process leads to growth in this narrow sense. But we must not be satisfied with this narrow view of human growth. Goals may very well change, even whilst the planner is engaged busily in identifying the means for their attainment, and many plans become irrelevant long before they are implemented. Nevertheless, even planning efforts that lead to no action may still result in human growth. This is because the rational planning process forces one to make assumptions explicit about oneself, one's environment, and how one relates to it, and it to oneself. In doing so, these thoughts become cast into the mould of an ordered argument thereby improving awareness of the structure of what, in Chapter 5, I shall term the action space, and the way its structure relates to preferences held. Ultimately, because in planning one must reflect on one's goals, it also increases awareness of oneself.

Awareness thus results from deliberations made during the process. It is improved as a result of feedback concerning the effects of actions on the environment. Overall, the result of engaging in rational planning is therefore learning, including self-learning, and hence an increase in the capacity to attain *future* growth.[7]

Lastly, the rational planning process is itself part of the *process* of growth, in line with that concept as outlined above. Following Diesing (1962), this process has been described as one of order being changed creatively into new order. However, this is precisely what the rational planning

---

[7]For instance, urban planners have learnt from the unintended consequences of urban renewal that a city does not only consist of houses, but that the people inhabiting them, together with these houses in their relative locations, constitute a "system". Similarly, as a result of deliberations following the publication of the Greater London Council's plan for a "motorway box" in and around London, planners, politicians and sections of the public have learnt that the problem of urban transport is inextricably linked with that of the distribution of life-chances amongst the inhabitants of a city. In both cases, the outcome is an enlarged concept of the end of planning but also of the nature of society, thus preparing the ground for action being taken with a view to further growth.

process does: it identifies a (future) order, together with the steps which must be taken to bring it about, based on knowledge concerning the present order of things. This order is constantly modified by newly received information.

In all this I see the rational planning process as analogous to another learning vehicle: *scientific method* meaning a set of procedural requirements which propositions must meet in order to pass as scientifically valid (Ackoff, 1962; Olsen, 1968). By imposing stringent requirements, scientific method forces the scientist to be explicit, to submit all his considerations to public scrutiny, thereby facilitating their testing. In doing so, science contributes to the solution of particular problems; it results in a general growth of knowledge; and, from a different standpoint, scientific pursuit may itself be regarded as another form which the process of growth takes.

HUMAN GROWTH AND META-PLANNING

There is a final gloss which one can put on this as it concerns planning theory. Since planning, like learning, is an information process, it is observable and, within limits, capable of manipulation and thus itself potentially the *object of planning*. Indeed, the basic idea underlying this book is that of providing a planning theory to guide this, what has been called meta-planning.

In one form or another, the authors quoted above have come to the conclusion that ways of going about decision-making may be improved on the basis of insights gained from consciousness. For instance, Diesing (1962) claims that, out of the five types of rationality which he identifies, *political* rationality concerned with "decision structures" (like planning agencies), is the most important:

> Negatively, a rational decision structure removes internal obstacles to decision, such as conflict, rigidity, and disproportionate influence. Positively, a decision structure so organizes a person's or group's perceptive, creative and communicative faculties as to enable him to reach effective decisions.

Deutsch (1966) and Buckley (1967) even provide models of "self-guiding systems" which incorporate highest-order feedback loops or consciousness. These models have their normative aspects. By identifying what a self-guiding system would be, they give a direction to the consciousness of any decision-maker. Finally, Etzioni (1968) links the same concern for increasing self-awareness of decision-makers with his belief in the potential of the social sciences for providing a firm basis for such awareness:

> As an intellectual process overlaying normative commitments, as a critical evaluator of existing social combinations, as an explorer of alternative combinations and their transformation, the social sciences are able to clarify basic commitments and to make them more realistic and, thus, more sustained.

The views of these authors converge with the concept of planning theory advanced. This convergence we may characterize as follows: the ultimate objective of planning theory is meta-planning. This must be based on the consciousness of planning agencies, that is on their awareness of their structure and procedures and their effects on planning, thereby taking cognizance of social-science findings. Meta-planning may thus be described as the most direct pursuit of human growth. Only where growth is based on consciousness is it truly deliberate. Therefore, the Promethean view of man as guiding his own growth may be interpreted as meaning man planning his own planning, thus underlining the importance of planning theory.

REFERENCES

ACKOFF, R. *et al.* (1962) *Scientific Method: Optimizing Applied Research Decisions,* John Wiley, New York.

AMOS, F. J. C. (1971) Presidential Address, *Journal of the Royal Town Planning Institute,* Vol. **57,** pp. 397–9.

*BANFIELD, E. C. (1959) Ends and means in planning, *International Social Science Journal,* Vol. **11,** pp. 361–8.

BEER, S. (1966) *Decision and Control,* John Wiley, New York.

BROADY, M. (1968) *Planning for People,* The Bedford Square Press, London.

BUCKLEY, W. (1967) *Sociology and Modern Systems Theory,* Englewood Cliffs, New Jersey.

CHADWICK, G. (1971) *A Systems View of Planning,* Pergamon, Oxford.

DAVIDOFF, P. and REINER, T. A. (1963) A reply to Dakin, *Journal of the American Institute of Planners,* Vol. **29,** pp. 27–8.

DAVIES, J. G. (1972) *The Evangelist Bureaucrat: A Study of a Planning Exercise in Newcastle upon Tyne,* Tavistock Publications, London.

DENNIS, N. (1958) The popularity of the neighbourhood community idea, *Sociological Review,* Vol. **6,** pp. 191–206.

DENNIS, N. (1970) *People and Planning,* Faber & Faber, London.

DEUTSCH, K. W. (1966) *The Nerves of Government—Models of Political Communication and Control,* 2nd ed. Macmillan, New York–London.

DIESING, P. (1962) *Reason in Society,* University of Illinois Press, Urbana.

DIMITRIOU, B. (1972) The interpretation of politics and planning, *The Systems View of Planning* (DIMITRIOU, B. *et al.*), Oxford Working Papers in Planning Education and Research, No. 9. Department of Town Planning, Oxford Polytechnic, Oxford.

*DYCKMAN, J. W. (1961) What makes planners plan? *Journal of the American Institute of Planners*, Vol. 27, pp. 164–7.

ETZIONI, A. (1968) *The Active Society*, Collier-Macmillan, London.

FRIEDMANN, J. (1969) Notes on societal action, *Journal of the American Institute of Planners*, Vol. 35, pp. 311–18.

*GLASS, R. (1959) The evaluation of planning: some sociological considerations, *International Social Science Journal*, Vol. 11, pp. 393–409.

GOULD, S. J. (1971) *The Rational Society* (August Comte Memorial Lecture) The Athlone Press, London.

*GRAUHAN, R. R. (1973) Notes on the structure of planning administration, *A Reader in Planning Theory* (edited by FALUDI, A.), Pergamon, Oxford.

GRAUHAN, R. R. and STRUDELT, W. (1971) Political rationality reconsidered, *Policy Sciences*, Vol. 2, pp. 249–70.

HUSSEY, D. E. (1971) *Introducing Corporate Planning*, Pergamon, Oxford.

KAHN, J. (1969) *Studies in Social Policy and Planning*, Russell Sage Foundation, New York.

KAPLAN, A. (1964) *The Conduct of Inquiry: Methodology for Behavioral Science*, Chandler, Scranton, Penn.

MARUYAMA, M. (1970) Cybernetics, *Planning Programming Budgeting* (edited by LYDEN, F. J. and MILLER, E. G.), 3rd ed. Markham Publishing Company, Chicago.

MCLOUGHLIN, J. B. (1969) *Urban and Regional Planning—A Systems Approach*, Faber & Faber, London.

MEADOWS, D. H. *et al.* (1972) *Limits to Growth*, Earth Island, London.

MEDAWAR, P. B. (1967) Scientific method, *The Listener*, Vol. 78, pp. 453–6.

MEYERSON, M. and BANFIELD, E. C. (1955) *Politics, Planning and the Public Interest*, Free Press, Glencoe.

OLSEN, M. E. (1968) *The Process of Social Organization*, Holt, Rinehart & Winston, London.

POPPER, K. (1961) *The Poverty of Historicism*, Routledge & Kegan Paul, London.

QUADE, E. S. (1968) Introduction, *Systems Analysis and Policy Planning* (edited by QUADE, E. S. and BOUCHER, W. I.), Elsevier, New York.

ROBINSON, I. M. (1972) Introduction, *Decision-making in Urban Planning* (edited by ROBINSON, I. M.), Sage Publications, Beverly-Hills-London.

YOUNG, J. Z. (1971) *An Introduction to the Study of Man*, Clarendon Press, Oxford.

*Included in FALUDI, A. (1973) *A Reader in Planning Theory*, Pergamon, Oxford.

CHAPTER 4

A Model of Planning Agencies

THIS chapter and the next develop the rationale of planning theory described in Chapter 3 by specifying, firstly, the components of agencies capable of engaging in planning, and then their relations to each other. These make the model of planning agencies. The next chapter will deal with the operations of planning agencies.

The claims made for this framework are: it explains planning phenomena by showing how they form part of a coherent whole; it creates a language in which to converse about planning; it is capable of being turned into testable propositions (as will be demonstrated in Part III); it forms the basis for ideal views about planning agencies and their procedures (as discussed in Part IV).

Basic to the framework is an analogy between planning agencies and an intelligent person contemplating and implementing change which affects his environment. I shall therefore develop step by step a model of the human mind as a *learning system*. This will form the basis of the model of planning agencies.

THE ANALOGY WITH THE HUMAN MIND

To be more precise, the model of planning agencies is based on an analogy between planning agencies and the *human mind* engaged in *operational (purposive) thinking*. My first reason for proposing this particular analogy is that we hold normative views of how an intelligent mind operates. The second is that much thought in the field of cybernetics has gone into building models of the human mind. I am therefore able to draw on shared ideals and on carefully constructed models explaining the operation of the human mind.

Of two possible objections to this parallel the first is that it simplifies reality, but this is precisely what all models do of necessity. The second objection is that to build models of the structure of planning agencies is futile because what really matters is the quality of the individuals who hold positions in that structure. This goes to the very heart of the type of planning theory concerned with the structure and the processes of planning agencies, and I shall take care to demonstrate that structure does matter.

An Intelligent Mind as a Normative Model

My first reason for putting forward an analogy between planning and an individual pursuing his ends is that most people hold views about how an intelligent mind would do this, and thus share normative ideas as well as commonsense notions of one agent pursuing human growth.

Let me specify what I mean by an intelligent mind engaging in operational thinking. In my view a person with such a mind:

—operates on the environment, drawing resources from it and transforming it. This does not necessarily mean exercising complete control, but does include the possibility of adaptation both to factors existing in the present, as well as to those which, unless taken account of, would affect the future. Thus, an intelligent person does not deplete his resources but uses them with careful foresight.

—operates consciously, that is he is aware of his own thoughts, commitments, the impact of his actions, and their interrelations. From this awareness he draws strength by including the changing of himself into the range of available options, and thus increasing his chances of growth.

—is aware also of his limitations, and in particular of the number of options which he can explore and evaluate. On the basis of this awareness, he devises strategies for coping with such limitations by directing his own thought processes to areas where they may achieve the best results, thus increasing his compound chances of attaining his ends.

—knows when to break off any process of search in favour of action which can invoke his facility of will by accepting the risks of proceeding on insufficient information. He thus strikes a balance between his longing for security and the desire to act out his commitments.

One may summarize this view by saying that it describes a person *whose knowledge, including his self-knowledge, and whose commitments result in action aimed at deriving the resources and the impetus for his growth from transforming his environment and/or himself.*

The analogy proposed is the more plausible, the more this ideal of an intelligent mind has actually been used in the past, albeit implicitly, whenever planners have formed planning agencies and devised procedures. As claimed in Chapter 3, planning has always been associated with the idea of intelligent action. In creating its preconditions in the way of organizational structure and procedures, planners make use of the model of intelligent action available to them. This is given by the way they perceive their own mind operating. To propose the following model of planning agencies only means to add sophistication to a concept of planning that is already built into its existing institutions.

Cybernetic Models of the Human Mind

The second reason for proposing the analogy is that a great amount of thinking in the field of cybernetics has gone into the exploration of the human mind, and thus models of it are available to explain, by way of analogy, how planning operates. There are, indeed, more sophisticated models in this field than I shall use, models which aim at simulating human thinking using computers (George, 1970; Stachowiak, 1969). Their application to planning opens a field for exploration which is far wider than the scope of the present book.

Cybernetics is the study of guidance and control. Since both planning and operational thinking are about the exercise of some kind of control, the relevance of cybernetics is really obvious. Originating from the fusion of concepts of biology and mathematics and their application in military technology during World War II, the message of cybernetics has now entered many disciplines. In a nutshell, this message is that very small amounts of energy in the form of information-flows guide the expenditure of substantially larger amounts by processes which have a physical basis and can thus be measured, analyzed and manipulated. The study of these information flows, cyberneticians claim, shows they follow similar patterns in individual organs, human beings, and simple social organizations, as well as in vast socio-technical systems. Since cybernetic thinking is being applied to such a range of apparently quite diverse phenomena, the use of its models to explain planning is hardly extravagant. On the contrary, it is very much in line with the intentions of this discipline.

The model which I shall choose below in explaining planning is that of a learning system incorporating higher-order feedback loops belonging to the family of controlled-feedback systems. A learning system is itself an elaboration of a simple feedback system. Some of its basic principles are best explained by using as an example a simple mechanical device such as the thermostat. From this we shall proceed to a more complex model of learning systems capable of adapting their ends as a result of new information. Much work has been done on these, because they resemble human thinking more closely than does a simple feedback system. In particular, the model of learning systems incorporates something vital for the exploration of human action: a memory. This memory contains something which is essential to any purposive operation including planning which I shall describe as the technology-image.

To make the model even more representative of human beings, as against animals or machines (which may also exhibit learning), the memory must be thought of as incorporating a reflective image of the person's own self. This enables him to change not only his ends, but also his own organization as a result of information received about the effects of various strategies on their attainment. The reason why this higher-order feedback based on a self-image is important for representing human beings, and subsequently also organizations like planning agencies, is of course that, drawing on notions as developed earlier following Deutsch (1966), Buckley (1967) and Etzioni (1968), such a feedback loop signifies the existence of the essentially human element of *consciousness*.

Models as Simplifications

Planning agencies are organizations with several individuals occupying their various positions. The obvious objection which one might raise against drawing an analogy between planning and individual thinking is therefore that it is a simplification. Planning agencies are indeed more complex than individual decision-makers to the extent that they ". . . are internally more differentiated, they can make use of larger amounts of knowledge and more sophisticated decision-making technology, and their process of decision-making is more institutionalized and organized" (Etzioni, 1968).

However, to describe something always means to simplify it, and models are no exception to this rule. Their advantage is that they are specific in the way in which they simplify. In my analogy I say precisely the following and no more: that planning agencies have components serving the same purposes as the components of the human mind engaged in operational thinking, and that the information processes occurring in a planning agency show patterns similar to those of operational thinking. There is no further claim involved. I do not claim that a planning agency relies on "eyes", on a "brain" or on "nerves". Nor do I claim that it has no other aspect but that described. Indeed, there are many facets of a planning agency: cliques of friends filling some of its positions; a sports club providing an arena for much informal contact; grades according to which positions are classified, and so forth. But, in drawing my analogy, none of these will come into play unless it has relevance to how a planning agency achieves its ends.[1]

Selecting particular aspects of reality for the purpose of constructing models is perfectly admissible. The ensuing simplification is a cost to be borne in exchange for the understanding which a model affords. To select obviously means to choose one alternative in preference to others. This choice has some voluntaristic element to it. Therefore, one cannot argue that the choice of one aspect of reality rather than another as the basis of building a model is wrong. Nor, for that matter, can such a choice ever be described as scientifically valid: to some extent its basis is always intuitive. The criterion to be applied is the usefulness of the models based on it: "Whether a model is right or wrong, true or false, is largely a matter of agreement; as long as two persons or more agree upon a model, they may draw interesting and useful conclusions from its development . . ." (Kreweras, 1966).

The second answer to the charge of simplification is that the distinction between planning and individual thinking which has been drawn, for instance, by Etzioni, is a matter of *degree*. Looking at it from a different angle, one can say that individuals are *similar* to planning agencies in that they too are differentiated, use certain amounts of knowledge, have a

[1] Furthermore, people with a different interest may develop a different model and use it for different purposes, just as there are at least two different models for explaining the phenomenon of light (Bross, 1953).

decision-making technology, and are organized, *only less so*. It is therefore possible to draw comparisons between the two. The charge of simplification could only be sustained if the critics either showed awareness of the inescapable need to simplify, that is if they indicated precisely a degree of tolerable simplification, or if they argued that planning and individual thinking were entirely different so that no useful analogy between them could be drawn. The latter view would run counter to current thinking on the logical structure of planning being the same whether the actor is a person or an organization (Meyerson and Banfield, 1955; Banfield, 1959; Dror, 1963; Rieger, 1967; Bolan, 1969).

Organizational versus Individual Factors in Planning

The claim is often made that, ultimately, what matters is the quality of the individual members of an agency rather than its organizational structure. People find it particularly difficult to see how agencies can perform *creative* tasks and argue that *decisions* must always be taken by individuals who are alone capable of shouldering the *responsibility* for what they do (Minett, 1971). Amos (1972) once made himself into their spokesman saying in relation to local government reform that ". . . the real success of reorganization does not depend so much upon the structures and processes which are adopted as the attitude of those who work in the authorities . . .".

I do not underestimate the importance of having well-trained and innovative minds in the planning situation. But to say that only individuals can make decisions is, at best, a truism. Emphasizing that the *locus* of decision-making is in the individual (which is deceptively obvious since individuals are at the nodal points of planning agencies) distracts from what should be of the foremost interest: the influences upon decisions. To a very considerable extent these do not come from *within* the individual but from *without* him, that is from the ". . . configuration of the communication channels and decision points in the political and social system in which they occur . . ." (Deutsch, 1966). When one is talking about agencies (metaphorically speaking) thinking, learning, being creative, and making decisions, one is therefore talking about the preconditions which the "configuration of channels and decision points" in agencies must fulfil before individuals filling their positions can take meaningful decisions. To divorce this influence which organizations have from that of individuals is therefore unjustifiable.

In a certain sense, organizations are even superior to individuals in decision-making. As mentioned before, they command a better decision-making technology and larger resources than individuals do. Their importance becomes evident when positions are filled by individuals who, in normal circumstances, would not be eligible. Armies, for instance, incur heavy costs in training officers. However, in combat, sometimes non-commissioned officers and privates must take decisions. Individuals may change, but agencies remain to some extent the same for as long as their structure remains unchanged. They may even exchange all their members and still carry on in much the same way. Therefore, the performance of agencies does not only depend on individuals, but also on the twin factors of their structure and the processes within them. Thus, agencies have an organizational existence which justifies referring to them as if they were individuals.

THE HUMAN MIND AS A LEARNING SYSTEM

At its very simplest, to exercise control over the environment means to maintain a steady state. Examples of this are steering a car along a straight road or maintaining water at a certain temperature. Indeed, the thermostat, which is the instrument performing the latter function, is quoted as an example of a "cybernetic" or "controlled feedback" system (Kuhn, 1966).

Because many of the processes in it aim at maintaining some variable in a steady state, a model of the human mind incorporates features of such a system. We shall now consider the components of a controlled feedback system, but human beings are more versatile. They can not only maintain steady states but also decide to aim for different ones involving changing ends. This is what is termed learning, and a system capable of changing its ends is a learning system incorporating, as it does, a memory, as well as a feedback system.

The components of a controlled feedback system are the *receptor* gauging the existing state of the environment and the effect of actions on it (feedback); the *selector* choosing between alternative responses on the basis of information received from the detector; and the *effector* producing changes in the environment on the basis of instructions from the selector

(Kuhn, 1966). The process which goes on inside such a thermostat is called *negative feedback* (Fig. 4.1): information concerning the effects of actions (for instance an increase in temperature beyond that required) is relayed back into the device and effects some change in the opposite direction.

As in all information, some small amount of energy must be spent on this process. In the case of the thermostat some minute proportion of the heat is diverted to expand a piece of metal which in turn closes an electric circuit and effects a change: the heater is switched off. Another example is

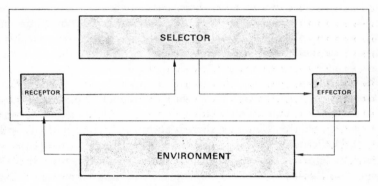

FIG. 4.1. A controlled feedback system

that of target shooting. One has to contend with the effects of factors which are, initially at least, unknown, such as imprecisions of the rifle. Therefore, it is common practice to indicate to the rifleman after each of a number of trials where the shot went. This enables him to counter the effects of these factors by aiming at an imaginary bull's eye which is the same distance from the target as his first shot but in the opposite direction. The rifleman, the rifle and the helper who indicates the amount of deviance constitute another example of a controlled feedback system.

The process which I have described is a lower-order feedback process with a fixed goal. The greater part of processes going on in the human mind as well as in planning agencies involves changing ends as a result of new information. The thermostat on its own does not exhibit this *learning*.

Learning requires an agent who resets the thermostat overnight with his latest electricity bill in mind.

The point about a learning system—the thermostat regulating the temperature of my room in combination with my regulating the thermostat with an eye to expense—is that it shows a "much higher average survival potential in the face of a changing or complex environment . . ." than ordinary feedback systems do (Kuhn, 1966). The thermostat would continue to maintain the temperature in my room at the level at which I set it for ever, or until the heat supply is switched off. It has no sensitivity for my overdraft but, clearly, its potential for survival is impaired by the possibility of the electricity supply being cut off (when my cheque bounces) in which case the thermostat would "die". Resetting the temperature not only saves me money and the embarrassment of my being in the red; it also "saves" the thermostat. The thermostat and I, taken together, constitute a good system for keeping me tolerably warm and both of us in business.

Learning is the basis for adaptation and growth in all living organisms. The principles of learning are always the same, though its mechanisms may differ. There are always links between the environment and the learning system via a *receptor*. Similarly, there is always an *effector*, much as in the case of the thermostat. Finally every learning device has a *selector* choosing between alternative responses. The difference is that, this time, the ends themselves are subject to change, as explained in the examples above. The mechanism which achieves this feat is a device for the preservation of useful information, that is a *memory* (Fig. 4.2). It enables the evaluation of alternative preferences against some higher criterion which is what learning entails. It is that part of the brain which "forms representations of the world and uses them for forecasting" (Young, 1971). Planning (meaning the formulation of a programme of action) always involves forecasting that the proposed steps will result in desired effects (Miller *et al.*, 1960). Representations of the world, and the forecasts based thereon, I shall describe as images and programmes, referring to both summarily as the technology-image.

THE TECHNOLOGY-IMAGE

To be more precise, the technology-image has three components: *images*, *programmes* and *goals*. Whenever any person engages in action, all these components of the technology-image come into play.

In the previous example of setting a thermostat, one end changed when weighed against another, higher-order end. In searching for a precise explanation of how this is done, one finds at least two distinct aspects to this process: an idea about the effects on higher-order ends resulting from certain decisions; and an idea of which action to take and in which sequence to remedy undesirable effects or to achieve those which are desirable. The first represents a *passive* element of human knowledge, passivity being expressed by calling it an *image* using a term coined by Boulding (1956) and applied by Miller *et al.* (1960) in their exploration of human thinking. The second represents its *active* element. Miller and his colleagues describe

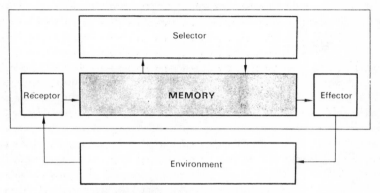

FIG. 4.2. A learning system featuring a memory

it as a plan, but since plan may also be taken to mean an image of the environment as it would be *after* action has been taken, I think it is more precise to refer to it as a *programme*.

Image and programme relate knowledge to the ends pursued by the actor. Together with these *goals*, they form a technology, that is a system for the purposive use of knowledge. I shall therefore describe goals, images and programmes as the *technology-image*. A term introduced by Rieger (1967), the technology-image simply describes everything which is involved when a learning system operates on the environment drawing on memory of past experience (Fig. 4.3). For instance, when driving a car and when approaching a bend, the driver of a car turns the wheel because he holds a technology-image containing the goal of accident-free driving; an image of the position of the steering wheel and the car as connected; a further image of the position of the car which is most likely to avoid accidents; a programme saying that turning the wheel to one side makes the car move into that direction. The learning system which I form with my thermostat can also be interpreted by reference to goals, images and programmes held by my memory. The image is one of causal relationship between the high temperature which is maintained in my room through the use of a thermostat and the likelihood of my bank account going into the red because of an

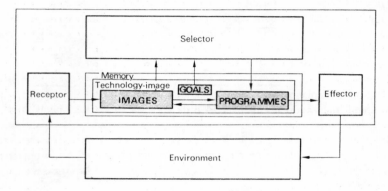

Fig. 4.3. The technology-image and the memory

excessive heating bill. This image I may transform into a programme of setting the thermostat at a lower temperature. I may reset it forthwith (a very simple programme) or wait until later tonight, shortly before I go to bed and can tolerate a lower temperature. The latter is a more complicated programme which involves remembering at a later point in time what one has decided. Heating engineers have recognized this and there is a timing device attached to my thermostat which enables me to programme it now, whilst I think about it. Similarly, in addition to knowing in which direction to turn the wheel one must also know when to turn it, and at what speed. Indeed, this is of the essence of the art of steering a car. A time-phased set of intentions relating to the kind, intensity, and timing of future actions aimed at achieving a set of goals, the programme is always based on an image of the part of the environment which the learning system acts upon.

IMAGES AND HUMAN KNOWLEDGE

Human beings hold many images, each somehow related to something outside them. Their total image consists of a set of partial images which are in some way organized. By implication, this total image is also somehow related to the environment and any knowledge concerning the environment is strictly limited to it.

This has consequences for the concept of what one calls objective knowledge. To explain this point, we must look at how images are formed. They are obviously formed by scanning the environment. Psychologists call what one receives from the environment sense-data. But the human eye does not perceive infrared and the ear cuts out ultra-sound, and even those data which one actually receives are too many to assimilate.[2] Therefore, selection takes place which is performed on the basis of previous experience, that is of images already formed, and of conscious choices. This is where goals come into play: in seeking ways to reduce spending, I develop an image of domestic heating which costs an excessive amount. The bill to which I paid scant attention this morning suddenly becomes important. From being a piece of unnoticed data, it is elevated to the status of meaningful information.

To be precise, this is not literally true and this is where the distinction between an active and a general memory comes in. One cannot recall sense-data which one has not noticed. Because of past experience, some part of the memory does register bank statements and other warning signs, and files them into a part of the memory which one may call the general memory which adds to, or changes, one's general image of the world. Similarly, one clearly holds general ideas about how to change the environment, again based on past experience. The general memory contains files full of programmes with wide applicability. It also contains goals, only part of which are relevant to any one problem. In action, some of the images held by the general memory are activated and lead to programmes relevant to the particular problem on hand.

[2]On the limitations of short-term memory see Chapter 6.

Now if goals have the importance for the formation of images described earlier, then any knowledge concerning reality can depend only partly on what that reality is, and partly on these goals. Everybody has, in the true sense of the word, blinkers or, better still, filters built into his perceptual apparatus. These are coloured by the purposes which he has in mind. For instance, the camel, to me, is an animal of less than vital interest. I have, on occasions, been inquisitive enough to find out about it, and with some effort could describe a few dozen or more of its special characteristics. But the Arabic language is said to contain 6000 words relating to the camel, obviously because it is of much greater interest to nomadic desert people than it is to me. (You will have to solve the problem of which of the two images of the camel, that embodied in the Arabic language or mine, is the more "objective" one!)

What holds true of images of the camel applies to all knowledge, namely that it reflects people's interests in manipulating that part of the environment from which the image comes. Objective knowledge which reflects exclusively what is does not exist.[3] Since "all knowledge [that is every image—A.F.] comes through the brain" (Young, 1971), it must be subject to its limitations. Two filters which sieve information before it is incorporated into an image represent these limitations. One of these comes before the receptor. It represents choices concerning the direction of any search for information. The other filter comes after the receptor. It represents the selectivity with which messages are transmitted from the receptor to the technology-image. Both these filters are "set" by the technology-image in turn, in particular its images and, even more important, the goals built into it (Fig. 4.4).

SHORT-CIRCUITING THE HUMAN MIND

The very simple model of learning systems in Fig. 4.2 has been refined considerably. The new model (Fig. 4.4) differentiates between a general and an active memory, with a technology-image consisting of goals, images and programmes. There are filters blocking the way between environment and receptor, and between receptor and memory which are set by the goals of the learning system.

[3]Which does not mean to say that people have not tried to achieve something approaching objective knowledge. Science is about how to do this, that is about how to draw valid inferences.

This section introduces a further refinement to the model. This is a short-circuit between the receptor and the effector which comes into operation whenever a person responds automatically. Keeping one's balance on a bicycle, greeting friends in the street, turning round when one's name is called, are examples. This will lead to introducing *automatic programmes* into the model, that is programmes which are not based on conscious images.

"Automatic" behaviour is what everyday language calls our "instincts", a definition not too far off the mark, though it is in the study of animal

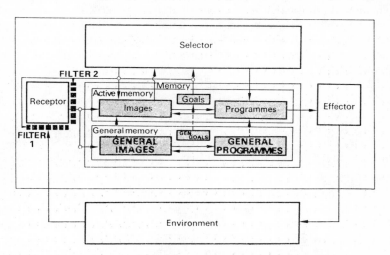

Fig. 4.4. Active and general memory and filters

behaviour that the concept of an instinct finds its proper use. One does many things *as if* guided by instinct, that is without making deliberate decisions.

Because all of us have some experience of these, it is easiest to explain automatic behaviour by talking about the way in which one acquires certain mundane skills like learning how to ride a bicycle, how to use Morse-code, how to drive a car, or how to type. Adults begin by receiving verbal instruction. Children tend to imitate what they see. In any case, the real learning process starts in *practising* the skill. Initially, one tries to follow verbal instructions, usually with little success. As time goes by, increasingly large blocks of behaviour begin to follow each other in an almost natural way. Teaching programmes for typing recognize this process by presenting the same groups of letters and words, and later the same sentences to the student who types them over and over again until he can do them almost without thinking (Miller *et al.*, 1960; Argyle, 1967). Once one has arrived at this stage some programmes which are contained in the memory can be activated with neither images and goals (the other components of the memory) nor the selector becoming involved any more. The flow of information is short-circuited from the receptor to the effector (Fig. 4.5). Where it occurs, such short-circuiting of the human mind greatly increases the speed with which reactions to clues coming from the environment are made. It also frees information-handling capacity for other, non-routine tasks.

SELF-IMAGES

To complete our description of the concept, an image must embrace an element of self-awareness. This reflective part of images makes for versatility in human beings: man alone can change himself (not just his immedi-

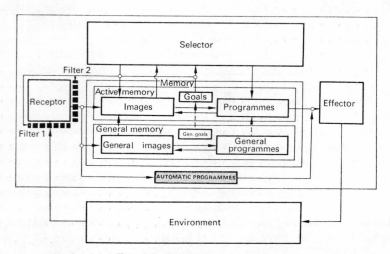

FIG. 4.5. Automatic programmes

ate aims as animals and learning machines do) on the basis of insights into the effects of his actions on his environment and, *via* that effect, on his goals. Including the self-image therefore turns the model into one that represents genuinely human behaviour.[4]

There are many ways in which a self-image is formed. People learn about themselves when they try to master difficult tasks—sailing across the Atlantic or climbing mountains. But, normally, interacting with the social environment provides more opportunity for reflection which is basic to the self-image. The simplest way to explain the rôle of self-images in coming to terms with the social environment is to consider the interaction between two human beings. Here, each of the two forms the (social) environment for the other.[5] Each has certain goals, and programmes for getting the other person to work towards them (Argyle, 1967). The self-image is formed during this process when each makes inferences about the way in which the other perceives him. From the other's reaction each forms an image about what he believes the image held of him by the other to be and adapts his programme so as to control his image. For example, you tone down your voice if you see the other person step back from it.

Experiences of this kind build up to the self-image. This self-image is relatively more stable than most of the other images, because one tests it over and over again by direct feedback from others, and compares it with impressions which other people make. Rôles which have been played in the past are another source for the formation of the self-image. All this information builds up to a view of the self which is central to the way in which a person perceives the environment. The more distinct, consistent and integrated it is, the more mature one says a personality is.

Self-images are subject to change, as all other images are, though, because of their importance, they are protected by more elaborate defences. Sometimes, a conversation about oneself is overheard which is very revealing; occasionally direct feedback from contemporaries brings about a change of the self-image. Comparison with others, or new rôles (say, after a promotion), may also achieve this change. Such change need not necessarily be painful. One can even learn to cast a different image. Quite

---

[4]On the importance of self-consciousness as distinguishing anthropomorphic models of man from others, see Harré (1971).

[5]Looked upon differently the two form a "system" which social psychologists call a dyad.

frequently this is all that is required in changing from one rôle to another. Certain professional rôles demand a superior, confident, inquisitive or smooth *persona*. Training for these rôles includes imparting of skills to make precisely the required impression (Argyle, 1967). However, more is involved than mere rôle-playing. These images have a tendency to reflect back on self-images, so that school masters behave exactly like school masters should, even out of school.

Figure 4.6 shows the addition of the self-image to the model of learning systems. A small example will help in understanding the diagram. This

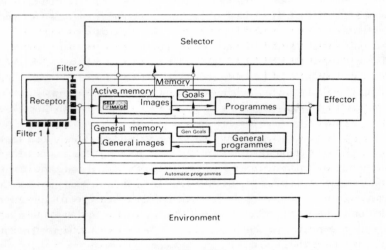

FIG. 4.6. The self-image

again concerns the meeting of two people, one talking to the other. The pitch of his voice and the speed with which the first talks are governed by his programmes for talking which he has chosen on the basis of his image of the situation in which he and his partner are: distance between them, size of the room, noise-level and hearing capacity of the other. The image of the situation thus provides the envelope of the self-image as depicted in the diagram.

Representing as it does a person's consciousness, the self-image is central to our notion of a mature person as one who is really master of himself. In addition to the possessing of a clear self-image, this means the ability to change it where necessary. During this process, the self not only adapts but also differentiates, it becomes more subtle and grows. Something of this is inevitably involved in the process of reaching biological maturity. But some minds continue to grow, rather as I hope mankind will continue to grow, by continuously changing its self-image. This is why I think this ideal of an intelligent person with a mind which grows throughout his life is a useful model on which to draw in conceptualizing planning.

CONSTRAINTS AND UNCERTAINTY IN THE ENVIRONMENT

I now introduce another refinement to the model to show why differentiation and growth are desirable. The environment is full of surprises, more than anybody could ever hope to anticipate. Diversification of images, including the self-images, resulting from growth, increases the number of alternative responses available to meet this variety of challenges from the environment.

To explain this, one must consider the environment in a new light. Thus far, I have treated it in a very passive manner, as if it were completely controlled by the actions of the subject whom the model represents. To be more exact, we have considered only those aspects of the environment which are controlled (the temperature of a room in the thermostat example). From now on, I shall refer to these as the *control variables* and distinguish them from those variables which one can *not* control.

For many purposes, it is sufficient to equate the environment with the control variables. This is particularly true where such variables can be separated easily from all the other variables in the environment. Normally, one disregards humidity in regulating temperature. Only when we question why the room should be warm, does humidity enter the situation, because real comfort depends both on temperature and humidity. Restricting our considerations to the thermostat and the temperature, what one calls the closure of the system (Kuhn, 1966) now appears to be artificial, which is precisely what *any* closed system is. It is still useful to employ such artificial constructs, but one should recognize that they are the results of limitations, both of the faculties of understanding all relevant variables (the image) and of the ability to control them (the programme). I may, for instance, be unable to afford full climatization in my home and must accept that a thermostat attached to a heater is all that my money can buy.

I shall modify the model in such a way that it will take account of the fact that the environment is neither totally controlled nor completely predictable in its reactions. This is very generally true, but again it is easier to explain the fact when talking about the social rather than the physical environment. In the example of my talking to another person, I have assumed that he will listen. But he may have only limited time or little sympathy with what he hears. To some extent, I am able to predict this and to contend both with the limitations of time and with his antipathy. I can treat them as *constraints* limiting what I say, and how much time I spend in saying it. Beyond this, there are always factors which I am not aware of, simply because the reactions of people are sometimes unpredictable. My partner may have had a bad night, a stroke of luck, or be suffering from toothache. These factors make for some *unknown variables* which introduce an element of uncertainty into our meeting.

Figure 4.7 reflects these considerations by showing two arrows representing constraints and unknown variables in addition to the control

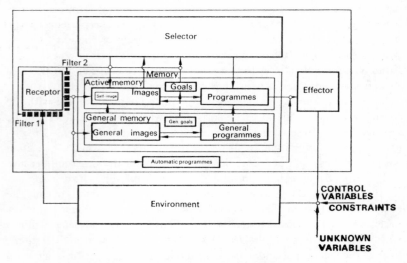

FIG. 4.7. Control variables, constraints and unknown variables

variables. The relative importance of these, as against the control variables, influences the way one operates. Thus, where the control variables are dominant, the subject is in command; where the constraints dominate, the subject merely adapts; where the unknown variables dominate, the subject drifts, waiting for the first clues from the environment, so that he can form an image of the situation. Clearly, any real-life situation is a mixture of all these, and, consequently, the subject's reaction to it will also be a mixture of control over the environment, adaptation to it, and search for more clues in his efforts to cope with uncertainties.

INTERNAL AND EXTERNAL TIME-LAG AND PREDICTION

Our last refinement concerns the introduction of a time-component into the model. There is a *time-lag* built into every process: it takes maybe a third of a second until one reacts to a new hazard on the road and puts the right foot down on the brake pedal. It usually takes the car even longer to stop because the brakes must transform its kinetic energy into thermic energy. The Highway Code therefore requires drivers to make allowance for both these time-lags by keeping a minimum distance from the next vehicle in front.

What I have just described is an example of what I term internal time-lag and external time-lag. Internal time-lag is the amount of time which it takes to act on information received from the environment. It is a feature of the internal make-up of the subject. External time-lag is the amount of time which it takes for his actions to take effect, that is the time which elapses between putting my foot down and the car coming to a halt. As any motorist knows, this depends on the quality of the car brakes combined with the road surface and weather conditions, that is, from my point of view, the environment.[6]

The implication of the existence of these time-lags is again profound. Changes may occur before actions have the desired effect. To counter this, one attempts to predict the state of the environment at the time when

---

[6]Properly speaking, the external time-lag incorporates another element which is the time which it takes for information concerning changes in the environment to reach my receptors. I am not really interested in changing the environment for its own sake, but in order to receive favourable information from it. Only when I receive information is the feedback cycle complete.

actions will come to fruition. For instance, when shooting at a moving target (say, clay pigeons) the rifleman does not aim at the *actual* position of the target, but at some imaginary point where he thinks the target will be at the time when the bullet crosses its path. Success depends on whether the rifleman aims properly *and* at the right point, that is on whether his prediction is correct.

In terms of the model, this means that the subject has two images in his memory: an image of the environment as it exists at the present (more precisely at the point in the past to which his information relates) and a hypothetical image of the state of the environment at some future point in time. This feat is achieved by mentally accelerating the development of known trends acting as constraints until that point at which the programme says that the controls might take effect. Figure 4.8 introduces this future image.

The example is a simplified one: I have only considered one variable: the path which the clay pigeon takes. This path is predictable only to a point: a sudden gust of wind may change it and the bullet will go astray. This is an example of unknown variables playing havoc with even the most reasonable prediction. Therefore, internal and external time-lags, predic-

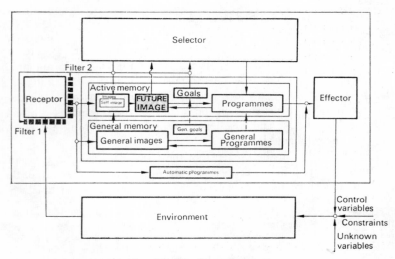

Fig. 4.8. The future image

tions and the operations of constraints and unknown variables in the environment are closely interdependent. Where, for instance, the time-lag is great, and the weight of unknown variables large, their predictions are unreliable. If I am interested in increasing their reliability, I may attempt to reduce the time-lag or to increase my knowledge of factors operating in the environment, whichever is the more feasible path to take. If, on the other hand, the importance of unknown variables is deemed to be small, then I can relax and let the time-lag increase to a degree where I do not even bother with searching for any feedback from the environment.[7]

The model of the human mind as a learning system is now complete. With variations, it has been used to represent the acquisition of motor and social skills (Argyle, 1967), the process of cognition (George, 1965, 1970), operational thinking (Stachowiak, 1969), complex defence systems (Stachowiak, 1969; Howland, 1966), and even political decision-making systems (Deutsch, 1966). It shows all the components of the model of planning agencies and is thus basic to the conceptual framework for planning thought which I present.

THE COMPONENTS OF THE MODEL

With the exception of the general memory which does not figure in the model of planning agencies (see below), the model is the same as shown in Fig. 4.8. All the components of a controlled feedback system like the thermostat are present: planning agencies, like a person, sometimes operate as if they were a thermostat with fixed preferences. In cases like this, automatic programmes are often used similar to those invoked by a person riding a bicycle. As in the latter case, these programmes are important in easing the planning load and in speeding up procedures.

But the more important cases are of course those where no such programmes are available. After all, the *raison d'être* of a planning agency is that it devises *new* programmes. As with an individual's mind this involves

---

[7]Consider a structural engineer designing a structure. He introduces safety factors of such a magnitude that there are very few things which could prove him wrong, even if they did not figure in the calculations. His control of the environment is so high that he can complete his calculations and, in routine cases, hand over to the builders because he *knows* that his prediction is safe. I shall return to this point in Chapter 7 on blueprint versus process planning.

drawing on past images held by the memory. It is as well, however, to note here two features of individual images which those held by planning agencies do not exhibit. The various images held by an individual are relatively well integrated into a total world outlook, and are also fairly well integrated with the goals which he holds. Stable and close-knit societies of the past provided their members with similar images, so that the discrepancy between one member's experiences and those of the community as a whole was not quite as dramatic as in modern society. The problems resulting from the fragmentation of modern society with its division of labour, and from the fracturing of the experiences of its individual members which this entails, are favourite concerns of social scientists from Durkheim's study on *The Division of Labour in Society* (1933) to the demands made by the German sociologist Habermas (1971) for re-instituting the public arena as a medium in which free citizens could come to an understanding of what society is about.

The problem is highly relevant to planning: where planning purports to proceed rationally, it claims to have selected the best course of action from all conceivable alternatives. This must mean that all the alternatives which could be constructed on the basis of the general image have been taken into account. Unfortunately, in contradistinction to a person, who is co-extensive with his total mind, no planning agency is co-extensive with the community it serves. Therefore, no single planning agency has access to the whole general image. On the other hand, planning agencies are subject to the same limitations as individuals are: their goals "set" two filters between their environment and their technology-image.

Three conclusions follow from this for planning and the model of planning agencies. One is that the notion of a general memory as held by individuals cannot be meaningfully transferred to the model of planning agencies. Though a planning agency has some access to the general image as held by the community (for the channels see Chapters 6, 13 and 14), it is therefore not shown as embracing that image, but only the active technology-image relevant to the particular purposes for which it has been set up.

The second conclusion is that, since the image on which any one planning agency can base its planning will always be more limited than the general image available to the community, its planning will by implication also be limited, in the sense of comprising fewer alternatives than could be devised in theory. Therefore, limitations of the technology-image, though variable, always constitute a constraint on planning, a factor which becomes important in a discussion of the rational-comprehensive versus the disjointed-incrementalist mode of planning in Part III.

Finally, whilst no one planning agency can hold an image which matches the general image as held by a community, a group of agencies may command a fair proportion of its content. The problem is, how can they be related to each other, and thus reduce their limitations? But relating technology-images is what happens when planning agencies form multiplanning agencies, and, thus, forming these may be one solution.

This one alteration concerning the general technology-image apart, the model remains unchanged: the self-image is an important element of a planning agency; indeed, the importance of planning theory for forming that self-image was emphasized before. Similarly, all the considerations concerning constraints and unknown variables operating in the environment, as well as time-lags, apply.

Figure 4.9 shows the model of planning agencies. Though the components of the model refer to, in the first instance, functions rather than parts (Kuhn, 1966), there is nevertheless some degree of correspondence between the two. For illustration, the components are renamed to make the model descriptive of a British Local Planning Authority. Thus, the receptor is now called the *survey unit*. In most cases, this will form part of the research section or, indeed, be identical with the research section which is, of course, an unduly narrow concept. Research must also be conducted into all the aspects of the technology-image. Nevertheless, many research sections nowadays seem to restrict their activities to collecting and sifting information for other sections.

Broadly speaking, the *development plan section* producing statutory development plans and programmes represents the technology-image. It draws on information from surveys, on its own memory, and on the guidelines received from the selector. Most important, it draws on its goals, which are built into it. These are the purposes for which the planning agency has been set up, and the rules underlying its very existence.

The selector may be identified with, in the case of public authorities, the legislature or with one of its committees. This body, most of the time, selects from amongst alternatives presented to it by the development plan section. Thus, it is the *decision-taker*, but it is only one of the participants in the process of decision-making (Friend and Jessop, 1969). Decision-taking does involve the specification of objectives, but only rarely are any of the goals modified. In view of the confusion about goal-setting, this is an important point and one which will be developed.

The effector is that part of a planning authority manipulating the control variables. There may be a special *development control section* administering planning permissions based on the development plan. Implementation may also involve the erection of physical plant or have other direct

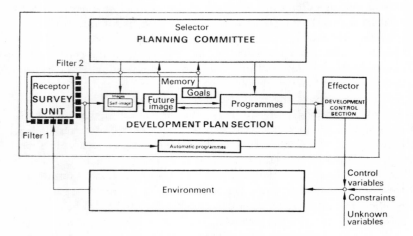

Fig. 4.9. The model of planning agencies as applied to Local Planning Authorities

effects upon the environment. In all these cases, implementation involves the application of power, be it the legal power conferred upon a planning authority, or its economic power as the financier of development. This is where the cybernetic process of planning comes to fruition, where the small amount of energy spent in producing a programme controls the application of large amounts of resources in moving physical structures as well as people, conferring benefits upon them or incurring costs, as the case may be. The control variables are all those effects which a planning agency may achieve by drawing on its resources: the power to control what is legally defined as development, compulsory purchase power, the power to give grants, the power to spend the ratepayers' money and others.

Evidently, the environment is influenced not only by the planning agency, but also by other forces operating independently. The environment contains many subjects with purposes and resources of their own, some predictable, others not, thus making for constraints and unknown variables.

Time-lag also becomes a factor. Many of the statutory obligations of a planning agency must be discharged within a specified period, because planning agencies show a tendency towards long internal time-lags. Planning is a complex business, and offices are notoriously understaffed, so that time-lag constitutes one important constraint.

This is then the model of planning agencies on which this book is based. Before it is put to use, first of all in working *Towards a Positive Theory of Planning* in Part III, I shall describe the operations of planning agencies.

REFERENCES

AMOS, F. J. C. (1972) Management of new local authorities: problems and opportunities, *Journal of the Royal Town Planning Institute*, Vol. 58, pp. 341–3.
ARGYLE, M. (1967) *The Psychology of Interpersonal Behaviour*, Penguin, Harmondsworth.
*BANFIELD, E. C. (1959) Ends and means in planning, *International Social Science Journal*, Vol. 11, pp. 361–8.
*BOLAN, R. (1969) Community decision behavior: the culture of planning, *Journal of the American Institute of Planners*, Vol. 35, pp. 301–10.
BOULDING, K. (1956) *The Image*, The University of Michigan Press, Ann Arbor.
BROSS, I. D. (1953) *Design for Decision*, Macmillan, London.
BUCKLEY, W. (1967) *Sociology and Modern Systems Theory*, Prentice-Hall, Englewood Cliffs, N.J.
DEUTSCH, K. W. (1966) *The Nerves of Government—Models of Political Communication and Control*, 2nd ed. Macmillan, New York–London.
*DROR, Y. (1963) The planning process: a facet design, *International Review of Administrative Sciences*, Vol. 29, pp. 46–58.
DURKHEIM, E. (1933) *The Division of Labour in Society*, Free Press, Glencoe.
ETZIONI, A. (1968) *The Active Society*, Collier-Macmillan, London.
FRIEND, J. K. and JESSOP, W. N. (1969) *Local Government and Strategic Choice*, Tavistock Publications, London.
GEORGE, F. H. (1965) *Cybernetics and Biology*, Oliver & Boyd, Edinburgh and London.
GEORGE, F. H. (1970) *Models of Thinking*, Allen & Unwin, London.
HABERMAS, J. (1971) *Towards a Rational Society*, Heinemann, London.
HARRÉ, H. R. (1971) The ethogenic way, *New Society*, 8 April, pp. 581–3.

HOWLAND, D. (1966) A regulatory model for system design and operation, *Operational Research and the Social Sciences* (edited by LAWRENCE, J. R.), Tavistock, London.

KREWERAS, G. (1966) Closing remarks, *Operational Research and the Social Sciences* (edited by LAWRENCE, J. R.), Tavistock, London.

KUHN, A. (1966) *The Study of Society*, Tavistock, London.

MEYERSON, M., and BANFIELD, E. C. (1955) *Politics, Planning and the Public Interest*, Free Press, Glencoe.

MILLER, G. A., GALLANTER, E. and PRIBHAN, K. H. (1960) *Plans and the Structure of Behavior*, Holt, Rinehart & Winston, Inc., New York.

MINETT, M. J. (1971) Is planning a profession? *Journal of the Town Planning Institute*, Vol. 57, p. 231.

RIEGER, H. C. (1967) *Begriff und Logik der Planung*, Otto Harrassowitz, Wiesbaden.

STACHOWIAK, H. (1969) *Denken und Erkennen im kybernetischen Modell*, Springer, Wien–New York.

YOUNG, J. Z. (1971) *An Introduction to the Study of Man*, Clarendon Press, Oxford.

*Included in FALUDI, A. (1973) *A Reader in Planning Theory*, Pergamon, Oxford.

CHAPTER 5

The Operations of Planning Agencies

THIS chapter will demonstrate how the model of planning agencies operates. We shall consider it in the terms of a subject formulating a rational programme for action. The operations so described apply to both individual and organizational choice. They evolve around the rational planning process: the generation of alternative programmes, their evaluation, and the choice of the one scoring best against a set of desired ends.

Unfortunately, to anybody with experience in planning, this must seem very remote from what actually happens. Planning is a messy operation. It is difficult to visualize it as proceeding in such an orderly fashion. But then, the rational planning process does not necessarily describe the way planning is done. In Chapter 3, I said rather that it prescribes how choices may be justified, that is by reconstructing an argument that appears to have gone through the steps of a rational planning process. The analogy with an individual is again an illuminating one. A person wishing to present conclusions convincingly outlines rational considerations that might have led to them in an orderly fashion. He does not normally claim that this is the actual process he used, but only that others should agree with his conclusions because they appear to be derived from reasoned argument. There are even rules for agreement: the rules of inference used in the deductive model of explanation. The analogy between the human mind and a planning agency may be extended to an analogy between these rules and the rational planning process. However, to reconstruct an argument is itself a process. In this respect the rational planning process corresponds to the deductive model of explanation, which is the final aim of the scientific enterprise but reflects back on all the stages of research.

Any criticism of this analogy between scientific method and the rational planning process is bound to focus on the nature of statements about the ends pursued in planning. In dealing with these objections, I shall try to be precise about different categories in which the ends of action may be described and, in so doing, will touch on the rôle of politics and planning.

In a first approximation, it is possible to identify three phases in the operations of a planning agency: the definition of the problem(s) to be solved; the formulation of a rational programme; implementation of that programme and feedback. The discussion follows this breakdown. The scheme does not indicate the links by which existing programmes may very well influence the initial definition of a problem. Also, the total process is certainly best seen as a continuous one (Fig. 5.1) consisting of round after round of problem definition, programme formulation and implementation, with refinements resulting from feedback on the effects of actions taken.[1] Since the process so described incorporates the facility for changing the ends of action, it represents a learning process. We shall see later that it is perfectly feasible to add a further feedback loop representing consciousness or the self-image.

WHAT IS A PROBLEM?

My definition of a problem crystallized during a debate which Barrie Needham and I conducted in the pages of the *Journal of the Royal Town Planning Institute*. This concerned, in the first instance, whether planning should be seen as "goal-seeking" or as "problem-solving" (Needham, 1971; Faludi, 1971). We resolved this part of our argument finding that there was no difference between these ways of describing planning.[2] We thereby accepted Chadwick's lucid formulation: Problem = Goal + Impediment to the Goal (Chadwick, 1971). This I translate into the definition of a problem as a *state of tension between the ends pursued by a subject and his image of the environment*. Such a statement implies that problems and goals are defined on the same level of specificity, a level which furthermore matches that of any empirical evidence held concerning

---

[1] This need not necessarily be the case, as I shall show in Chapter 7.
[2] This resolution occurred whilst we continued our debate privately. See also Faludi and Needham (1973).

"impediment to that goal". Sometimes a statement of a problem fulfilling these requirements can only be formulated after several rounds of analysis during which the end statement and the image of the environment are adapted to each other.

I take this argument as my starting point, adding the *caveat* that what we called a goal during that debate is not identical with the goal component of the technology-image as identified in the previous chapter. Because it aims to be a relatively specific statement, it is rather of the nature of an *objective*.

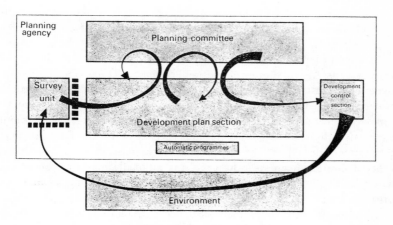

Fig. 5.1. Problem definition, programmeformulation, implementation and feedback

The definition of a problem as a state of tension has three advantages: it relates problems firmly to the *subject* experiencing them, thus dispelling any ideas that problems are like objective facts; it applies whether the subject is an *organization* or whether he is an *individual*; it diffuses the debate concerning whether planning deals with situations occurring in the *present*, or whether the dimension of the *future* plays a prominent part in planning.

Sometimes people question whether planning means to act upon the environment. They argue that planners merely react to what happens outside their sphere of influence. The definition of a problem as a state of tension allows one to accept both views. There may be changes in the environment which result in new impediments to the attainment of some end, or the definition of these ends itself may change, thus elevating some quite innocuous image to the status of highly relevant information. Whichever way, tension arises (and thus a problem exists) in the subject's *mind*, and it is only here that a problem may exist. The environment has no problems, a fact expressed succinctly by the American saying: "Houses have no problems, people have"!

This definition of a problem as a subjective state of tension applies to individuals as well as to organizations, and is consistent with the view expressed in the previous chapter that there is an analogy between individuals and planning agencies. Organizations exist for the attainment of certain ends. When they perceive impediments to their objectives, they experience tension much as individuals do. Indeed, such tension may be viewed as motivating both organizations and individuals to attempt to remove their sources, which is what problem-solving means.[3] A planning agency is simply an organizational unit specialized for the formulation of programmes designed to solve problems in the most effective way. Every organization trying to solve its problems rationally may thus be viewed as a planning agency and not just those described officially as planning organizations.

This definition of a problem also helps in tackling the question of whether planning should be dealing with the future. It is sometimes argued that enough problems already exist, and that one should attend to these rather than to an elusive concept of future problems. Conversely, people argue that planning is distinguished by its very future-orientation (Broady, 1972; Dimitriou, 1972). But all processes are embedded in time. The time dimension, however, is continuous. Remedying a problem inevitably means taking action based on a future image, as Figs. 4.7 and 4.8 show. Even where the future image is not different from the image held of the

---

[3]When psychologists talk about motivation or drive as underlying individual problem-solving, they often talk about tension; see Stachowiak (1969). For the application of this concept to organizations see Deutsch (1966).

environment as it exists at the present, that too amounts to a prediction of no change. To maintain that there is a useful distinction to be made between different types of planning along this dimension of time would thus require the distinction between planning for different time horizons, not between planning for the future and for the present. This, too, proves somewhat difficult. All images are four-dimensional, that is they incorporate a notion of how what they depict develops and perishes over time. But different images have different dynamic characteristics. Some are extremely volatile, and some develop very slowly. In some cases the future image is clear, in other cases it is fuzzy, and this has implications for programmes based on them. But all this depends on what the image represents and not on the time horizon *per se*. The usefulness of planning for any specific time horizon must therefore not be decided *a priori* but only after investigating the dynamic aspects of those images on which planning draws.

But even if one were to concede that the distinction made in common parlance between the present (that is the immediate future) and the future (the long-term future) was a meaningful one, future problems would still be felt in the same way as existing ones. The view that present problems are somehow more "real" is namely based on the assumption of problems existing *independently* of the subject. However, problems only exist at the interface between the ends pursued by a subject and the images he holds. As humans, we have the peculiar faculty of accelerating the time dimension of any of our images, thus forming future images. Indeed such future images are indispensable, even, as we have shown, for such a straight-forward "planning" task as shooting at clay pigeons. These future images, however, can be the source of tensions which are as real as those resulting from present conditions, as anyone who has ever suffered from the fear of anticipation might agree. Problems may therefore stem from anticipating conditions which will occur at any time in the foreseeable future, and there is nothing to distinguish between a future problem and any other.

If one regards a problem as a state of tension between a subject's ends and his images, then it follows that problems originate from changes to either. Little can be said about a subject changing his ends except that it is an *autonomous* process of man deciding on what he wishes the world to look like. But one can say something about the way images change to create problems.

P.T.—D

CHANGING IMAGES

If images are patterns of information, it is obvious that they can only change when *new* information becomes available. In this section, I distinguish between three different ways in which a message may change an image.

Any message received by a planning agency first passes through a filter representing its orientation towards particular aspects of its environment. It is then received by the receptor and passed on to the technplogy-image, thereby passing through a second filter representing the disposition of a planning agency to accept only certain types of messages even about those aspects of its environment with which it is concerned. These two filters are set by the goals and images held by the memory (Figs. 4.4–4.8).

In the technology-image box, the message comes up against the image which may be changed by the new message in three alternative ways:[4]

Radical change. A message may require abandoning an image, often a painful process. Images are related to goals, and become part of oneself. People are loath to change them. Evidence to the contrary notwithstanding, they pretend that their holiday is marvellous because of an idea developed throughout the year that this is how it should be. Similarly, scientists sometimes cling to their images. But, by and large, scientists and ordinary men, as well as planning agencies, do change their views drastically when bombarded with evidence which penetrates the defence perimeter around images. When ships returned from the east having sailed to the west, the image of the world as flat finally collapsed, learned arguments to the contrary notwithstanding.

Adaptation. In many cases, changes are less significant. During the course of time, people come to accept human weaknesses in their spouses without in all cases completely abandoning any favourable images which they hold of them. They make small adaptations to an initially somewhat unrealistic image by adapting, instead of abandoning, them. Images have an inertia, which is as well because one needs to retain some images in order to be able to act at all purposively.

[4]Rieger (1967), on whom I draw, distinguishes four ways, but he counts "no change" as one of them.

Addition. The message can add to the image. This happens when one explores some aspects of an image into depth. Sometimes, such an addition is a literal filling in of gaps, as when one walks down a road seen many times before, but never taken in, and thus experiences its visual qualities for the first time. The image of the road network does not change, but one of the images forming part of it becomes more specific.

Changes to images may bring about changes to future images. These occur when analysing new images for any laws and regularities which may allow one to predict by accelerating their time-dimension. It is these new future images that may cause tension and thus result in a problem. Problem definition is the process of a subject determining whether, and in which way, a future image causes a problem.

PROBLEM DEFINITION

It is simpler to start discussing problem definition with a new future image being perceived as an impediment to one or more of the subject's goals, though it should be remembered that the process could equally well start with the subject changing his ends (thus taking us beyond the behaviouristic assumption of man as merely reacting to his environment). When a future image is formulated, the selector comes into play, and must determine whether the image is in any way problematic. Now, the subject may already have dealt with a similar image before, and thus hold some views, or it may have to form new ones. As mentioned above, these views need to be formulated precisely so as to match the image, that is as operational objectives.

We shall consider objectives and how they derive from goals later. Suffice it to say now that objectives are *descriptive statements of a hypothetical but conceivable situation (or of any part of that situation) in which the tension resulting from impediments to one or more goals has disappeared.* Objectives thus provide a bridge between the way in which the subject perceives the world and his goals. Only when a subject has formulated a set of objectives (implying the perception of those features of the image which constitutes impediments to his goals and which would thus disappear in a future world) may we say that he has defined his problem.

To define a problem is often very difficult indeed. Only rarely will it be possible to formulate a relevant set of objectives at once. The process by which objectives are formulated is, rather, an iterative one, involving successive rounds of more and more specific descriptions of a world free from tension. During each round, a provisional statement of objectives is compared with the relevant features of the image in order to determine whether they relate to each other—that is whether the objective removes the tension generated. When it does not, then either the objective is reformulated or a similar image is sought to fit the objective. Where suitable images are still not available from the stock held by the memory, and where the objective cannot be restated so as to match existing images, whole new search procedures must be instituted until an image is found which fits the bill.[5]

Only when objectives have been formulated which match the image is the problem properly defined. However, it is not always possible to reach this stage. Where there are major difficulties, it may be advisable to proceed on the basis even of an unsatisfactory definition. New light may be shed on the problem during future attempts to solve it, as well as during the implementation of solutions even to tentatively defined problems. This is what the experimental approach to planning advocated by Meyerson and Banfield (1955) entails. I shall turn to this below.

FORMULATING A RATIONAL PROGRAMME

Ideally, the process of problem definition provides statements of objectives, that is descriptions of how a world would look in which one or more sources of tension have been removed, together with a description of the relevant features of the image. A problem is solved when ways are found of influencing the environment so as to create the world described by these objectives.

As we have seen, three types of forces operate on the environment: control variables, constraints and unknown variables. For the time being, I shall concentrate on the first two only. The constraints obviously circumscribe what I can achieve. Where there are severe constraints, these may have repercussions on problem definition. To find that the source of some tension cannot be removed in any circumstances often leads to a reformu-

[5]The same routine also helps in finding images to fit objectives which the subject conceives autonomously, that is without being stimulated by messages from the environment.

lation of objectives. Objectives describe *possible* worlds, not fantasies. But often there are at least some means available for bringing about change: some variables are what I described as control variables. To formulate a programme means to *devise a set of intentions concerning the type and intensity and the timing of actions aimed at manipulating the control variables of a problem situation so as to achieve a set of objectives.* Programmes may be based on others used in the past. For recurring problems automatic programmes exist (Figs. 4.5–4.8). But when no routine solutions are available, then new ones must be formed.

Here, one must distinguish between two cases. In the first, the problem has been formulated with sufficient accuracy for one programme to be derived unambiguously from a comparison between objectives and the future image. We may invoke once more the very simple example of a central heating system where the problem is to reduce the heating bill by X pounds to avoid an overdraft. The image which we hold of the system may say that it costs Y pounds per hour to run. The answer to the problem is then quite evidently that we must keep the system running for X/Y hours less than at present. The formulation of the problem is therefore sufficiently precise to allow the *deduction* of one programme which achieves our objective.

In the second case, as the problem has not been formulated in quite so much detail, we may be able to deduce more than one programme from what we know about the attainment of our objectives. Clearly, one needs some guidelines for coping with this situation which occurs far more often than the first. In both cases though, deduction plays a central rôle. There is some confusion concerning what deduction means in this context. Therefore, I now turn to a discussion of this vital aspect of the formulation of programmes.

Deducing Programmes

It is not uncommon to talk about planning as the deduction of programmes. For instance, Braybrooke and Lindblom (1963) identify the "rational-deductive" method as one of the "concepts and ideals of evaluative method" in decision-making. Likewise, Dimitriou (1972) describes the "logic of planning" as deductive. Underlying this is an analogy between the formulation of programmes taking into account any known laws and regularities (for instance unit costs) and the deductive model of explanation presented in Chapter 2. I think that an analogy between planning and this indeed exists, but that it merits more discussion than either of the two works referred to above provides. There are, in particular, problems concerning the position of ends and how they lead to the formulation of programmes, the mistake being that end statements are identified with laws in the deductive model of explanation.

The analogy between the formulation of programmes and the deduction of events from laws or regularities may be drawn, firstly, on the level of the aims of doing one or the other. Secondly, a formal analogy exists. Thirdly, one can draw an analogy between each of the components involved in formulating a programme and in the deductive model of explanation.

The aim of any explanation is to present an event as something one should rationally expect. Likewise, to formulate a programme means to present it as something one should rationally choose. Thus, the first analogy between formulating a programme and providing an explanation is that both activities seek to communicate some finding in a convincing manner so that other people feel bound by reason to accept it.

The deductive model of explanation explains events by subsuming them under general empirical laws, showing that these laws and some initial conditions must lead one to expect precisely what one has observed (see pp. 22–23). Commonly, deduction is presented in the following form:

$$\frac{\begin{array}{ll}\text{Empirical laws} & L_1 \ldots L_n \\ \text{Initial conditions} & C_1 \ldots C_m\end{array}}{\text{Event(s) to be explained } E_1 \ldots E_k}$$

The argument is that the choice of a programme (an intention to take certain steps) may be explained using the same format as does deductive explanation. To demonstrate the formal analogy between deducing programmes and events, we must first of all identify the analogies between the various components of the formulation of programmes and the deductive model of explanation.

If one wishes to explain the choice of a programme, then surely that programme must be the equivalent of the event(s) to be explained in the deductive model. Since I defined a programme as the intention to take a set of specific actions spaced out over time (that is as the intention to bring about a series of events) there can be no formal objection to drawing this analogy: both programmes and events to be explained are strings of specific statements.

As against these, laws are statements of a general kind indicating how two or more variables are thought always to co-vary. In explaining some event, these laws are of the kind provided by the empirical sciences. In explaining the formulation of programmes, they are supplemented by another kind of man-made laws meaning legal powers. As empirical laws, legal powers are general statements of what a decision-taker may or may not do, or expect other subjects to do. Much as empirical laws do, they limit what is possible in terms of action.

When explaining a programme for future action, "initial conditions" refers not to present conditions, but to the predicted future image with respect to which the programme is being formulated. "Initial conditions" are those features of the future image which, when compared with the subject's ends, cause him tension. In Chadwick's formulation, they are the impediments to the subject's goals.

No set of intentions for forming a programme may be deduced simply from laws and the features of a future image. One also needs a subject to whom that future image causes tension. His reaction to tension (his definition of the problem) requires formulating a set of objectives describing a world where tension has disappeared. Adding this set of objectives to the "initial conditions" derived from the future image, one now has two sets of descriptive statements: one describing a future problematic world as it would be without any action taken; the other describing the same world but without its problems. One may visualize these two sets as the images of the beginning and the end of an intended process of change turning a problematic world into one which, in certain ways, is ideal, in line with Dakin's view of planning as: ". . . a technique we employ to render the ideal real . . ." (Dakin, 1963).

Having identified what the analogies between the components of programme formulation and deductive explanation are, I return to the analogy between their respective forms. One can now see that to explain a programme (the intention to implement a time-phased set of actions) means to deduce it from a set of relevant empirical laws and legal powers for bringing about change and from the description of that process of change which the programme is meant to bring about, this description taking the place of initial conditions.

| Relevant empirical laws and legal powers for change | $L_1 \ldots L_k$; $P_1 \ldots P_l$ |
| Intended process of change (initial conditions + objectives) | $C_1 \ldots C_m$; $O_1 \ldots O_n$ |

Programme steps $S_1 \ldots S_p$

The analogy between programme formulation and deductive explanation therefore holds on all three levels: their aims, their form and their components. It may be observed that the ends of action figure as the objectives under "initial conditions". There is no question, therefore, of programmes being deduced from some designated ends, though, to be certain, statements of ends do figure in the process of formulating programmes alongside with empirical laws, legal powers and future image.

I am of course not claiming that programmes are produced in this way. But then, this not only holds for the explanation of future intentions, but also for that of past events. As emphasized above, these are ways of presenting programmes and explanations, not of formulating them. What l am claiming is merely that the logic of explanation and of the formulation of programmes is the same.

Finding the "Best" Programme

As shown by the example of a central heating system, it is possible to construct cases in which one programme is deduced from such "empirical laws" as unit-costs. But such examples are rare in the world of planning. In most cases it is possible after the first attempt at problem definition to formulate a number of programmes that seem to meet the objectives. In formal terms this means that, instead of being able to deduce one programme from laws and initial conditions, all that one can deduce are some *indications of the area of choice*. The programme must still be identified within that area of choice or what I shall term the *action space*, using a word translated from the German *Handlungsraum*.[6]

---

[6]I came across this concept whilst participating in a joint project between the Institute for Operational Research, London and Coventry, and Professor Dr. F. Scharpf of the University of Constance in the Federal Republic of Germany. Subsequently I found that Friedmann (1966/7) had been using it. Beer (1966) uses the similar concept of phase-space drawn from mathematics.

How does one identify one programme out of many? The first answer may be that one takes the first one within the action space that comes to mind. If the action space is defined correctly, then this must be a feasible programme. Indeed, as Simon argues (March and Simon, 1958), this strategy of *satisficing* (identifying one programme that satisfies all requirements instead of searching for the one which is optimal, see Chapter 6) is the procedure used by many decision-makers.

If decision-makers were dealing with isolated problems, there would be little objection to this. But they have to cope with many problems occurring both concurrently and in sequence. Since effecting change always means to expend resources, the resources spent on one problem may not be available to solve another. A reasonable actor will therefore try to economize in his use of resources so that he can address himself to as many problems as possible. He can do this by seeking the most favourable ratio between the attainment of objectives and the expenditure of resources, that is by *optimizing* his programme. Assuming that the objectives are defined precisely, and that they are within reach of the subject, this means minimizing expenditure.

Optimization is merely another way of saying that, whilst attending to any one problem we also preserve our chances of attaining other ends now or in the future. It is thus a formal expression for the maximization of the chances for further growth. This introduces a new element into programme formulation which is termed a decision-rule, this decision-rule being invoked in all those cases where the action space contains more than one programme.[7]

Amongst approaches to the formulation of rational programmes one can distinguish two groups: *optimization techniques* and the *rational planning process*. The distinction is similar to those drawn between algorithms and heuristics (Longton, 1966; Miller *et al.*, 1960) and between solving "small", routine, and "big", non-routine and ill-defined problems in operational research and systems analysis (Hitch, 1957; Enthoven, 1970; Harris, 1968/9). Only the one made below between approaches dealing with *quantitatively* and *qualitatively* defined variables is more basic: although problems which can only be defined qualitatively tend to be complex and

[7]Statistical decision-making distinguishes between several formulations which this decision-rule may take. These incorporate the notion of risk. See Bross (1953) and Ackoff (1962).

P.T.—D*

ill-defined (thus requiring heuristic approaches to their solution) this need
not necessarily be the case. The rational planning process is a search procedure, but this is its secondary (though, practically speaking, more
important) use. Logically prior is its application to solving qualitatively
defined problems. The distinction is as follows:

Optimization techniques. When the variables describing a problem
situation are defined quantitatively, then ". . . each possible set of values
along the relevant scales specifies a possible course of action" (Ackoff, 1962).

This usually means that one need not list all the alternative courses of
action: alternative "product mixes", alternative replacement schedules
and so forth. Techniques like linear programming exist which allow one to
identify the optimal programme (subject to specified constraints) directly.
Because of the great precision and certainty which they afford, these
represent an, albeit often distant, ideal for planning.

The rational planning process. The same facilities are not available where
the variables describing a problem are defined qualitatively instead of
quantitatively. This applies in the great majority of cases. Here, one must
go through the rational planning process: enumerate the finite number of
alternative programmes,[8] evaluate them, and select one, thereby invoking
a decision-rule like optimization. This process is at the heart of rational
planning.

The rational planning process may involve several rounds of attempted
programme formulation and new problem definition, until one can identify
the optimal programme. This is where the link between the rational
planning process and human growth becomes evident. The decision-rule
of optimization provides the conditions for more growth as a *product;* the
refinements to images and objectives resulting from repeated cycles of
problem definition and the attempted formulation of rational programmes
represent *learning* or growth as a *process.* The second benefit accrues during
the process of search rather than when it is accomplished and may be
derived even when (as is so often the case) it proves impossible to identify
an optimal programme with much confidence.

[8]Finite because, being defined qualitatively, they are measured on a discrete
scale and within a certain range.

Solving an Ill-defined Problem

The main reason for this failure to identify an optimal programme is that problems are ill-defined. In many cases we cannot formulate a precise future image. This is what Friend and Jessop (1969) characterize as one type of *uncertainty* affecting planning: uncertainty concerning the environment (UE). In the previous chapter, this was indicated by the addition of the unknown variables to the control variables and constraints influencing the environment in Figs. 4.7 and 4.8. The use of "planning assumptions" (Hussey, 1971) and of various techniques described by Friend and Jessop may alleviate the problem, but it is impossible to remove it completely.

If the future image is fuzzy, it is obviously difficult to formulate a set of objectives. Difficulties are compounded by the fact that the relationship between goals and objectives is usually also anything but clear-cut. To formulate a set of objectives, even on the basis of agreed goals, is not a completely analytical process but requires political decisions (see pp. 100–103). The process is fraught with a second type of uncertainty as identified by Friend and Jessop, namely uncertainty concerning values (UV).[9]

Add to this that usually our knowledge of any laws which might have a bearing on programme formulation is very fragmentary indeed and it becomes plain that it is impossible to formulate a very clear notion of the limits of the action space. Even in this situation, however, the rational planning process provides the best approach to formulating a rational programme. With an ill-defined problem, instead of objectives precisely describing a world in which one source of tension has been removed, one must accept the idea of proceeding on the basis of statements concerning the *direction* into which one ought to move to reduce that tension. To move as far as possible into that direction (for instance to build as many houses as possible; to create as many jobs as possible; to preserve as much open space as possible) then replaces an achievement described in terms of X number of houses built, Y number of jobs created and Z acres of open land preserved as the one to be pursued.

[9]Rightly speaking, it should not be values, since values are recurring preferences (Deutsch, 1966). In a new version, Friend *et al.* (1972) refer to uncertainty concerning policies rather than uncertainty concerning values.

Obviously, one must still have an eye on resources. However, instead of minimizing the amount of resources spent on the attainment of fixed objectives, that is on the attainment of an ideal world free from some tension, one now seeks the most favourable ratio between the extent to which one moves towards that ideal (measured in terms of some *standard* like number of houses, or jobs, or acreage of open land), and the amount of resources spent. This is another, more sophisticated, form which the decision-rule of optimization takes.

In tackling an ill-defined problem, this decision-rule is therefore introduced even before the limits of the action space are properly identified. At face value, this seems paradoxical: optimization means finding the best of all possible programmes; where the limits of the action space are not properly identified, one cannot be certain of having enumerated all possible programmes; since there will always be unidentified programmes, one can therefore never be certain that one has chosen the best. The very attempt to optimize seems to be futile.

But in a world where knowledge is scarce, the jump from an imperfectly perceived action space to an, albeit tentative, "optimal" programme is a more promising approach than not presenting a rational programme at all until it can be formulated with certainty (meaning never). The former at least requires assumptions to be brought into the open, and like the deductive model of explanation in science, invites and facilitates their investigation. The argument engendered by a proposed programme is therefore likely to bring forward additional knowledge if it is available, and to encourage further research. Also, once this argument is tentatively resolved (tentatively because of the element of uncertainty which always remains), and once implementation gets under way, incoming information may be related with benefit to these prior assumptions. Thus by imposing stringent requirements on the explicitness with which programmes are presented, defended, tested and reviewed, the rational planning process as the means of identifying an optimal programme results in learning. During the ensuing learning process, the subject explores his action space from its centre (where the most obvious programmes are to be found) to its fuzzy edges, gaining progressively more knowledge of its structure whilst he proceeds.

As argued in Chapter 3, the fact that the rational planning process, by the very demands which it makes on the precision of images, objectives and the subject's perception of his action space, results in learning, provides a *raison-d'être*, even beyond that of finding an optimal programme. One can now see why this is so. Benefits in terms of increased knowledge do not only accrue from actually accomplishing the formulation of an optimal programme, but may be derived over and above and before all other advantages. Above all, they are ones which are much more certain to arise. This is as well because, as any thoughtful planner might agree, it is usually impossible to identify such a programme with very much confidence, and an optimal programme may never be found. The least one must do is to make a fair number of assumptions to simplify the problem before any "optimal" programme can be identified. And even when these assumptions prove just about adequate at the time of formulating the programme, some unforeseen turn of events may invalidate them within no time at all. Therefore, were there not the benefits of increased knowledge it would be doubtful whether rational planning would be worth the effort. As things are, they constitute the most powerful argument for the rational planning process. We may visualize it as propelling the process of human growth along more quickly than any hit-and-miss approach to the formulation of programmes.

IMPLEMENTATION AND FEEDBACK

With an optimal, or presumed optimal, programme identified, in theory, the rest seems simple enough. As I shall say in Chapter 15, in practice the implementation of programmes is a sore point with planners. Here I shall merely argue that the difficulties of implementation must stem from inadequate problem definition and programme formulation and that these may be alleviated over time by the use of feedback.

Basically what happens during implementation is that some resources are mobilized in order to influence the environment. These resources need not be held by the effector of the planning agency, but it must have access to them. In physical planning terms, the legal powers conferred upon Local Planning Authorities by the planning acts are, figuratively speaking, held by the planning agency itself. The development control section, by interpreting the law, provides access to them. The financial resources for implementing any positive proposals for development are held outside the Local Planning Authority, for instance by the housing department or by developers. As long as the effector can influence them to release the right amount of money at the right time for the right purpose, this does not affect the argument.[10]

When the effector converts resources into action as prescribed by the programme, the aim is to change the environment. Effects which are totally different than those anticipated indicate error during problem definition and programme formulation. For instance, the image may have been a false one, for the circumstances anyway. Alternatively, the deduction of the limits of the action space may have been at fault. In other cases, the results may fall short of target, but can still be meaningfully related to the original intention: perhaps the constraints operating in the environment have been underestimated, and the image needs to be adapted. Alternatively, some unknown variable may become evident as a result of the implementation of the programme, this leading to further adaptations of the image. In most cases, there will be a mixture of various results: intended ones, short-falls and deviations from the target, but within the action space, and unintended consequences occurring outside it.

In feedback, unintended consequences are much more important than messages signalling success: there is nothing to be learned from the latter and a very great deal from the former. Success may confirm what is already known, but failures induce more learning. To this end it is important to analyse failures for what they entail for the image. Changes to the image may then trigger off a wholly new process of problem definition, programme formulation and implementation.

CHANGES TO THE SELF-IMAGE

A special kind of feedback relates to the subject himself. As indicated in the previous chapter, it is easier to conceive of changes of the self-image in terms of people interacting because impressions gained during interaction of how others see the self are a prime source for formulating the self-image.

---

[10]But, where this is the case, it usually involves some "give and take" during the previous phases of problem definition and problem-solving: obviously, it will be easier to induce the holders of the purse strings to do as the programme says, if they can legitimately regard that programme as fulfilling, amongst others, their objectives. The point is of vital importance for implementation and will figure in the relevant chapter.

Let me put myself into the situation of the speaker. Whilst speaking, I scan the face of my partner for small clues. The first decision which I make is whether he understands me. If I think he does understand, then I continue. But if he listens with strain, if he bends forward or turns his ear towards me, then I begin to wonder whether I have defined the situation correctly. Perhaps the background noise level is too high, or my partner rather deaf. If so, then I shall speak louder. But if the room is quiet, and I have no reason to suspect that my partner is deaf, and if the same reaction is repeated, then I may be forced to conclude that I am not speaking loudly enough. To some people, this is a matter of professional concern. They must evaluate their changed self-image against their goals and decide to do something about it. Receiving such information is called a higher-order feedback.

Higher-order feedback is internal to the system. Some people are better at attending to it than others and certainly sensitivity to the needs of others is involved. The skill can to some extent be acquired by engaging in reflection about what images one casts. Techniques have also been devised to help the process, and various forms of this "sensitivity training" are being used in training managers and similar professionals who have to be highly effective in working with other people.

The need for such special sensitivity training shows that it is a skill which it is difficult to exercise and acquire. With the self-image occupying such a central position in our world outlook, the obstacles in the way of changing it are formidable. It may be preferable to me to assume that I have assessed the situation incorrectly rather than that I have misjudged myself. The raw information does not tell me precisely what is involved, and I am thus open to self-deception.

Planning agencies have a self-image similar to the individual self-image. By way of illustration one may show how the process of changing a corporate self-image as a result of feedback from the environment might occur, similar to changes to the individual self-image occurring.[11] Suppose a planning agency finds that people do not listen to it; that, at best, they only react adversely to published proposals. It may first of all ask whether people receive the information which it has given, and whether its meaning is what

[11] The idea of a corporate self-image figures prominently in one recent textbook on corporate planning: the "Corporate Appraisal", in Hussey (1971).

is intended. It can use a variety of means to ensure this, from mounting more and better exhibitions to calling in experts in public relations to write its brochures. But suppose that, as a result of all this, reaction becomes, if anything, more hostile. Clearly, the planning agency must ask itself questions, such as which objective it pursues and with what means, and how its programmes are being formulated and how an obviously unhappy situation may be changed by changing its procedures and its structure. This is precisely the process of soul-searching which has been going on in planning (especially over the last years) leading to changes of various kinds, including changes to the way in which planning agencies and the public interact. These changes are motivated, amongst others, by a new self-image of planning.

POLITICS AND PLANNING

The example of people reacting strongly against planning proposals is one which can frequently be observed. One reaction to it must be that people do not see planning proposals as serving their own ends. Since planning agencies usually think that the objectives pursued by them are in the interests of the people they see themselves as serving, this reaction is disturbing. It requires a discussion of the way objectives are determined.

Let me begin by taking stock. Thus far, I have introduced the terms goals and objectives, occasionally referring to both summarily as ends. The concept of an end always relates to a feedback process. From the observation of this feedback process one may namely infer that it will end (*sic!*) when it reaches a certain state. With simple feedback processes, this end may be brought about, observed and described, and that is that. It is not necessary to differentiate any further between goals and objectives. Such a differentiation is only important when talking about learning systems. In the previous chapter, the human mind was described as such. The key-feature of this learning system is that it may change its ends as a result of new information received from the environment (Kuhn, 1966). In these cases, it is necessary to differentiate between two types of ends: that which is being changed, and that in the name of which change takes place. These are objectives and goals. To return to the well-worn example of my domestic thermostat, the temperature at which I set it is the objective, to keep warm is my goal.

Two things may now be said about goals and objectives. One is that they must *relate* to each other: turning up the radiator tap in my bathroom will not increase the temperature in my study. The second is that the objective (the temperature at which I set the thermostat) relates to *specific operations* by which the goal, or goals, may be achieved. An objective is, as one says, an operational definition of a goal.

For any goal, or any set of goals, there may be several paths to its successful attainment. I might do exercises, or drink tea, instead of resetting the thermostat. The formulation of an objective usually requires a choice between alternative ways of achieving the goal to which it relates. This choice may itself be represented as a planning problem, that is as the identification of an optimal course of action out of the number of possible courses. I might for instance care to list all possible ways of warming up (my goal): push-ups, the acquisition of a paraffin heater, drinking tea, resetting the thermostat and so forth. Only, this time, the programme does not result in immediate action relating to the environment. It is rather in the nature of a directive for the next-lower "planning process": the thermostat should keep the temperature at 65°, I must perform push-ups, counting till I have done twenty-five, and then stop, or some such instruction.

In making a choice between these directions, one invokes other criteria than the two original goals. For instance, I might introduce a personal preference for physical exercise, thus committing myself to doing push-ups. However, one very quickly comes up against the problem of evaluating the original goals in turn: how much is it "worth" keeping warm, or out of the red, or physically fit? It seems apparent that there is either no end to this argument, or that one must invoke some notion of "ultimate" goals: keeping fit is good for you and that is that!

This is a dilemma because on the one hand there seems to be no basis for declaring anything as beyond argument. On the other hand, it is clearly impracticable to go on questioning the reasons underlying the choice of ends indefinitely. Firstly, one might find that there is not the *time* available to do so; secondly, one very quickly meets the problem of a *lack of knowledge* to base one's answers on. Therefore, under pressure people simply become dogmatic. However, dogma is opposed to reason.[12]

---

[12] For a further elaboration of this argument see Albert (1969).

Professionals seem to be particularly prone to succumb to ultimate goals. Apart from pressure of work, the reason, in their case, is that ultimate goals promise to provide a rock-solid basis for basing programme proposals on. They thereby enhance the status of their professional guardians and increase their autonomy *vis-à-vis* other participants in the process of decision-making, politicians in particular. But even apparently unquestionable goals can always be questioned. It is only because of recognized limitations of time and knowledge that one has to accept some things as given: in any particular choice situation, certain assumptions need to be made which must not be questioned, *but only within the context of that choice.* They are thus *provisional* assumptions and do not involve declaring anything as absolute. These assumptions may be changed from one choice situation to the next, as new evidence becomes available or new preferences are formed. In this way, assumptions may supplement analytical knowledge in goal-setting (as well as in the identification of the action space available to the subject).

Which assumptions to make, and when to make them, are decisions which the subject makes as a *free and responsible agent*. He can choose because there is no evidence available to guide him (not even evidence of constraints upon his choice) so that he might as well act out his preferences. But he must also hold himself responsible to accept whatever flows from that decision. He must, in other words, be prepared to take *risks*.

I suggest that the same holds true even where the subject is not an individual but a collectivity, or even a whole community, making decisions. This amounts to saying that, from the point of view of decision-making, political choice is that process by which a community agrees to make those assumptions required to underpin and supplement knowledge so as to arrive at decisions. It does not mean that those assumptions are sacrosanct, that they must not be criticized, but merely that there are ways of temporarily resolving issues which otherwise could not be resolved for lack of time and/or empirical evidence.

The division of labour indicated between rational argument and criticism based on knowledge on the one hand and the making of choices based on preferences and the acceptance of responsibility for what might ensue from them on the other, is based on an appreciation of the inherent characteristics of rational and political choice. It allows for a change of emphasis as new knowledge becomes available, without arguing that the need for political choices would ever disappear. It thus allows for a further expansion of knowledge as a firm basis for decision-making: nobody would seriously argue that political choices should disregard evidence. They should, rather, supplement analytical knowledge where there is not enough of it available to make a final decision.

This may seem an unduly narrow view of politics and an unduly imperialistic one of the rôle of knowledge. But knowledge, by its very expansion, always creates new problems both of a theoretical as well as of a practical kind. The expansion of knowledge, far from doing away with the need freely and responsibly to formulate choices and take risks, perpetually re-establishes the need for political choices. Rather than to infringe upon each other's territory, rational argument, and political choice concerning how to change the world, can thus grow together!

There are other views of the relationship of politics and planning. In particular, political scientists argue that the political process has some sort of primacy over rational argument, though it is not always quite obvious on what basis. But, from the perspective of this book, which examines how rational decisions are made in order to promote human growth, the rôle of the political process is that of generating the willingness to take the risks involved in every assumption leading to action. In my submission, this is by no means an unimportant rôle. Any planning decision is based on some political choices, and during most planning operations the need for more choices is revealed. Thus, there is a need for constant interaction between the political process and planning. The end of promoting this interaction is served best, not by claiming supremacy for either planning or politics, but by identifying what one or the other ought to do, which is what the final section of this chapter has tried to do. The implications of this view of planning and politics will be one of my major concerns in Part IV.

REFERENCES

ACKOFF, R. *et al.* (1962) *Scientific Method: Optimizing Applied Research Decision*, John Wiley, New York.
ALBERT, H. (1969) *Traktat über kritische Vernunft*, 2. Aufl., J. C. B. Mohr (Paul Siebeck), Tübingen.
BEER, S. (1966) *Decision and Control*, John Wiley, New York.
BRAYBROOKE, D. and LINDBLOM, C. E. (1963) *A Strategy of Decision—Policy Evaluation as a Social Process*, Free Press, New York.

BROADY, M. (1972) Social administration: some current concerns, *Inaugural Lecture of the Professor of Social Administration*, delivered at the University College of Swansea on 9 May 1972.

BROSS, I. D. (1953) *Design for Decision*, Macmillan, New York–London.

CHADWICK, G. (1971) *A Systems View of Planning*, Pergamon, Oxford.

DAKIN, J. (1963) An evaluation of the "choice" theory of planning, *Journal of the American Institute of Planners*, Vol. 29, pp. 19–27.

DEUTSCH, K. W. (1966) *The Nerves of Government—Models of Political Communication and Control*, 2nd ed. Macmillan, New York–London.

DIMITRIOU, B. (1972) The interpretation of politics and planning, *The Systems View of Planning* (DIMITRIOU, B. *et al.*), Oxford Working Papers in Planning Education and Research, No. 9, Department of Town Planning, Oxford Polytechnic, Oxford.

ENTHOVEN, A. (1970) Systems analysis and the navy, *Planning Programming Budgeting: A Systems Approach to Management* (edited by LYDEN, F. J. and MILLER, E. G.), Markham Publishing Co., Chicago.

FALUDI, A. (1971) Problems with "problem-solving", *Journal of the Royal Town Planning Institute*, Vol. 57, p. 415.

FALUDI, A. and NEEDHAM, B. (1973) Planning and the Public Interest, *Journal of the Royal Town Planning Institute*, Vol. 59, pp. 164–6.

FRIEDMANN, J. (1966/7) Planning as a vocation, *Plan Canada*, Vol. 6, pp. 99–124, Vol. 7, pp. 8–26.

FRIEND, J. K. and JESSOP, W. N. (1969) *Local Government and Strategic Choice*, Tavistock Publications, London.

FRIEND, J. K., YEWLETT, C. J. L. and POWER, J. M. (1972) *Public Planning: The Inter-corporate Dimension*, Unpublished manuscript.

HARRIS, B. (1968/69) People, problems and plans: the purpose and nature of design, *Transactions of the Bartlett Society*, Vol. 7, pp. 9–53.

HITCH, C. (1957) Quoted by LINDBLOM, C. E. (1959) The science of muddling through, *Public Administration Review*, Vol. 19, pp. 79–88.

HUSSEY, D. E. (1971) *Introducing Corporate Planning*, Pergamon, Oxford.

KUHN, A. (1966) *The Study of Society*, Tavistock Publications, London.

LONGTON, P. A. (1966) Introduction and commentary on models, decisions, and operational research, *Operational Research and the Social Sciences* (edited by LAWRENCE, J. R.), Tavistock Publications, London.

MARCH, J. G. and SIMON, H. A. (1958) *Organizations*, John Wiley, New York.

MEYERSON, M. and BANFIELD, E. C. (1955) *Politics, Planning and the Public Interest*, Free Press, Glencoe.

MILLER, G. A., GALANTER, E. and PRIBHAN, K. H. (1960) *Plans and the Structure of Behavior*, Holt, Rinehart & Winston, New York.

NEEDHAM, B. (1971) Concrete problems not abstract goals, *Journal of the Royal Town Planning Institute*, Vol. 57, pp. 317–9.

RIEGER, H. C. (1967) *Begriff und Logik der Planung*, Otto Harrassowitz, Wiesbaden.

STACHOWIAK, H. (1969) *Denken und Erkennen im kybernetischen Modell*, Springer, Wien–New York.

CHAPTER 6

Rational Planning—Limitations and Approaches

In this chapter I propose to take the analogy between planning and a person engaged in operational thinking even further. My starting point is the observation that people engaged in formulating programmes are subject to certain limitations, and that similar problems exist in planning. Ways in which people cope with their limitations are therefore a source of ideas for how planning agencies might cope with theirs. I shall discuss these ways under the headings of planning strategies, creative planning,[1] and balancing commitment against criticism, suggesting that some of the approaches to planning which are presently taken make perfect sense when a planning agency is seen as analogous to a person.

Deficiencies of planning may be described as the inability to use any one or all of these approaches to combat limitations. I shall describe the reasons for such an inability as planning pathologies. As regards these, I can go no further than giving a few indications. It is precisely in this area of identifying planning pathologies that empirical research is badly needed. Part III will provide a basis for such research.

THE PROBLEM OF RATIONAL PLANNING

The key-problem of all rational planning is that of coping with the limitations of information-handling capacity from which every conceivable subject suffers. These pose the riddle of how people cope at all, let alone

[1]Planning strategies and creative planning are similar to two of the "normative models of public policymaking" identified by Dror (1968): the economically rational, and the extrarational model. Eddison (1973) refers to these as models of the planning process.

engage in rational planning. The answers suggest ways in which planning agencies might cope with *their* limitations, thus showing how the analogy drawn in the two previous chapters may be put to practical use.

At first glance, to describe the perennial problem of planning as information *overload* seems to conflict with an alternative view of the difficulties which planners face as evolving around how to *obtain* information. These difficulties may be used unwittingly to deflect from the more demanding question of how information informs decisions taken. Development plans adopted since surveys have become statutory requirement in Great Britain are far from explicit about the way in which their recommendations flow from the facts collected. The folklore of planning is full of stories of surveys being conducted by research sections, and plans being drawn up quite independently by people who have taken neither a hand in designing the surveys nor much notice of their results. I suggest that these results are not used because there are limits to the amount of information which people can handle.

Why is the capacity for handling information (and thus for formulating rational programmes) limited? The reason is quite simply that humans have a limited channel capacity and that the human memory is also limited. What is even more important is that this same memory is differentiated into a short-term memory, containing all that information which is required for solving an immediate problem, and the memory at large, from which that information can be drawn. The short-term memory, however, is *very much more limited in its capacity than is the memory itself.*

Its limitations are very severe indeed. There is a strict limit on the number of syllables or figures which one can immediately grasp and recall, as one might well remember from efforts to learn a complicated word in a foreign language, or to memorize a telephone number. Psychologists have found that, by and large, the capacity of the short-term memory does not exceed the recall of more than seven items at once (Miller, 1968).

Planning agencies deal with many more items simultaneously. The prescriptions of the rational planning process are that they must evaluate *all* alternative programmes against *all* the objectives pursued. The rational planning process is *comprehensive*. But, though planning agencies may draw on the faculties of many individuals, and thus pool their memories, even the most successful team still has a far too limited capacity for simultaneously holding the mass of information required to fulfil this prescription. Therefore, criticisms of "rational-comprehensive" planning focus on the sheer impossibility of fulfilling its recommendations (Lindblom, 1959; Braybrooke and Lindblom, 1963).[2] Relative to the complexity of their problems, limitations of information-handling capacity as the key-problem of rational planning therefore applies to all subjects, whether they are individuals or planning agencies.

But surely individuals cope with these limitations? Despite the proven limit of their short-term memories, people succeed in memorizing more than seven items; they evaluate a great amount of information simultaneously, for example, when they drive cars, fly aeroplanes with dozens of instruments, or write books! In most everyday situations, people deal reasonably successfully with large amounts of information. If we find out how, then we may learn something about the way in which planning agencies might cope with their problems.

For any feat of memory beyond a very small number of items, individuals must use certain strategies. These find their parallels in what I shall term *planning strategies*. Planning strategies are *approaches which enable a subject to take rational decisions precisely by paying due regard to the limitations of his ability to handle large amounts of information.* In accepting these limitations as facts of life which, in making choices must be included with other relevant information, a subject has more chance of success than he would enjoy by following the impossibly complex prescriptions of the rational planning process. Planning strategies accept limitations either by pre-structuring problems, that is by imposing patterns on the information which a subject holds concerning them with the aim of narrowing the field of choice to what is manageable; or by the controlled suspension of the requirements of the rational planning process until the field of rational choice coincides with that which is analysable, taking into account the available resources for research.

Planning strategies are greatly assisted by previous experiences. But, if these are so important in prestructuring a subject's perception of his problem, then one must first of all ask how he can respond to entirely new situations where he has no previous knowledge; and, secondly, how he may change a technology-image that has become unsuitable as a basis for problem-solving. Individuals capable of developing adequate responses

[2]See the discussion of these criticisms in Faludi (1973) and p. 153.

to novel situations are commonly described as *creative*. Further below I
shall investigate what psychologists mean by creativity hoping, as in the
case of planning strategies, to inspire some thoughts about the design of
planning agencies which will allow them to engage in creative planning.

PLANNING STRATEGIES: IMPOSING PATTERNS ON INFORMATION

To understand how the limitations referred to in this section may be
circumvented by imposing patterns on the information received, one must
examine how human beings operate through an ability of pattern recognition, all the limitations of the short-term memory notwithstanding. Let us
begin with the fact that, obviously, one can remember many more than
the seven letters which the short-term memory is said to be able to hold.
The alphabet has twenty-six and everyone can remember that! One can
memorize whole sentences or even paragraphs, which consist of a very
large number of letters. If one knew how, then one would be much closer
to understanding how the human memory copes with complexity.

Here, research into the nature of memorizing helps us: Miller (1968)
found that most people can remember syllables as easily as letters, although,
obviously, syllables contain several letters each. He concluded that it does
not matter to the short-term memory whether the limited number of items
which it contains are simple or complex. The human brain has a facility
called pattern recognition, or the ability to recollect configurations with
much the same ease as individual items. In memorizing tests, subjects use
this facility to cope with strings of items that would, in the first instance,
exceed the capacity of their short-term memory. They break them up into
groups of letters, memorize those, and then link them together.

The importance of this ability of the human brain to assign patterns to
information coming from the environment is evident when one looks at its
most striking achievement which is human speech. Language is based
precisely on this ability to recognize patterns. Words are nothing but
symbols for such patterns. When I utter a word, I refer to a pattern of
information which I have received about something in the outside world.
In doing so, I activate the memory of other people sharing my experiences.
In this way, language becomes the basis of human culture. It enables man
to express his thoughts, to share them with others, to cross-check on results

and improve on their validity and relevance to his problems. It is the basis of any division of labour, or co-ordination, of virtually every social activity.

Pattern recognition reveals something about the human brain and the way in which it enables man to cope with the environment. To show this, linguists have examined ways in which infants learn to speak and have found that, if the brain was not purpose-made for acquiring human speech, it would be impossible for human beings to become proficient in the use of something as rich and complex as language. But the human infant sucks in language as a dry sponge sucks in water, with amazingly little effort. In particular, infants are able to learn not only words (that is small patterns) but also larger patterns like sentences. This enables us to infer that some order must be built into the structure of the brain, just as one can make inferences about the structure of a sponge from the way it absorbs water. We may therefore evade the thorny problem of whether there is order in the environment (which we cannot resolve) in favour of saying that there is definitely order in the human brain, and that it is by imposing this order on the environment that the human brain copes with it, for better or for worse, but certainly in ways which seem to improve all the time.

Take, for instance, the problem of recalling an article read the other day: this carries too much information for the short-term memory and is therefore too complex to be remembered word by word. But what one does instead of memorizing it is to remember what the gist was, thus recalling the general pattern. One then concentrates on specific parts, trying to develop the argument in detail, sometimes even remembering individual words. As every student knows, this is a skill which can and must be learned when taking notes and reconstructing arguments from them.

Imposing patterns on information coming from the environment is basic to at least three different planning strategies which I shall describe under the headings of *routinization, sequential decision-making* and *mixed scanning*. In the first and second case, the overall pattern or framework imposed on the information received from the environment is relatively stable, whereas in the last this framework itself is subject to change.

Routinization

When describing the model of planning agencies in Chapter 4, I referred to a certain class of programmes as automatic. In human beings, the equivalent of these automatic programmes is a short-circuit from their receptors to their effectors. In understanding how humans cope with the environment, this short-circuit is important. Automatic programmes ease the load on the short-term memory, especially where speed is essential and exacerbates the problems of handling information. The learner driver, because he has to decide which foot to put down to stop the car, does not react quickly enough, which is why the instructor has a second set of controls. It is only when his response is short-circuited from his sensory organs to the right foot, and when the exact pressure and timing of this reaction are ingrained into this process (that is, when the automatic programme has been firmly established), that he can stop the car smoothly and effectively. Clearly, programmes of this kind are not only useful but often essential for survival.

It is not only small programmes which are acquired and used in this way. Fire drills, large sections of military training, some strategies in swotting for exams, as well as the study of planning techniques are all ways of ensuring that the right actions are taken in the right sequence when time is short and pressure great. By practising these programmes, one "automates" their performance, for human beings, individually or in groups, do not have to rely only on those skills which are already built into their psychic make-up, but can also manipulate their habits in purposive ways.

In all these cases, the overall pattern into which these routine programmes fit is represented by the rules which determine when a programme should be invoked. These overall patterns themselves may be very elaborate and involve many considerations of the appropriateness of response. Nevertheless, the rules are couched in the form of brief, imperative statements the purpose of which is to reduce the decision-maker's problem. The final aim is the formulation of precise processes ". . . which even an unintelligent human being can perform effectively, arriving at a successful answer without understanding the details of the process, or the purpose for which it is used" (George, 1965). As long as the decision-maker is confident that these are well thought out, that they form part of a strategy and are not mere rules of thumb or, even worse, biased prescriptions masquerading as technical rules, he need not worry about not investigating the reasons underlying routine solutions. He should merely be aware of the fact that he *has* to make compromises, and that developing, prescribing, and accepting routine solutions to problems is one of the strategies for obviating limitations on information-handling capacity.

Sequential Decision-making

In the study of the rational planning process in Chapter 14, I shall describe how a choice was made out of eighty alternatives. The procedures used there are fairly typical and may thus serve to illustrate sequential decision-making which is used frequently in dealing with limitations of information-handling capacity.

The problem of handling information in making a choice out of eighty alternatives is that they grossly exceed the capacity of the short-term memory. To make things worse, each alternative in the case to be discussed was analysed against fifteen criteria as held by twelve interest groups, giving a total of thirty assessments per alternative or two thousand four hundred in all. Instead of resorting to despair, what was done was to evaluate one alternative after the other, to score each, and finally to select the one with the highest score. The total problem was thus broken down into a sequence of like problems which could be solved one after the other, none of which exceeded the information-handling capacity of the decision-maker.[3]

The precondition on which this rests is that one can formulate the rules for codifying and ordering judgements. These again represent the overall pattern imposed on information. Obviously, the choice of any one pattern may always be criticized as being inadequate. But there is no escaping the fact that some pattern must be imposed to reduce demands on information-handling capacity.

As in routinization, sequential decision-making is a planning strategy not without cost. It means to make up rules and stick to them, at least until a better one is found, even if this means taking risks.

Mixed Scanning

The last of the planning strategies based on pattern recognition, mixed scanning (Etzioni, 1967, 1968), is the most versatile of the three. It involves

[3]In actual fact, the group concerned broke the problem down into further subroutines: they organized the total process such that each member of the group specialized for one criterion only. He could then deal with each individual evaluation more quickly and more reliably. The total process thus took twenty-odd people a couple of hours.

imposing patterns on information received (making *fundamental* decisions), formulating a programme within this framework (making *bit* decisions), and going back to *changing that framework* whenever one gets stuck on the more detailed level.

With its feature of oscillation between two (or more) levels, mixed scanning again describes how individual human beings operate. As an example I may refer to a problem of which I am beginning to accumulate some experience: writing a book. I have written many frameworks since starting the book because, while I am writing individual chapters, these frameworks have a peculiar habit of changing. The same may be said about chapters and sections, sections and paragraphs and so on, right down to the choice of particular words within the framework of any one sentence: I oscillate more or less rapidly and frequently between the broader and the narrower level of formulating my "programme" until, hopefully, my chapters will fit the framework, the sections the chapters and so forth, the sum total providing a solution to the problem which I set for myself.

Similarly, an architect faced with a design problem, rather than decrying his incapacity of solving that problem instantly, first decides on the *kind* of solution to propose: tall blocks, low rise-high density development, or bungalows and terraced houses. This reduces his problem. In finding a solution, he need not worry about the details of the general patterns which he rejects; he can proceed to consider the structure of his particular type of building. Again, he does not normally consider the details of where to provide, for example, the requisite ducts for cables (though occasionally this may impinge on the structure of a building). Normally, he leaves the ducts until later, by which time his problem will have narrowed down to such a level of detail. Thus, by hierarchical organization of programme formulation, men can create enormous buildings, imposing themselves prominently on the environment, sometimes on the basis of a small sketch on the back of a cigarette packet. This is another example where approaches to the formulation of programmes outlined in the previous chapter have been adapted to the limitations of information-handling capacity from which the human mind suffers. With such adaptations, the human mind can cope better with problems than by trying to follow the rational planning process to the letter. However, to be able to cope better is surely the ultimate measure of rationality.

Hierarchical organization of the formulation of programmes is ubiquitous as a method. By its use, planning seems more successful than by trying to understand every detail of a situation before attempting a solution. Etzioni (1968), who coined the term mixed scanning, provides an example: describing a group of infantry men moving into hostile territory, he argues that a comprehensive investigation of the field may be dangerously slow, and a detailed investigation of specific areas only (for instance those from where fire might be expected such as bushes, houses and ridges providing cover) risks the danger of surprise attack from elsewhere. The men therefore scan the field, thereby establishing the general pattern of the problem, and only then proceed with the detailed investigation of specific areas. In this way, the composite chances of survival increase.

The strategy is never foolproof. It may fail you at any time when the patterns which you have invoked are unsuitable. Were the architect to decide to erect a tall block only to find, on the next level of planning, that the ground was unsuitable, and that the costs of building elaborate foundations was too great, the strategy would not have prevented him from doing this. But the point is that he has now *learnt* something vital impinging on his final choice. He can go back and choose another solution which is more suitable, given the conditions of the site. One could also say that he has restructured his general problem which, for technical reasons, now includes these conditions.

Mixed scanning is the final example of a planning strategy based on the facility of the human mind for pattern recognition. Besides being more versatile than routinization and sequential decision-making, it yields a very important return: a structure within which learning can occur. The architect, or any other decision-maker, is provided with a framework on which to hang the notices of his failure as warning signs: unsuitable site conditions, no tall blocks!

PLANNING STRATEGIES: CONTROLLED SUSPENSION OF RATIONAL PLANNING

There is a second range of approaches which decision-makers use in coping with their limitations: they simply suspend rational argument. This is rational for three reasons: firstly, when a problem cannot be tackled by exercising rational choice, then even the effort of trying to do so is not only pointless but positively wasteful; secondly, by concentrating planning resources on what can be planned, the compound chances of success increase, even though parts of the operation may be left to chance; thirdly, to suspend rational argument in a controlled manner depends on one's knowing about the problem and which parts one may tackle by using such argument and which not. It thus represents a rational decision in itself.

There are again three strategies which one can name. In an ascending scale of the degree to which they suspend rational judgement, they are the following: *satisficing, a-priori decision-making, random decision-making.*

Satisficing

The prototype of this kind of approach is the way in which a structural engineer solves many of his problems. If he wishes to optimize the design of a beam, he must calculate exactly how much various available beams could take, and choose the cheapest of these. However, this is not very easily done because the forces generated by a load on a beam are very complex. Also, even if the engineer were to identify all these, there would be little point in basing his construction on complete and thorough calculations because the material which he uses and the methods builders employ are highly unreliable. If he really wishes to go to the limits of what his beam could actually take, the engineer will have to investigate the actual beam and personally supervise the building operations. Of course, his sense of economic realism prevents him from doing this. One might also say that the problem of optimizing the construction of a beam is too complex for the amount of resources which one should spend on its solution, in normal circumstances anyway. What the engineer does instead is to use standards of, for instance, maximum stress and pressure which incorporate security factors of up to ten! Having done this, he is then satisfied, not that he has *optimized* anything, but that the beam will not collapse.

This strategy is called *satisficing*. It means to accept any programme which happens to meet the objectives (often expressed as minimum standards) and to refrain from invoking additional decision-rules.

Satisficing is often used in combination with optimizing. This combination occurs in linear programming, and also in physical planning where a wide range of planning standards exist. Standards such as residential density, sun light, provision of open space and so on are minimum requirements which any solution to a physical planning problem must meet. Within the constraints imposed by these, the physical planner may still seek to find an optimal solution.

A-priori Decision-making

Suppose a decision-maker found it beyond his capacity to make a rational choice. Suppose further that he had tried other strategies, but that there still was a hard core of choice left which he could not resolve. Suppose finally that he has a preference for one of the remaining alternatives. It would be entirely reasonable to say that the decision-maker should follow that preference. The point is that, where there is no evidence on which to base his choice, following his preferences, or even his whim, is still better than inaction through lack of decision. For example, imagine having to determine what the opinion of individuals is worth. Clearly, there is an infinite variety of people, and the problem is an impossible one to solve analytically. Instead, what one does is to impose an *a-priori* decision on the problem, namely that, in certain fundamental decisions, each individual's opinion is worth the same, such as is the case in elections.

Decision-makers who are constantly faced with situations like this may develop patterns of preferences or *values*. Their choices will thus be, if not rational, then at least stable. Emery and Trist (1969) show that this is an approach which institutions take when operating in what they call a turbulent environment. This environment, from the point of view of institutions operating in it, poses precisely this kind of problem: a lack of understanding of the forces operating in it so that choices cannot be made rationally. Making choices on the basis of values which are commonly held and understood is described by Emery and Trist as making it "possible to deal with persisting areas of relevant uncertainty", and hence as a planning strategy in the terms of this book.

Random Decision-making

When not even preferences exist (quite apart from information concerning the choices to be made), then a *random* decision is an entirely rational one. Simon (1956) shows this by the case of a hypothetical organism moving around in an environment which gives no clues as to where to find food. Random movements are the best it can do.

Though randomization procedures are perfectly respectable in advanced mathematical techniques, I have heard only one planner suggest tossing a coin seriously as a method of making choices (Branch, 1969). But then he was not talking in his capacity as a planner, but as a planning commissioner for Los Angeles who had been trying to persuade his planning counterparts to accept that the tossing of a coin still gave a fifty per cent chance of success, quite apart from the saving in terms of time and effort in vain attempts to research an intrinsically insoluble problem.

Besides these six alternative planning strategies, there are other approaches to coping with his limitations to which a subject may turn, which I shall now explore.

CREATIVE PLANNING

The planning strategies identified in the previous section rely on knowledge gained previously. In organizations, this accumulated experience leads to a division of labour. This in turn results in programme formulation which relies on convergent thinking strictly within the confines of one narrow technology-image. Where programmes cannot thus be formulated, we have the problem of relaxing the rigidity of thought.

There is a parallel to this in individual thinking. A person capable of relaxing the rigidity of his thinking and of searching for solutions outside the standard range we describe as creative. The analogy between individuals and planning agencies may be further extended to one between creativity in individuals on the one hand and creative planning as performed by planning agencies on the other. I shall show that the informal networks occurring in planning agencies, as in other organizations, provide channels through which they may engage in the type of divergent thinking which is essential to creative planning. How this happens (and how it may be facilitated by taking heed of the information coming through informal channels of communication) I shall try to elucidate by using a case study of creative planning.

To suspend rational planning in a controlled manner, and even more so to impose patterns on information received, depends on some preconception of the nature of the problem. In most cases, such preconceptions are informed by previous experience. Knowledge concerning the environment is arranged in certain patterns or *disciplines* reflecting such experience. However invidious this may be, some distinction into disciplines is inevitable in order to narrow the field from which images may be drawn in any particular case. The general pattern thus imposed is therefore the first step in programme formulation leading to division of labour with all its resulting difficulties and benefits. The distinction between an active and a general technology-image drawn in Chapter 4 builds on this basic feature of any advanced human civilization.

Every so often the active technology-image proves inadequate as a basis for solving a problem. Under the mixed scanning strategy, one should go to the next-higher level of programme formulation and select a new general solution. But what if that has been tried already? Should one continue to proceed systematically, going from one level to the next? Ideally, perhaps; but again there are limitations of time. This is where creativity comes into play. Creativity ". . . means to produce a relevant combination here and now which on the basis of probability . . . should have been found only in the . . . distant future" (Deutsch, 1966).

This concept emphasizes that a creative solution is certainly one that must be judged rationally. Indeed, the criterion is whether the proposed solution stands up to criticism in the same way as one that was reached by systematic procedures. This is why Deutsch emphasizes that creativity means to produce a *relevant* combination, the standard of relevance obviously referring to the fact that the solution must be a justifiable one. Rationality and creativity are therefore not opposed to each other. That the rational argument assessing its relevance is only constructed after the solution has been found is not significant; what counts is whether it holds water.[4]

How do people arrive at "relevant combinations" earlier than by using systematic procedures? One aspect of this question seems to be most relevant to the analogy of creative planning and individuals engaging in creative thinking—that there are *two different kinds of thinking involved*. One takes place within a relatively well-ordered framework and conforms to our views of rational thought, but cannot cope with situations *outside*

---

[4]As suggested in Chapter 3, rational arguments are, anyway, best seen as reconstructions for the purpose of justifying choices.

that particular framework. The other type is less orderly but may lead to surprising solutions and ultimately to the choice of an entirely new technology-image. When combined, these types of convergent and divergent thinking enable truly creative responses to an ever-changing environment in a way which neither of the two would be capable of providing on its own:

> .... in convergent thinking, the aim is to discover the one right answer to a problem set. It is highly directed, essentially logical thinking of the kind required in science or mathematics. It is also the kind required for the solution of most intelligence tests. In divergent thinking, on the other hand, the aim is to produce a large number of possible answers, none of which is necessarily more correct than the others though some may be more original. Such thinking is marked by its variety and fertility rather than by its logical precision (Zangwill, 1966).

Convergent and divergent thinking have been thought of as describing two different personality types with different aptitudes, for instance for scientific as against "creative", artistic work. But Hudson (1966), having reviewed the literature on creativity, finds:

> The platitudes which ache to be released from this complex literature are the ones about the original scientist being the scientist who possesses some of the divergent qualities of the artist; and the successful artist being the one who enjoys some of the rigor and dedicated single-mindedness of the scientist. The notion accords neatly with Kuhn's analysis of scientific invention—that it depends upon a tension between the forces of tradition and revolution.[5]

The same type of argument is also made by Deutsch (1966) in his distinction between child and adult learning. One may conclude that man possesses a facility for relaxing the rigidity of convergent thinking, of making the boundaries between his active and general technology-image permeable, so that his thoughts can cut across them. My proposition is that the same may be said about planning agencies. But because (for reason given in Chapter 4) we must visualize planning agencies as embracing only

---

[5]The parallel to Kuhn's thesis concerning *The Structure of Scientific Revolutions* (1962) is indeed striking. Kuhn points in the same direction of the combination of two different ways of thinking as being essential to growth. His thesis applies to a social system, the system of knowledge production, or science. He distinguishes between two types of science. The activity of "normal science" is "puzzle-solving", that is the solution of albeit difficult problems within one framework, one "paradigm". Occasionally, however, "normal science" fails to deal with recurrent problems so that it breaks down and a "paradigm change" occurs. After a while, this paradigm change is completed and a new "normal science" emerges.

the active technology-image and not the general one as held by the community at large, creativity on the part of planning agencies requires that they should keep themselves open to information coming from *outside* their institutional boundaries. This would enable planning to become creative by oscillating between convergent and divergent thinking.

Convergent thinking is represented by the normal operations of planning agencies.[6] The question is obviously: through which channels and by which procedures does a planning agency engage in divergent thinking? Here, a new look at the model of planning agencies will help. Every rôle in the model is occupied by one or more people. Figure 6.1 shows a hypothetical situation with circles representing councillors, planners and members of the public in their respective positions.

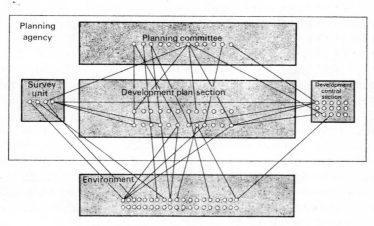

FIG. 6.1. Channels for divergent thinking

There are many relationships cutting across boundaries, *each representing a potential channel for divergent thinking*. These relationships are based on the fact that every person plays more than one rôle; the councillor is not only a "selector", he is also a party member, representative of his constituency, chairman of an amenity society, small shopkeeper, father of school children, and so forth. Indeed, everybody occupying any of the

[6]They represent what Kuhn calls "puzzle-solving".

rôles of planning agencies is also in some sense outside them: the shɔp
owned by a councillor may be threatened by a central area development
scheme; a planner may have to apply for planning permission. These
relations of personal identity apart, there are numerous other links such as
friendships or allegiances which cut across boundaries. It is therefore
possible to represent the rôles involved in planning as being enmeshed in
a complex network of relations cross-cutting the boundaries separating
individual components of planning agencies as well as planning agencies
from the outside world. For planning agencies to engage in divergent
thinking, they must activate the informal network of relations cutting
across boundaries and listen to relevant information which comes through
its multiple channels.

I shall now illustrate this proposition with reference to a case study of
how planners failed to listen, or listened only reluctantly, to the information
coming through this network. In interpreting this case study, I shall argue
that public participation in planning is one way of ensuring that they do
listen. Quite apart from views about the improvements to democratic
control which may flow from its introduction, public participation thus
provides the preconditions for creative planning: the public possesses a
mass of varied information which a planning agency by itself cannot provide, not only technical information, but also information about the way
in which interests are affected by planning proposals. It is a kind of *political
intelligence* built on a personal interest, either of a direct or of an altruistic
type. Persons with such an interest are highly motivated and usually have
access to means for alternative ways of solving problems. They thus provide
a source of *variety* in planning which goes far beyond that provided by a
less interested planner.

The case study concerns a proposed road in the salt-mining village of
Hallstatt in Upper Austria.[7] This is a small village situated on a steep
mountain slope by the side of a beautiful lake. The slope is so steep as to
make access difficult, and until quite recently the only access has been by
boat.

Hallstatt is very picturesque. The view from the lake is particularly
famous because of the roofline of the boathouses along its shores. Consequently, there was an uproar when it was proposed that some of these

[7]For a German version of this and two other case studies see Faludi (1970/1).

boathouses be pulled down so that a bypass could be built along the shores of the lake.

Ṫ ie government of Upper Austria had an interest in building the road as it would give access to a cable car in which they had invested money. Since many of the buildings in Hallstatt itself were listed, and since the slope was far too steep to build a road above the village, planners thought their solution was the only sensible one. Even then, considerable technical difficulties would have to be overcome because there was not enough land to build the bypass on, and stilts were needed to carry it above the surface of the lake. For reasons of cost, the alternative of building a tunnel through the mountain was dismissed out of hand.

The public outcry did not deter the planners. They were utterly convinced that the road would eventually have to be built their way. They went ahead with detailed plans, even entering into financial commitments. However, some people taking part in the discussions had access to information of a highly detailed technical kind which the planners could hardly be expected to possess: an outspoken opponent, the director of the local museum, could point out that there had been a landslide in 1808 making the underground conditions just off the shore of the lake treacherous. The director of the salt mines could argue that the rock above Hallstatt was soft but solid, so that tunnels could be cut very easily without much further support. He also happened to know of a similar project where the considerable ventilation problems of such a tunnel had been solved by building two one-way tubes instead of one two-way tunnel, so that the passing vehicles acted as compressors and took care of most of the ventilation.

These two committed experts published articles in a local paper, mobilized national groups and involved outside experts. On the face of it, their success was not very great. All that they achieved was the concession that, when the official project was put out for public tender, alternative proposals could be submitted for consideration. In the event, most of the submissions were not for the official project at all. Hard-headed businessmen had calculated that the risk introduced by the conditions of the ground off the shore, coupled with knowledge of the relatively favourable constitution of the rock, made a tunnel the more financially acceptable proposition. Eventually, two one-way tunnels were built, though at a higher cost than would have been incurred had the proposal been taken up originally. This was because of rising building costs, but was also due to the costs of working out the official project and the purchasing and demolition of buildings in anticipation of its implementation.[8]

This example shows how planning decisions could be improved by public involvement. Had the intention of building a bypass been published earlier, and had the planners been prepared to listen to whatever local expertise was available (and of course also to ordinary citizens both in Hallstatt and elsewhere who felt very strongly about its scenic beauty), the project could have been built much earlier and at a reduced cost. As it happened, without an awareness of the existence of this peculiar mixture of technical and political intelligence which members of the public have, and without the existence of statutory procedures for public participation, the planners were simply not attuned to accepting that vital information could be obtained simply by listening to what people had to say.

It is possible to generalize from this case and say that the more prepared planners are to listen, the better the chances of finding creative solutions to complex problems such as these. In this context highly committed groups are probably the most valuable sources of the "political" intelligence which I talked about earlier. Planning agencies should therefore look upon pressure groups as a source of creative planning. They provide access to parts of the general technology-image with which planning agencies themselves do not have many links. Planning agencies should therefore become receptive to being influenced, especially at the formative stages of planning, and the more so, the less clearly their problem relates to any specific technology-image held. As with individuals described as *open-minded* when they are ready to accept new information about their environment and themselves, keeping an open mind is a mark of distinction in planning.

BALANCING COMMITMENT AGAINST CRITICISM

Having highly committed groups operating in the environment of planning agencies providing sources of variety through criticism has a disadvantage. They hinder decision-taking, for to make a choice always means to cut out a great variety of possible alternatives and to disregard

---

[8]The two parallel case studies confirmed the availability of great amounts of highly relevant technical information outside planning agencies, and the likelihood of costs resulting from their reluctance to pay attention to this.

some criticisms. Choices therefore require something which one may liken to individual will-power. This brings us again into that area where the previous chapter ended: the rôle of politics in planning.

Deutsch (1966), in introducing the concept of will-power into his discussion of decision-making, posits that will is the putting into operation of data proposed from the past in such a manner as to override most information received after a certain deadline. To do so is only feasible where the actor commands resources which he is prepared to mobilize so as to influence the environment.

This will-power and scepticism are opposed to each other. Nevertheless, they are part of what makes a mature person, who therefore needs to strike a balance between the two. Similarly planning agencies have to strike a balance between fostering criticism and commitment because, in planning agencies too, these are in opposition. The problem is one which Diesing (1962) regards as the key issue of what he describes as "political rationality", that is rational thought directed towards maintaining and improving decision structures. It is, furthermore, one which can never be resolved once and for all. The balance between criticism and variety on the one hand and commitment on the other is constantly threatened. The operation of many different critical minds results in knowledge which is imperialist in nature. There are no known limits to its expansion.

This creates two related problems for the maintenance of balance between knowledge and commitment. Firstly, knowledge nibbles away on normative commitments. It is foolish to be committed to how the world ought to look when there is evidence of how it actually looks. The Catholic Church, for instance, had to concede in the end that Galileo's views based on observations were superior as a cosmic image to its own teaching. Secondly, knowledge transforms the environment, sometimes resulting in quite severe stresses which nowadays erupt in the form of technological obsolescence and an ensuing social dislocation. Knowledge thus continuously creates new situations of which we do not have appropriate technology-images. In coping with new situations, there are always risks to be taken, and there must be decisions to end enquiries and to move into action.

Unfortunately, because problems created by knowledge tend to be new, the appropriate commitment may not exist. Coping with change thus becomes as much a problem of formulating preferences (that is of politics) as it is one of increasing our understanding: knowledge, via what is commonly called automation, appears to create a world of widespread abundance on the one hand and technological unemployment on the other. This meets with a value system emphasizing the virtues of thrift, competition and individual achievement. Unless changed, this value system may prevent man from adapting to a situation where most goods and services could be distributed irrespective of individual merit (Webber, 1968/9).

Since understanding is the prime mover behind this type of turbulence in the environment, it is impossible in principle to combat it by increasing understanding of the environment. More understanding would simply create yet more turbulence. Never will it be possible to cope without values and the continuous formation of new commitments through politics.

But one can not only have too little commitment but also too much. This leads to calling a halt to the search for alternatives, and to disregard criticism and information about the failure of one's chosen course of action. The balance between criticism and commitment is therefore always threatened from both sides, because there is always the danger of too much criticism and too little commitment or too much commitment and not enough criticism. The maintenance of this balance is a recurring problem for planning agencies: some thought must always be given to adjusting their own structures and procedures. This is the concern of *The Politics of Rational Planning.*[9]

PLANNING PATHOLOGIES

The politics of rational planning is a politics of a second order concerned with how ordinary political processes relate to planning. Likewise, the rationality involved is a second-order rationality: to plan successfully does not necessarily mean to plan in a completely rational way. Given the limitations on their capacity for handling information neither individuals nor planning agencies can do that. As Kahn (1969) says so aptly: "True

[9]In one form or another this problem of balancing commitment and criticism has concerned a number of writers. Thus Diesing (1962) talks about the need to maintain a balance between unification and diversification, Buckley (1967) about an optimum mix between stability and flexibility in complex adaptive socio-cultural systems, and Grauhan and Strudelt (1971) about "the conflict between the opening of the full range of choice through an extensive 'socialization of conflict' and the necessary capacity of any choice structure to eliminate, at least for the actual choice situation, all possible alternatives which in the end are not chosen".

rationality . . . always allows for the irrational". Therefore, planning cannot be measured solely against the standard of rationality. Its criterion of success is whether it copes with limitations by invoking planning strategies, engaging in creative planning, and striking a balance between commitment and scepticism. Planning pathologies are the reasons *why planning agencies do not take any one or more of these approaches.*

Again we invoke our analogy with the human mind. This idea of transferring experiences concerning pathologies from the individual to organizations is thus consistent with the basic idea of this book and has its parallels in the work of Deutsch (1966):

> A good many decisions depend in part on the configuration of the communication channels at decision points in the political and social system in which they occur. . . . In such situations, insights applicable to the pathology of the decision system of an individual personality may offer at least some general policy suggestion for preserving and safeguarding the autonomy and long-run existence of larger organizations . . . .

Deutsch himself suggests that the ethical imperatives of the great religions of this world may be interpreted as rules designed to remedy pathological aspects of decision-making. Thus, he equates humility with the demand for openness of decision systems, faith with commitment, reverence with the high valuation of information, love with respect and grace, and receptivity for it, with the acknowledgement of the possibility of unpredictable events. Miller *et al.* (1960), in their work on *Plans and the Structure of Behavior* proposing a psychology based on the notion of man as engaging in planning, also pursue this line by interpreting various psychological illnesses as the effort to cling to plans or to parts of plans. Beer (1966) similarly talks about "thought blockages" as the reasons for ineffective management, thus drawing the analogy between individual and organizational thinking.

In introducing the concept of planning pathology I indicate an area of future research, for there are not enough empirical studies available to do more than suggest the connection between planning pathologies and planning limitations. Research into this must treat planning as an observable phenomenon. Therefore, before launching into the final part, where some very general notions will be given of how planning pathologies may be obviated by properly designing planning agencies and their procedures, I shall in Part III venture to provide the tools for research into planning.

REFERENCES

BEER, S. (1966) *Decision and Control*, John Wiley, New York.

BRANCH, M. C. (1969) Comprehensive planning, Lecture at the American Yugo-slav Project, Ljubljana.

BRAYBROOKE, D. and LINDBLOM, C. E. (1963) *A Strategy of Decision-Policy Evaluation as a Social Process*, Free Press, New York.

BUCKLEY, W. (1967) *Sociology and Modern Systems Theory*, Prentice-Hall, Engle-wood Cliffs, N.J.

DEUTSCH, K. W. (1966) *The Nerves of Government—Models of Political Communi-cation and Control*, 2nd ed. Macmillan, New York–London.

DIESING, P. (1962) *Reason in Society*, University of Illinois Press, Urbana.

DROR, Y. (1968) *Public Policymaking Reexamined*, Chandler, Scranton, Penn.

EDDISON, T. (1973) *Local Government: Management and Corporate Planning*, Leonhard Hill Books, Aylesbury, Bucks.

EMERY, F. E. and TRIST, E. L. (1969) The causal texture of organizational environments, *Systems Thinking* (edited by EMERY, F. E.), Penguin, Harmonds-worth.

*ETZIONI, A. (1967) Mixed scanning: a "third" approach to decision-making, *Public Administration Review*, Vol. 27, pp. 385–92.

ETZIONI, A. (1968) *The Active Society*, Collier-Macmillan, London.

FALUDI, A. (1970/1) Pluralismus im Planungsprozeß, *Informationen der Arbeits-gemeinschaft für interdisziplinäre angewandte Sozialforschung*, Bd. 2, S. 75–92.

FALUDI, A. (1973) *A Reader in Planning Theory*, Pergamon, Oxford.

GEORGE, F. H. (1965) *Cybernetics and Biology*, Oliver & Boyd, Edinburgh.

GRAUHAN, R. R. and STRUDELT, W. (1971) Political rationality reconsidered, *Policy Sciences*, Vol. 2, pp. 249–70.

HUDSON, L. (1966) *Contrary Imagination—A Psychological Study of the English Schoolboy*, Methuen, London.

KAHN, J. (1969) *Studies in Social Policy and Planning*, Russell Sage Foundation, New York.

KUHN, T. S. (1962) *The Structure of Scientific Revolutions*, University of Chicago Press, Chicago.

*LINDBLOM, C. E. (1959) The science of muddling through, *Public Administration Review*, Vol. 19, pp. 79–88.

MILLER, G. A. (1968) *The Psychology of Communication*, Penguin, Harmonds-worth.

MILLER, G. A., GALANTER, E. and PRIBHAN, K. H. (1960) *Plans and the Structure of Behavior*, Holt, Rinehart & Winston, New York.

SIMON, H. A. (1956) Rational choice and the structure of the environment, *Psycho-logical Review*, Vol. 63, pp. 129–38, and *Systems Thinking* (edited by EMERY, F. E.), Penguin, Harmondsworth.

WEBBER, M. (1968/9) Planning in an environment of change: Beyond the indus-trial age; Permissive planning, *The Town Planning Review*, Vol. 39, pp. 179–95; Vol. 39, pp. 277–95.

ZANGWILL, O. L. (1966) Quoted after HEATH, T. (1971) Creativity in design systems, *Architectural Association Quarterly*, Vol. 3, No. 2, pp. 4–9.

    *Included in FALUDI, A. (1973) *A Reader in Planning Theory*, Pergamon, Oxford.

PART III

TOWARDS A POSITIVE THEORY OF PLANNING

In this part I shall try to indicate ways in which a positive theory of planning may be developed. The reasons for talking about a positive theory were explained in Chapter 2: once developed, it allows one to invoke explanations following the deductive model: particular instances of planning can then be explained by subsuming them under relevant laws of planning.

Part V of the companion volume to this book presents three out of the relatively small number of published papers devoted to the aim of developing a positive theory. In the introduction to that section of the work, I strike a note of scepticism about the possibility of achieving the target of firm knowledge about planning based on extensive research (Faludi, 1973). Even if the difficulties which bedevil all social-science research did not warrant scepticism about developing positive theories, the likelihood of extensive programmes of research into planning getting under way quickly, and of their findings becoming available as and when needed, is small.

The same scepticism is justified *vis-à-vis* the proposals made in the following pages. I can only hope that readers will find what I have found in the work of others working towards a positive theory of planning: that the discipline of the attempt to formulate researchable hypotheses reflects back on their own clarity of thought—a benefit to be derived over and above, and independently from, any findings based on empirical research. This of course does not mean that one should not aim for research into planning, but that one should not rely on its solving all the problems of planning theory. In the following three chapters I shall therefore give the outlines of a research design with every hypothesis, this design indicating the variables which one would probably be looking for in testing them.

The concepts around which the following hypotheses are built have been derived from a synthesis of my reading of the planning literature, and from the conceptual framework for planning thought (in particular the components of the model of planning agencies) built in Part II. The best way of explaining this is to relate how I came to develop this part of the argument. It all started from an attempt to bring conceptual order into my perception of what the literature said about planning. Firstly, I noticed that certain of the recurring terms used to describe issues in planning (for example blueprint planning, the process approach, comprehensive planning, allocative planning) referred to opposite extremes. I then linked these pairs together by the concept of dimensions of planning, "dimension" referring to observable features of the conduct of planning agencies.[1]

Each of the pairs thus referred to one dimension of planning, and consisted of extreme types of planning. I shall now call these extreme types modes of planning.[2] Actual instances of planning always fall somewhere between them.[3]

The three dimensions of planning discussed in the part are as follows:[4]

the blueprint versus the process mode of planning (Chapter 7);
the rational-comprehensive versus the disjointed-incrementalist mode of planning (Chapter 8);
the normative versus the functional mode of planning (Chapter 9).

There is an issue underlying each of these three dimensions, the nature of which affects the order of presenting them. The first is the extent to which planning should (and could) get away from the inflexible approach inherited from its engineering tradition. The second is the extent to which

[1] This use of the concept of a dimension follows suggestions made by Zetterberg (1962). Dror (1963) uses the more general concept of a "facet".

[2] Friedmann (1967) describes these as "forms of planning".

[3] A number of other authors have used opposite extremes to describe planning indicating that planning would in reality fall between the two; see Friedmann (1967), Madge (1968) and Kahn (1969a and b).

[4] LeBreton and Henning (1961), who also use the concept of "dimensions of planning", identify nine: complexity, significance, comprehensiveness, time, specificity, completeness, flexibility, frequency, confidential nature, formality, authorization, ease of implementation, ease of control. However, most of these are really "issue attributes" in Bolan's sense (Bolan, 1969) rather than dimensions of the way planning agencies go about their business.

planning could (and indeed should) plan as the ideal of rationality suggests: by comprehensively evaluating all conceivable alternatives. It can only do so by adopting the process approach defined under the previous dimension. The last issue is whether or not to extend the area of scope of rational choice from means to ends.

Before launching into the first of these, I shall show how I came to see these dimensions in relationship to the model of planning agencies. I developed this model quite independently in order to understand the structure of planning agencies but whilst doing so perceived that the modes of planning corresponded to certain typical ways in which planning agencies act. If this was indeed so, then it should be possible to explain the modes of planning in terms of the components of the model of planning agencies. More specifically, I tried to identify those factors which led to a planning agency operating in a certain way, and those which limited its ability to do so. In the subsequent chapters, I shall differentiate between these as determinants of, and constraints on, planning. A determinant should encourage the tendency to engage in a certain mode of planning whilst a constraint counteracts that tendency.

I shall now present this idea of modes of planning. By couching it in terms which enable research to be conducted, I hope to show how one moves from models to testable hypotheses. These, in due course, may become laws of planning or even the elements of a positive theory of planning. This is of course subject to the reservations made above, and subject also to the fact that I am, obviously, in no way claiming to cover the *whole* field which a complete positive theory of planning would have to span.

Why should one present the terms of a positive theory without being able to present the fully fledged theory? The answer is that the process of deriving these terms proved interesting in itself. Furthermore, it was sometimes possible to throw light on certain planning issues. Also, during the process, new questions were cast up. Some of these required the elaboration of the conceptual framework of planning thought by the introduction of new concepts. I shall end Part III with a chapter dealing with these, despite the fact that they are not strictly speaking part of the positive theory of planning, in order to demonstrate my point that the benefits which accrue from the rigor of working towards a positive theory are not limited to obtaining thàt theory.

REFERENCES

*BOLAN, R. (1969) Community decision behavior: the culture of planning, *Journal of the American Institute of Planners*, Vol. **35**, pp. 301–10.

*DROR, Y. (1963) The planning process: a facet design, *International Review of Administrative Sciences*, Vol. **29**, pp. 46–58.

FALUDI, A. (1973) *A Reader in Planning Theory*, Pergamon, Oxford.

*FRIEDMANN, J. (1967) A conceptual model for the analysis of planning behavior, *Administrative Science Quarterly*, Vol. **12**, pp. 225–52.

KAHN, A. J. (1969a) *Theory and Practice of Social Planning*, Russell Sage Foundation, New York.

KAHN, A. J. (1969b) *Studies in Social Policy and Planning*, Russell Sage Foundation, New York.

LeBRETON, P. P., and HENNING, D. A. (1961) *Planning Theory*, Prentice-Hall, Englewood Cliffs, N.J.

MADGE, C. (1968) Planning (Social), *International Encyclopedia of the Social Sciences*, Vol. **9**, pp. 125–9.

ZETTERBERG, H. (1962) Theorie, Forschung und Praxis in der Soziologie, *Handbuch der empirischen Sozialforschung* (Edited by KÖNIG, R.), Enke Verlag, Stuttgart.

*Included in FALUDI, A. (1973) *A Reader in Planning Theory*, Pergamon, Oxford.

CHAPTER 7

The Blueprint versus the Process Mode of Planning

THERE is a growing feeling that planning is not about the production of glossy plans and the unswerving execution of proposals they contain, which is what *blueprint planning* means. Rather, the current mood stresses the continuous nature of the planning enterprise or the *process approach* to planning. This chapter is about the dimension of planning to which these two concepts refer. In their pure form, they represent the two modes of planning at the opposite ends of this dimension. Observable instances always fall somewhere between these.

THE MODES DEFINED

The central feature of the very concept of planning is often seen as that of a "... *plan*, which will formally consist of one or more goal statements that are successively reduced to more specific policies, programs, and projects, all spaced out over a limited period of time and related to sets of priorities, standards, investment needs and financial arrangements" (Friedmann, 1966). To keep within the terminology introduced in Chapter 4, such a *programme* must build on a great deal of thinking performed *in advance* of its implementation so that there remain no uncertainties about its leading to the desired effects. This blueprint mode of planning is therefore an approach *whereby a planning agency operates a programme thought to attain its objectives with certainty*. Because of this certainty, a decision-taker committed to the objectives is bound to execute the programme. Also, modification during implementation is not anticipated. A prototype of blueprint planning is the design of large-scale engineering projects like barrages.

Where this very stringent condition applies, blueprint planning is the proper approach. But obviously few such instances exist. As Friend and Jessop (1969) demonstrate, there are many sources of uncertainty which make it impossible to derive programmes in which one can be confident enough to execute without anticipating later modification. Where blueprint planning is practised, uncertainties notwithstanding, it is based on grossly simplified assumptions making for its inefficiency and heavy-handedness.

The process mode of planning, on the other hand, is an approach *whereby programmes are adapted during their implementation as and when incoming information requires such changes.* In process planning, the plan document itself, where this programme is laid down (which is of central importance in blueprint planning—hence its name), becomes far less significant, perhaps even ephemeral, a daily computer printout. Process planning becomes an approach in which strategic information and feedback impinge directly on action, providing signals that lead to incremental adjustments to its direction and intensity (Friedmann, 1966). However, process planning does not necessarily mean that the time horizon is a short one. Nor does it mean that the interdependence between various objectives, and the actions leading to their attainment, are disregarded as in disjointed incrementalism (to be discussed in Chapter 8). In process planning, any action taken may very well form a consistent part of longer-term, comprehensive policies which are themselves subject to review in the light of new information so that process planning operates simultaneously on several time horizons.

A process approach is best taken whenever a programme cannot be expected to result in the attainment of the objectives with certainty: and whenever such certainty cannot be attained economically either by firming up the underlying image or by increasing the control exercised by the planning agency. In this situation, rather than lapsing into inaction while striving to provide a firm image, process planning proceeds by implementing some elements of a programme and hopes that the information thus generated will result in more knowledge concerning the next stages.[1] This requires accepting the risks attached to action in a world of uncertainty and facing up to them; it needs the courage to proceed whilst still waiting

---

[1] A strong point for this approach of experimenting simply in order to find out what the effects of a proposal are has been made by Meyerson and Banfield (1955).

for the messages which will signal errors; it means accepting these with humility when they come and analysing them impartially for the changes they may bring to one's original assumptions. In short, process planning requires the spirit of enquiry and criticism which characterizes science.

BLUEPRINT PLANNING CRITICIZED

In the first instance, blueprint planning is justified only where the condition of complete certainty is met. Failing that, it must proceed on the basis of simplifying assumptions and implement its programmes by exercising relatively high degrees of control. Criticisms of planning as being blueprint-oriented concentrate precisely on these points: gross simplification and heavy-handedness. Urban planning provides an example. Its blueprint orientation is partly explained by the dominance in its early days of architects and engineers. The latter frequently use satisficing strategies (see Chapter 6) involving simplifying assumptions and thus blueprint planning, with reasonable success. Additionally, the problems with which, at the outset, urban planning was faced, were of a relatively simple kind, as Webber (1968/9) pointed out:

> ... the early city planners could usefully interpret solutions to problems as standing in direct one-to-one relations to demonstrated causes, typhoid to a water-carried salmonella, traffic breakdowns to unpaved muddy streets, rodent infestation to accumulated garbage, and so on. The science of the times supplied the explanation that in turn led to direct technical solutions . . . .

The tools with which this kind of planning operates are, again in Webber's words, ". . . directly from the kit-bag of civil engineering". They are the technical standards, the master plan, and the land-use regulation. They certainly *did* help to alleviate some of the problems of their time, where simple, "mechanistic", assumptions concerning the causes of problems, and the firm images based on them, were adequate, and where these problems were urgent enough to make the necessary controls available for acting on the basis of these images. The success story of this kind of blueprint planning is the way in which the large-scale epidemics of the nineteenth century came to an end through the achievements of sanitary engineering.[2]

[2]For an argument suggesting that improvements preceded advances in medical knowledge see p. 16.

Unfortunately, the same type of image was extended to other kinds of urban problems. If epidemics had an identifiable cause which could be removed by assuming certain powers of control, then so, it was believed, had other problems. A derivative of this belief was the assumption that a single determined intervention directed against the root-causes of a problem could alleviate it once and for all. Much of the early talk about housing and planning was therefore accompanied by the assurance that the measures proposed would be short-lived.

As an example of an extension of unsuitably firm images, one can quote investigations into the correlation between death rate and the number of rooms in tenements (Denyer and Hand, 1906). The inference drawn was that the high rates resulted from overcrowding; if only overcrowding were stamped out, death rates would decline. To reduce overcrowding, it was deemed sufficient to legislate against high density, in line with Charles Booth's contention ". . . that interference by administrative action and penalties at each point at which life falls below a minimum accepted standard is the way by which the problem must be approached . . .".[3]

Thus, it was thought that a solution had been found based on empirical investigations, with clear implications for policy. Ever since, the concern to reduce density has been a prominent one with town planners. The first "Housing, Town Planning, Etc., Act" of 1909, limited though its powers were, was expected to bring such a reduction about, with one of its promoters, John Burns, saying: "I trust the chief benefits of this Act will be, first fewer houses per acre, more space and gardens about the dwelling . . .".[4] Later, Raymond Unwin was to concern himself most prominently with proving that there was *Nothing Gained by Overcrowding* (Unwin, 1912), and, as Foley (1960) shows, the planning policies of the post-war period were still held together by this very same belief: that new towns, green belts and industrial relocation, taken together, would help reduce overcrowding.

There are many parallels to this way of thinking. The Victorians believed in the seductively simple theory that poverty was caused by individual laziness, and built a whole system of social policy, the Poor Laws, on this theory (Pinker, 1971). Peterson (1966) quotes another example: the

---

[3]Quoted by Denyer and Hand (1906).
[4]Quoted by Jenkin (1910).

rationale of early Western economic aid to developing countries, namely that industrialization would lead to democratization. Nowadays it is said that inflation is caused by excessive wage demands, and policy implications are drawn from this view. The idea of an "efficient cause", an identifiable prior event standing in a clear relation to the phenomenon to be explained, has a very powerful appeal to our common sense which is largely conditioned by the apparent success of the mechanical sciences. One accepts all too easily any explanation that provides such a cause, especially when it can be translated into a snap solution to a problem which one would dearly love to forget about as quickly as possible.

Throughout most of its history, urban planning has accepted such explanations and based policies on them. The views that slums resulted from deteriorated houses; lack of community feeling from too large and amorphous urban areas; and the absence of neighbourliness from the failure to provide corner shops are cases in point. The prescriptions derived from these images are as compellingly simple as the one derived from the correlation established between death-rate and overcrowding: pull "substandard" houses down, and you get rid of slums; split urban areas up into small neighbourhood units, and there will be revival of the village community; provide corner shops in new housing areas, and people will be as friendly to each other as they are in Bethnal Green. The spirit of this type of prescription is summed up by Davidoff's sardonic remark about physical planners who ". . . cope with the problem of alienated man with the recommendation of reducing the time of the journey to work" (Davidoff, 1965).[5]

Every single one of these policies, and the simplistic images on which they are based, have been subjected to extensive criticism coming, in the main, from social scientists. The tenor of these criticisms ranges from the claim that simplistic assumptions must lead to ineffective policies to the view that policies based on such assumptions are positively harmful. This is the basis of much of the criticism of urban renewal. Its discussion has certainly helped to make urban planners more circumspect concerning their planning policies (Webber, 1963). The single most important result of this barrage of criticism was the shift towards a process mode of planning.

[5]However sardonic, the remark is almost word by word what Gutkind (1964) asserts.

THE SHIFT TOWARDS THE PROCESS MODE OF
PLANNING

A good example of the way in which a process approach has replaced
blueprint planning is that of urban renewal. The problem was originally
defined merely as one of improving the physical fabric of towns and cities,
and ignoring completely the social dimension of the urban community
(Davidoff, 1965). Where programmes were devised simply to increase the
standard of housing provision or, worse still, to increase the rateable value,
this had the most devastating effects on certain sections of the community
who were uprooted, pushed around and often deprived of cheap accommo-
dation of the type they could afford (Frieden, 1965; Hartmann, 1964).

As a result of criticism, urban planners have become alert to unexpected
side effects of renewal projects, and alternatives to comprehensive redevelopment are being considered. Urban renewal is being recognized as a
problem which extends far beyond the realm of physical planning. More
recent policies also deal with employment, with education and with more
general improvements to the quality of life. The assumption is that physical
standards are secondary to these, and will follow suit if improvements are
made to the quality of life generally. These improvements include economic
opportunities and the exercise of citizenship.

The images underlying planning are therefore becoming more comprehensive. I shall turn to this in the following chapter. Here, we shall simply
note that more comprehensive images spanning a wide field including
physical improvements and measures in the areas of employment, social
provisions and institutional structure are necessarily characterized by much
greater degrees of uncertainty than are partial images. By welding partial
images together, uncertainty accumulates. It is therefore no surprise that
planners are becoming much less convinced of the success of comprehensive policies, and much more interested in their actual effects. This is
reflected in a growing interest in monitoring. They hope that success, or
failure, of policies (not only of those in the field of urban renewal) will
become measurable, and that unexpected side effects may be detected at
an early stage.

Likewise, planners are less content nowadays to deliver a blueprint and
wait for its implementation. They are much more concerned with having
an impact on day-to-day policies. Blueprints for a twenty- to thirty-year

period are therefore distinctly out of fashion, and the preference is for plans for several time horizons and different degrees of specificity from the most general, long-range type of "goal planning" down to the annual budget (Friedmann, 1966/7). Also, thought is being given to the inter-relations between these various levels of planning, and to the way revision should take place. For instance, in the companion volume, attention is drawn to the impact which Meyerson's paper (Meyerson, 1956) has had not only on American planning thought, but also on planning legislation. Similar progress in the direction of process planning may be observed in British planning legislation since the report on *The Future of Development Plans* (Ministry of Housing and Local Government, 1965). Development plans are now differentiated into more general structure plans and more specific local plans. Of these, structure plans are in any case becoming less of a blueprint: firstly, they are less detailed than development plans; secondly, they may be reviewed as and when required; and thirdly, the relevant act incorporates public participation as a statutory requirement, thus generating some pressure for flexibility.

However (and this is most evident in the case of monitoring and review), there are limitations to process planning which it is difficult to overcome. There is an inevitable time-lag between actions taken and information concerning their effects (this has been described as the external time-lag in Chapter 4). This time-lag may be so long that process planning becomes far less continuous than people would like to think. Such considerations lead into the key part of this chapter where I shall argue that there are determinants and constraints which make for a certain mode of planning. Understanding these will help in providing a research design on the one hand, and more insights into the difficulties encountered in process planning on the other.

DETERMINANTS AND CONSTRAINTS

There are three factors we shall consider as determinants and constraints of planning along this dimension of the blueprint versus the process mode of planning. They are the image, the extent of control exercised by a planning agency, and the time-lag built into all planning operations. The first and the second act as determinants, the third as a constraint. Table 7.1

gives a preview of the argument. It summarizes the hypothesis that blue-print planning is brought about by a firm image and complete control over the environment, subject to the constraint of small time-lags; and process planning by uncertain images and incomplete control, subject to great time-lags acting as constraints.

TABLE 7.1

DETERMINANTS AND CONSTRAINTS OF BLUEPRINT VERSUS
PROCESS PLANNING

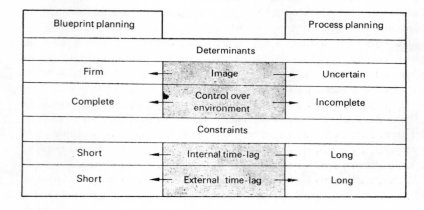

Blueprint planning		Process planning
Determinants		
Firm	Image	Uncertain
Complete	Control over environment	Incomplete
Constraints		
Short	Internal time-lag	Long
Short	External time-lag	Long

Images

The argument will be that a firm image creates a potential for blueprint planning and an uncertain one for process planning. The first offers a description of the environment from which precepts may be derived for manipulating it in order to achieve desired objectives *with certainty*. An uncertain image simply does not offer the same facilities. It only gives an indication of the type of intervention which might lead to a desired effect.

An example of a firm image might be an engineer working on an exten-sive irrigation project. Once he embarks on his project, he is not normally concerned with human reactions. His problems are those of soil mechanics and hydraulics. To overcome these he can use knowledge acquired previously and add to it by experiment, even using small-scale models of his project. Thus he satisfies himself completely about the technical feasibility of his project before building starts. Consequently, he is certain that building barrages, excavating canals, and making other earth movements will have the desired effect.

In keeping with this firm image, the ideal of the engineer engaged in planning irrigation works is that of completed projects designed to the full satisfaction of the specification to which they have been built. By the same token, sanitary engineers envisaged an environment without cholera, one which fortunately now exists in many areas. But because the ideal environment is one in which a certain problem has been removed, this ideal is a *static* one. Indeed, the picture of the ideal environment becomes identical with the blueprint. This is the most characteristic feature of blueprint planning.

As an example of an uncertain image we could take new management styles. The old image of employees being motivated only by their need to earn a living (the firm image underlying old-style management) is being replaced by much more subtle but less certain images of what motivates people to work. Management feels a need to keep much more in touch. This is reflected in co-operative styles, especially in high-skill research and development establishments where job satisfaction is very important for the attainment of satisfactory results. Compared with older management styles, these new approaches are much more like process planning as participatory styles of planning are relative to older planning styles.

Uncertain images are indeed more congenial for dealing with people. Firstly, they are indeterminate as far as individual cases are concerned. Consequently, they incorporate the notion that the individual may react in ways different from the majority of his fellow-men. By recognizing this possibility, process planning tends to leave room for individual autonomy, and directs attention more to the framework within which individuals operate than to controlling their actual conduct. Also, as a complement to the less firm image of process planning, the view of the ideal environment where relevant problems are solved is much less specific. It is tempered by an awareness of complexity in the environment which leads to more caution. Solutions are perhaps seen in terms of a limited number of strategic variables. Policies resulting from process planning tend to be diffuse, general and "permissive" (Webber, 1968/9): negative income tax instead of specific welfare benefits, rent subsidies to individuals instead of rent control on property and so on.

Degree of Control

The second determinant is the degree of control exercised by a planning agency. Complete control leaves no room for the environment, or any part of the environment, to act in ways other than those set by the planning agency. Hence, there will be no unanticipated consequences, and also no feedback to wait for (which is what blueprint planning means). The irrigation engineer who physically changes the landscape of whole regions (as in the building of the Aswan Dam) provides one example of the exercise of complete control. Milder examples of blueprint planning are development corporations of new towns and major town expansions with their relatively great spending power for physical development. New-town planning is therefore closer to the blueprint side of the dimension than is the planning of existing towns. Similarly we have factory managers and staff officers planning the deployment of men and resources with complete confidence that their orders will be carried out.

However, in these examples, more clearly than in others previously quoted, a dilemma of control becomes evident. Control gives a sense of security which may be spurious: where it is complete there is inevitably little reporting back; inefficiency creeps in and a factory organization or army division becomes rigid. Not only do they become ineffective instruments, but the people subjected to control are allowed little say in vital concerns affecting them. This seems to be at the heart of the problems of industrial relations and, by way of analogy, of new-town planning, where there has been much talk about the so-called "new-town blues".

Conversely, incomplete control means that planning agencies must anticipate what other agents will do, striking bargains with them and responding to opportunities as they arise. This requires seeking information through many channels, and flexibility in responding to new situations (which is what process planning means).[6]

[6] A low degree of control does not necessarily mean little influence though. Small amounts of resources may be used strategically in setting a *framework* for other actors to operate within. This type of framework control is the only way in which rational-comprehensive planning can be made to work (as will be demonstrated in the next chapter).

Time-lag

In Chapter 4, the difference between internal and external time-lag was seen as the time which elapses between information being received from the environment and the planning agency response to it and the time which passes between its actions and their effects being reported back to it. These two elements of the total time-lag will be treated separately. In both cases a long time-lag acts as a constraint on the process approach and a short time-lag on blueprint planning.

Time-lag affects the mode of planning in the following way: first of all, the greater the *internal time-lag*, the less frequent the review of plans. The more complex and costly the operation, the more internal time-lag itself increases. The planning of some great engineering works may take years, sometimes longer than their execution, and relates to very complex undertakings involving immense amounts of capital. Engineering works are therefore prototypical examples for blueprint planning, partly because of the internal time-lag involved. But complex planning studies also have a considerable internal time-lag which is why there are limits on the extent to which structure planning, for instance, will be able to engage in process planning.

There is little that can be done about internal time-lag. Except for innovations in the field of planning technology, the scope for which is limited, contingency planning seems to be the only answer. But contingency planning is costly and only feasible where the costs of not having a plan prepared as and when needed appear to be even greater than those of preparing it in advance. There are probably few examples of this kind of contingency planning outside the fields of defence and industry.

Where planning is not a unique operation, where many decisions of a similar kind and of comparatively lower degrees of complexity have to be taken in succession, and where they do not involve major increments of expenditure, the tendency will be for shorter internal time-lag. But the need for immediate and intelligent responses from planning agencies is not limited to repetitive problems of minor significance. On the contrary, it is very often the unforeseen event which requires an immediate reaction. This results in planning agencies being slow, precisely where quick action is needed. Planners perceive this problem well very, and their efforts to build overall models of the system which they can manipulate is motivated largely by their desire to provide immediate answers.

The second element of time-lag is *external* to the planning agency. Again, engineering works are the prototype of projects which take a very considerable time to complete. They may very well take so long that feedback becomes meaningless, for in the interval the planning agency itself may have changed so completely that it has little ability to benefit from feedback. Therefore, in the case of such projects the only *raison d'être* of a planning agency is often that of delivering a blueprint. Most project teams are disbanded once implementation is under way.

Also, projects which take a long time to complete and cannot easily be curtailed or diverted during their implementation must necessarily be of a blueprint kind, creating their own momentum for completion once they get under way. A further constraint on process planning is the state of the art in monitoring. Its methods and techniques are such as to delay reviews of plans for years: hardly a comfortable prospect for process planning whose need is to react quickly to new information concerning its original assumptions and to changes in client preferences!

On the other hand, short external time-lag acts as a constraint on blueprint planning by making information concerning the actual effects of programmes available relatively soon after measures have been taken. This by itself facilitates making comparisons between actual and anticipated results, and often leads to questioning the certainty with which plans are thought to work. Where such questions are to the point, as they probably are in most cases, this affects the technology-image in turn, and the mode of planning moves towards the process end of the dimension.

A RESEARCH DESIGN

The concepts developed in the previous three sub-sections will help in clarifying some of the problems which process planning faces. Before exploring those, let me give a summary of the concepts discussed, and the variables which may be used in doing research into the relations prevailing between them. Table 7.2 provides this summary. It should be read in conjunction with Table 7.1.

From this and Table 7.1 a hypothesis may be formulated concerning the way in which planning varies along the dimension of blueprint versus process planning. Thus an uncertain image (as indicated, say, by a great number of qualifications in a planning report) and incomplete control (as indicated by the legal powers available) will probably result in process planning (as indicated by expectations of frequent changes of direction, or even by the sheer absence of a detailed plan for the long-term future[7]) subject to the constraint of internal and external time-lag (as indicated in flow charts and planning reports). This hypothesis is testable (as is the

TABLE 7.2

VARIABLES FOR RESEARCH INTO BLUEPRINT VERSUS PROCESS PLANNING

Concepts	*Variables*
Mode of planning (blueprint vs. process)	Existence or non-existence of definite programme covering considerable time spans; confidence expressed in it; frequency of reviews and changes.
Image (firm or uncertain)	Indications in planning reports and from planners of firmness of assumptions underlying programmes.
Internal time-lag (long or short)	Time taken for programme formulation extracted from reports, case studies, interviews, statistics.
External time-lag (long or short)	Time earmarked for completion of projects; time after which first results are expected to become available.
Control (complete or not)	Legal powers; administrative resources; financial assets; type of power structure and administrative system; informal controls.

corollary for blueprint planning): It would be possible for a researcher to observe the variables indicated (no doubt modifying the research design from experience) and to say with some confidence whether the mode of planning actually depends on the factors suggested. The result of such research would then build up to what this part purports to lead towards: a positive theory of planning.

[7]When Friedmann joined the staff of the Tennessee Valley Authority, one of the fine examples of a wide-ranging planning venture, he was surprised to find that no comprehensive plan for the development of its area existed (Friedmann, 1966).

PROBLEMS OF PROCESS PLANNING

To proceed with due caution where knowledge is insufficient, and to react flexibly to challenges, are certainly worthy ideals for planning. Process planning therefore has a much greater appeal than blueprint planning. In this section, I shall sound a cautionary note by describing some of the problems which planning faces in trying to engage in this desirable mode of planning. The concepts described above, and the assumptions made concerning the way they affect the mode of planning, will help in clarifying these, demonstrating my earlier point that there are immediate benefits to be derived from working towards researchable hypotheses. This, of course, does not mean that the hypotheses do not need testing: had they been tested, the following points could be made much more forcefully.

There are two separate problems. One is that of the disparity between the image held and the control exercised by a planning agency. The second is much more evident: the way time-lag militates against process planning. Given the limitations of information-handling capacity this is really no surprise. The only way out is that process planning must employ some of the planning strategies outlined earlier.

As regards any disparity between images and control, here again two cases may be distinguished. One exists where a firm image is available concerning the root causes of a problem, and ways of solving it, but where the powers of control lag behind. Pollution is a case in point. Though I do not wish to underestimate the extent of the problem caused by delays in introducing controls, I think that, by and large, this situation has a self-correcting element built into it, as the host of legislative measures taken (as well as the historical example of sanitary control) indicate. A more difficult problem arises when control is greater than the image would justify. Here, the self-correcting element is absent. If anything, control is self-enhancing, resulting in a vicious circle of more and more control which cannot be broken easily unless there is a crisis. The American urban renewal programme, for instance, spent enormous sums on transforming the physical fabric of towns and cities. Critics had pointed out the effects of this on the poor, and on ethnic minorities in particular. Thus, an image was available from which inadequacies of the current policy could have been deduced. It appears, however, that an urban crisis was needed to effect any changes, some of which very sensibly aim at sharing out resources (including professional skills) and reducing overall control which was the issue in the New York school strike (Skjei, 1972).

The constraints of a relatively long time-lag are always very much in the mind of planners. If it only promises to save time, they will leap on almost any technological bandwagon. Such improvements may certainly help in reducing the time spent on survey work. Aerial photography, various sensors, and even satellites may serve this purpose. More conspicuous even than these are the changes occurring at the technological base of information systems. Social indicators hold similar promises of reducing time-lag by providing instant and comprehensive information from the environment, though the expectations held with respect to both these developments seem exaggerated (Fehl, 1970, 1971; Fehl *et al.*, 1972).

There are corollary strategies on the organizational side. Opening additional channels of communication to the planning agency increases the chances of the reporting of unexpected side effects. Public participation may therefore improve the quality of planning by reducing the time elapsing between undesirable side effects and their detection, at least to the extent that relevant sections of the public are "tuned in" into the decision-making process.[8]

Other methods of reducing time-lag involve compromise in the requirements of continuous adaptation to new information, or planning strategies. Here we meet the paradox of process planning. In order to be able to react quickly to new information the planning agency must stabilize at least some part of its image because of its inability to take simultaneous decisions on several levels. Therefore, time-lag can be reduced, either by creating a framework for detailed decisions (similar to mixed scanning) or by holding

[8]On the other hand, planners may hold that public participation *increases* time-lag. In Britain, for instance, an enquiry has been held into the Greater London Development Plan lasting two years in the wake of which the statutory requirements for public participation have been changed so as to speed the proceedings up. However, it is not entirely certain whether their misgivings are based on an adequate appreciation of the case for public participation. To start with, a development plan for the area of Greater London must be judged an exceptional case. Secondly, and most important, the enquiry has proved to be a great learning experience for the planners during which the content and the character of the plan have changed (Eversley, 1972). This may, however, be interpreted as a sort of *anticipatory feedback* and thus as an indication of process planning. Indeed, the kinds of changes which have occurred in the plan are in the direction of more flexibility and less specificity and thus seem to confirm this view.

small images constant within a larger, more fluid decision-making situation (routinization). As explained before, this is rather like the problem of language. You either think about the choice of words in the context of sentences, or about the structure of sentences, holding the meaning of words constant.

In planning, the equivalent of the first approach is that of trying to model the system as a whole. McLoughlin (1969) describes how he sees development control decisions (decisions on a detailed level) being made speedily by reference to a whole family of models describing the overall situation, and the way in which alternative decisions would affect it. Clearly, in order for this approach to be meaningful, the overall image of the system built into the models must be held constant, at least during any one cycle of development control operations. This framework then takes on something of the character of a blueprint.

The second approach is used even more frequently. It involves building certain ready-made solutions to repetitive problems into the very structure of the planning agency by devising administrative rules, technical standards, internal classification systems and routines and more informal understandings about the way in which detailed decisions ought to be made. In terms of the model of planning agencies, this refers to the automatic programmes which are invoked without involving decision-takers. They are obvious, if only small, examples of blueprint planning.

There is a further intractable problem which process planning faces. This is the long external time-lag in the execution of large-scale projects. A conspicuous example is that of urban motorway programmes. From a technical point of view, their planning tends towards a blueprint approach. Motorway systems cannot normally be divided into many independent elements but rather depend for their effectiveness on the completion of large parts, if not the complete network.[9] Also, in order to effect the tremendous changes which they must bring to the physical fabric of towns and cities, legal powers have to be assumed, large amounts of administrative resources assembled and great sums of money mobilized, thus giving the planning agency concerned tremendous control over the environment and the people living in it.

[9]Donnison (1972) argues the same about comprehensive education: "Some policies cannot be tried out incrementally on the geographical and financial scales at which we are obliged to operate."

The problem is this: assuming even that an urban motorway programme fitted the present and foreseeable requirements of urban living (which is open to doubt, as one is becoming increasingly aware), unknown variables may change this fit even during their construction, not to speak of the long useful life which roadworks have. Such changes may result from the introduction of new technologies, or from shifts in popular preferences. They may even result directly from the upheaval created by the destruction of many thousands of homes in the cause of motorway construction. Though motorways must themselves evidently be built on the basis of firm images, the prior decision of whether they ought to be built or not therefore must be based on another image, that of an urban community being *served* by roads. This image is, however, much less firm. The dilemma is such that large-scale road building programmes had to be abandoned recently in the United States, with fly-overs ending in mid-air as monuments to blueprint planning.

The nearest that one may come to avoiding similar results is to introduce uncertainty of future preferences and future technologies as an explicit cost into evaluation. Airports, motorways, canals, pipelines, container terminals, and power lines are parts of our civilization. But once their implementation has begun they constrain future choices. They certainly cannot be ruled out from the start. They therefore ought to prove themselves in the light of the possible costs imposed by their inflexibility and indivisibility, that is in the light of all the risks involved.[10]

These are the problems of process planning. Some may be contained more easily than others simply by introducing technological improvements. But the problems of possible biases in the assumptions underlying models and administrative rules, and those of the long external time-lag involved in large projects, seem very difficult indeed. Planning has a poor reputation for the arrogance with which such problems were brushed aside in the past. Much of the criticism of planning is directed against an inflated concept of it rather than against the idea of planning as intelligent action, as one of the most vociferous critics of planning, Hayek (1962), points out himself:

[10]For a similar argument see Plowden (1972). The problem is not necessarily limited to infrastructure investments. Grossner (1971) lists major research projects in atomic physics and armaments programmes as examples where decisions are likely to constrain future choice.

> (The) question is whether ... it is better that the holder of coercive power
> should confine himself in general to creating conditions under which the
> knowledge and initiative of individuals is given the best scope so that they can
> plan most successfully: or whether a rational utilisation of our resources
> requires central direction and organisation of all our activities according to
> some consciously constructed 'blueprint'. The socialists of all parties have
> appropriated the term planning for planning of the latter type and it is now
> generally accepted in this sense.

Today planners are struggling bravely towards much more flexible
approaches, and towards exercising their powers in ways closer to Hayek's
first alternative. They must recognize where the limits of these efforts lie,
and where they reach them, be that much more humble.

REFERENCES

*DAVIDOFF, P. (1965) Advocacy and pluralism in planning, *Journal of the American Institute of Planners*, Vol. **31**, pp. 331–8.

DENYER, C. H. and HAND, J. E. (1906) Science and physical development, *Science in Public Affairs* (edited by HAND, J. E.) pp. 1–44. George Allen, London.

DONNISON, D. (1972) Ideologies and policies, *Journal of Social Policy*, Vol. **1**, pp. 97–117.

EVERSLEY, D. (1972) Lecture at the Department of Town Planning, Oxford Polytechnic.

FEHL, G. (1970) Towards a project-oriented information-support system, *Oxford Working Papers in Planning Education and Research*, No. 5, Department of Town Planning, Oxford Polytechnic.

FEHL, G. (1971) *Informations-Systeme, Verwaltungsrationalisierung und die Stadtplaner*, Stadtbau Verlag, Bonn.

FEHL, G. *et al.* (1972) *Planung und Information—Materialien zur Planungsforschung*, Bertelsmann Fachverlag, Berlin.

*FOLEY, D. L. (1960) British town planning: one ideology or three? *British Journal of Sociology*, Vol. **11**, pp. 211–31.

FRIEDEN, B. J. (1965) Towards equality of urban opportunity, *Journal of the American Institute of Planners*, Vol. **31**, pp. 320–30.

FRIEDMANN, J. (1966) The institutional context, *Action under Planning* (edited by GROSS, B. M.), McGraw Hill, New York.

FRIEDMANN, J. (1966/7) Planning as a vocation, *Plan Canada*, Vol. **6**, pp. 99–124, Vol. **7**, pp. 8–26.

FRIEND, J. K. and JESSOP, W. N. (1969) *Local Government and Strategic Choice*, Tavistock Publications, London.

GROSSNER, C. (1971) Wenn Zukunft verplant wird, *Die Zeit*, 9. April, S. 8–9.

GUTKIND, E. A. (1964) *International History of City Development*, Vol. **1**, Free Press, Glencoe.

HARTMANN, C. (1964) The housing of relocated families, *Journal of the American Institute of Planners*, Vol. **30**, pp. 266–86.

HAYEK, F. A. (1962) *The Road to Serfdom* (first published 1944), Routledge & Kegan Paul, London.

JENKIN, C. J. (1910) Some thoughts on town planning, *Housing and Town Planning Conference of the Institution of Municipal and County Engineers* (edited by COLE, Th.), pp. 173–89. London.

MCLOUGHLIN, J. B. (1969) *Urban and Regional Planning*, Faber & Faber, London.

*MEYERSON, M. (1956) Building the middle-range bridge for comprehensive planning, *Journal of the American Institute of Planners*, Vol. 22, pp. 58–64.

MEYERSON, M. and BANFIELD, E. C. (1955) *Politics, Planning and the Public Interest*, Free Press, Glencoe.

MINISTRY OF HOUSING AND LOCAL GOVERNMENT (1965) *The Future of Development Plans: A Report by the Planning Advisory Group*, HMSO, London.

PETERSON, W. (1966) On some meanings of planning, *Journal of the American Institute of Planners*, Vol. 32, pp. 130–42.

PINKER, R. (1971) *Social Theory and Social Policy*, Heinemann, London.

PLOWDEN, S. (1972) *Towns Against Traffic*, André Deutsch, London.

SKJEI, S. S. (1972) Urban systems advocacy, *Journal of the American Institute of Planners*, Vol. 38, pp. 11–24.

UNWIN, R. (1912) *Nothing Gained by Overcrowding*, Garden Cities and Town Planning Association, London.

*WEBBER, M. (1963) Comprehensive planning and social responsibility, *Journal of the American Institute of Planners*, Vol. 29, pp. 232–41.

WEBBER, M. (1968/9) Planning in an environment of change: Beyond the industrial age, Permissive planning, *The Town Planning Review*, Vol. 39, pp. 179–95; Vol. 39, pp. 277–95.

*Included in FALUDI, A. (1973) *A Reader in Planning Theory*, Pergamon, Oxford.

CHAPTER 8

The Rational-comprehensive versus the Disjointed-incrementalist Mode of Planning

THE second dimension of planning is that of the rational-comprehensive versus the disjointed-incrementalist mode of planning. The latter term will perhaps not be readily understood. This is because, in the minds of most planners, planning is firmly associated with rational and *ipso facto* comprehensive approaches (even if they admit that this is a distant ideal). The mere suggestion of proceeding in piecemeal fashion (for which disjointed incrementalism is the less familiar but more descriptive technical term), and of presenting this as a deliberate strategy rather than as a regrettable deviation, is therefore likely to meet with some disbelief. A short account of the argument leading to such an alternative will therefore be helpful.[1]

CRITICISMS OF RATIONAL-COMPREHENSIVE PLANNING

The following is a summary of the criticisms of rational-comprehensive planning as provided by Lindblom. An analysis of these and of the alternative approaches suggested in his disjointed incrementalism will show that the real bone of contention concerns the scope of the problems to which rational planning should be applied.

Lindblom (1965) summarizes his points concerning rational-comprehensive planning (or what he variously calls the rational-deductive or the synoptic ideal) under the following propositions:

[1] I have replied to the argument of the most prominent of the critics of rational-comprehensive planning, Charles Lindblom, at some length in the introduction to the part of the companion volume containing one of his seminal papers.

The synoptic ideal is not adapted to man's limited intellectual capacities . . .
The synoptic ideal is not adapted to inadequacy of information . . .
Nor is it adapted to the costliness of analysis . . .
The synoptic ideal is not adapted to failure, which must be anticipated in many circumstances, to construct a satisfactory set of criteria, as for example, in the form of a welfare function . . .
The synoptic method is not adapted to the closeness of observed relationship between fact and value in policy-making . . .
The synoptic ideal is not adapted to the openness of systems of variables with which it must contend . . .
The synoptic ideal, lastly, is not adapted to the diverse forms in which policy problems actually arise . . .

What is evident in these criticisms is that they apply to blueprint, but not necessarily to process planning. Rational planning may therefore proceed cyclically, as the process approach suggest and answer these criticisms.

Based on this conception of rational planning as necessarily proceeding in a blueprint manner, Lindblom argues against rational-comprehensive planning that decision-makers cannot follow its prescriptions in actual fact (which is true for the majority of cases where blueprint planning is indeed doomed to fail). He says that the very attempt to plan rationally distracts decision-makers from more feasible approaches, such as strategies of simplifying decision problems. These he summarizes as the alternative to synoptic planning, his disjointed incrementalism. As will be seen, some of its features remind one of the planning strategies proposed in Chapter 6. None of them states that rational choices should not be made, but only that the range of alternatives included, and the range of ends considered, should always be limited.

The features of disjointed incrementalism are (Braybrooke and Lindblom, 1963):

Margin-dependent choice.
Restricted variety of policy alternatives considered.
Restricted number of consequences considered for any given policy.
Adjustments of objectives to policies.
Reconstructive treatment of data.
Serial analysis and evaluation.
Remedial orientation of analysis and evaluation.
Social fragmentation of analysis and evaluation.

Of these, four have already been mentioned in different contexts before and are therefore incorporated into the notion of planning presented in this book, which is nevertheless opposed to the disjointed incrementalist position. Firstly, "adjustments of objectives to policies" and "reconstructive treatment of data" are both in line with the notion of process planning: the model of planning agencies as learning systems is very well capable of performing these operations, and indeed will perform them regularly as part of the formulation of its programmes. Secondly, "serial analysis and evaluation" has been presented as the planning strategy of sequential decision-making in Chapter 6. Lastly, "remedial orientation of analysis and evaluation" refers to the non-issue of whether planning is goal-seeking or problem-solving: in Chapter 5 I argued that there was no difference between these ways of describing planning.

Of the others, numbers (1) to (3) indicate various strategies for cutting back on the complexity of rational choice by limiting the scope of its application. They are of the same kind as the planning strategies proposed in Chapter 6. Used wisely, they may *increase* the chances of rational planning:

Margin-dependent choice. According to Lindblom, the dominant characteristic of decision-makers in action is that they focus on increments by which alternatives differ from the *status quo*, that is their choices are based on an assessment of margins. For instance, they ask themselves not whether liberty is precious, and whether it is more precious than security, but rather whether an increment of one is worth an increment of the other. The strategy is then *to limit the number of alternatives put forward for evaluation to a handful which do not differ widely from what is being done at the present.*

Restricted variety of policy alternatives considered. Here, Lindblom suggests that non-incremental alternatives are often politically unfeasible. Also, hardly ever is there adequate information available for choosing rationally between such alternatives. This is even true for the greatest part of incremental alternatives which are theoretically feasible. On the whole, decision-makers therefore restrict consideration of alternatives to those which are not only incremental but for which they also possess adequate information, thus limiting the range of alternatives from which their choice is being made. The strategy is then *to further limit the number of alternatives put forward for evaluation to those on which adequate information is available.*

Restricted number of consequences considered for any given policy. In considering any given course of action, the decision-maker usually eliminates those consequences which are uninteresting to him. He furthermore omits the remote, the imponderable, the intangible and the poorly understood consequences, no matter how important they are. The strategy is then *to perform evaluation in the light of only a few well-understood ends.*

There is no doubt that disjointed incrementalism is highly descriptive of real-life planning. Who would deny that decision-makers have to compromise on the range of alternatives and of ends considered? The problem is, how do these become prescriptions? How does Lindblom arrive at the view that decision-makers should employ strategies which limit the area of rational choice rather than extend it? He gives two reasons. One could be tested, although he does not do this. Lindblom says that decision-makers will be successful when using his strategy, but he neither indicates variables by which degrees of disjointed incrementalism could be identified, nor defines "success" in decision-making.[2] The other reason for putting disjointed incrementalism forward is an assertion. One must first of all note that what Lindblom is against is making rational choices of a fundamental kind affecting large parts, or even the whole, of a community. Here, the eighth and last of the features of disjointed incrementalism becomes relevant because it reveals Lindblom's basic perspective: that such choices should not be made at all. "Social fragmentation of analysis and evaluation", in his terms, means that analysis and evaluation in a democratic society take place at a very large number of points. Each of the many different approaches is being taken simultaneously by more than one decision centre. Whilst this is couched in the form of descriptive statements, it is clear from Lindblom's writing that it is at the same time a prescription.

In this case, whatever direction the community as a whole takes, it cannot be the result of deliberate choice. Rather, it is the resultant of the operation of various forces. The significance of this feature of Lindblom's strategy is reflected in its name: *disjointed* incrementalism. It reveals his

---

[2]See, for instance, Etzioni's criticisms of disjointed incrementalism (Etzioni, 1967, 1968).

image of society as an aggregate of individuals and groups in competition. The obvious model on which he builds is the market, where many small decisions are taken with a view to individual advantage. These nevertheless automatically result in developments which are (allegedly) to everybody's long-term advantage.

This assertion of one image of society over all others is at the heart of Lindblom's strategies. These are all intended to limit the scope of rational decision-making to what relates to the ends and alternatives which clearly identifiable (or self-identifying) groups would consider. There are no "macro-decision-makers" making fundamental choices in Lindblom's image of society, so that it has been characterized as *atomistic* (Etzioni, 1967, 1968).[3]

Lindblom's thesis created a great deal of controversy which Etzioni's paper in the companion volume summarizes. In particular, he was attacked for the inherent conservatism of a position where only the more powerful groups in society would normally get their way in a free-for-all (Etzioni, 1967, 1968; Dror, 1964, 1968; Donnison, 1972). I do not wish to pursue this aspect but rather to use Lindblom's concept as a basis for suggesting lines of empirical research into planning which would incidentally also highlight the merits and disadvantages of Lindblom's thesis.

Rational-comprehensive planning versus disjointed incrementalism as a basis for empirical research is founded on the fact that, methodological and philosophical merits of Lindblom's views apart, people hold alternative images of society and act accordingly. When this occurs, planning agencies and their procedures are built on views which are the opposite of Lindblom's. In such cases one may expect planning to show the tendency to move away from disjointed incrementalism towards a more comprehensive approach (subject of course to practical limitations). Where, on the other hand, planning agencies and their procedures are designed on the basis of Lindblom's views, disjointed incrementalism will be even more descriptive of actual planning than is normally the case (though, again, there are limitations as I shall try to show). It is to a discussion of this idea that we turn, beginning with a definition of the two modes of planning concerned.

---

[3]Even on a sub-societal level where, clearly, decision-makers with a corporate identity exist, Lindblom advocates that they should fragment their decision-making, thus again reflecting his preference for aggregates of small over big decisions; see Lindblom (1959).

THE MODES DEFINED

Advocates of rational planning say that *all* conceivable courses of action must be identified and evaluated against *all* relevant ends. Thus, they suggest that rational planning must necessarily proceed *comprehensively* (leading to the identification of rational with comprehensive planning). Otherwise, one could never be certain that the chosen course of action might not only be "sub-optimal" but positively harmful in areas left unconsidered. In the terms introduced in Chapter 5, the rational-comprehensive mode of planning is therefore that approach *whereby the programmes put forward for evaluation cover the available action space and where the action space has itself been derived from an exhaustive definition of the problem to be solved.*

Against this, the critics of rational-comprehensive planning consider it neither possible nor desirable to perform such a comprehensive evaluation. Their preference is for a disjointed-incrementalist mode of planning *where the programmes considered by any one planning agency are limited to a few which deliberately do not exhaust the available action space, and where that action space is itself ill-defined.* It will be remembered that to limit the range of alternatives and fragment decision-making between various agencies are the chief strategies on which disjointed incrementalism builds.

Observable instances of planning will always cover only part of the available action space, and thus be to that extent disjointed incrementalist. But, firstly, this is a matter of *degree*. Secondly, some planning agencies are making efforts to cover larger segments of their action space than they have been able to cover hitherto. Thus, they are *moving towards* rational-comprehensive planning. Therefore, observable instances of planning will always fall somewhere between the two extremes. The following sections develop a hypothesis as to where that is.

DETERMINANTS AND CONSTRAINTS

There are again three factors which I shall consider as the determinants and as constraints of planning along this second of the dimensions. The determinants are various images held of society which, as indicated before, underlie different types of institutional structure and procedures used in planning. By way of these, images of society create a potential for either rational-comprehensive or disjointed-incrementalist planning.

The two other factors acting as constraints are the scope of images and the relative autonomy of planning agencies. Table 8.1 summarizes the hypothesis advanced which is that holistic images of society, as reflected in the structure of planning agencies and in their procedures, make for rational-comprehensive planning subject to the constraints of narrow images and small relative autonomy, whereas atomistic images do the same for disjointed incrementalism, subject to the constraints of wide images and great relative autonomy.

TABLE 8.1

DETERMINANT AND CONSTRAINTS OF RATIONAL-
COMPREHENSIVE VERSUS DISJOINTED-INCREMENTALIST PLANNING

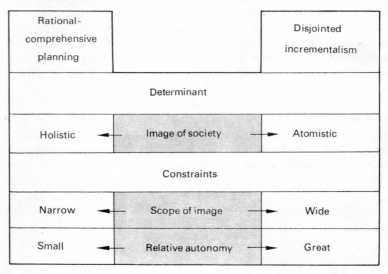

Images of Society

The argument is that different images of society make for either one or the other mode of planning. To be precise, these are images of the way individuals relate to society; whether it is a mere aggregate of individuals (the *atomistic* view) or whether it is something beyond, something which has a standing of its own (the *holistic* view). In the Epilogue I shall reveal my qualified holistic stand. Here, I merely argue that there are people taking both positions and planning on the basis of their respective views.[4]

How can an esoteric concept like images of society influence the mode of planning? Few people may be aware of which image they hold, and still fewer of these may be planners. How, then, can images of society influence what they do? The answer is that they are built into different institutional structures and procedures from which they can be inferred. Since institutional structures greatly influence planning, it may be said to be influenced by the images of society they contain. As will be seen, both the proponents of rational-comprehensive planning, as well as their critics, appear to agree about this.

To start with, rational-comprehensive planners desire a government to be an *organization* with centralized decision-making and a common purpose which mirrors the common (or public) interest of the community. On the other hand, incrementalists perceive government as a collection of agencies, each having its own clientele, with perpetual conflict between them reflecting the ongoing struggle between various groups in society, each with an interest of its own.

The two modes thus described are clearly reflected in planning thought on both sides of the Atlantic. The holistic view and its derivatives tend to be more popular with planners and the atomistic view with social-science critics of planning. For instance, the response of American planners to criticisms of the ineffectiveness of physical planning in the fifties and sixties was to extend their area of concern to *all* factors affecting the achievement of their ends. From the following quotations, the stance regarding "city life" as one identifiable whole becomes evident. To Haworth (1957) what distinguished the then current phase of planning was ". . . a concern to bring within the orbit of the planning venture all of those aspects of the urban complex which affect the quality of city life . . .". In a similar vein, Perloff (1965) writes that ". . . the breadth and difficulty of the social problems that communities face today strongly suggest that social planning should include all pertinent socio-economic and human behavior considerations which are of central significance in governmental

[4] For an alternative statement of the same proposition see Hyman (1969).

and voluntary agency decisions. It would thereby provide the human esources counterpart to physical city planning . . .".

Such holistic notions of "city life" and its problems are clearly reflected in some planners' preferences for certain types of institutional structures and procedures. In the case of structure, they incline towards centralized forms of decision-making with strong chief executives or "city managers". As early as 1941, Robert Walker thus argued in America that the place of the planner was on the staff of the chief executive instead of the independent board under which many American planners still serve (Walker, 1950). The complementary notion for procedures was that of the "policies plan". This was because the apex of planning, and its logical conclusion, appeared to be the overall co-ordination of *all* the facets of the activities of government: "A policies plan would be a unified document expressing the general goals, specific plans and programmes for urban growth and change. It would guide the evaluation of the particular area of governmental jurisdiction by expressing in one plan the social, economic, physical and political policies intended" (Fagin, 1959).

British planners and administrators now take the same line. Until fairly recently neither British central nor local government were centralized internally, and in both administration was fragmented between independent departments which, in the case of local government, served different committees of the councils. This sometimes approached the widespread American practice of independent boards performing different functions of local government. But, increasing concern with local government organization resulted in a major review undertaken in the sixties. This began with the Royal Commission on Local Government in Greater London (1960), continued with the report of the Royal Commission on Local Government in England (1969) and in Scotland (1969) and finally led to reforms of major proportions. As part of this review, two committees were formed to deal specifically with organizational problems (Ministry of Housing and Local Government, 1967a, b). Since then, an experimental form of local authority organization similar to that of the city-manager type in the United States has been spreading.

A parallel process of realignment of central government departments into larger units may be observed. These units (for instance the super-department of the environment) deal with wide areas of governmental responsibility under the authority of one overlord. Such centralization is enforced by the tendency of centres of decision-making to have their own staffs. The Cabinet in Britain as the highest centre of decision-making has been strengthened by the creation of a "Central Policy Review Staff". Similarly one of the recommendations of the Committee on the Civil Service (1968) was that each central government department in turn should create its own planning staff to give expert advice on future policy.[5] On the local level too, staff planning units are being established under chief executive officers. The policies plan has also been introduced. The following quotation strongly reveals its underlying holistic assumption.

> A local authority needs a general planning framework within which specialised planning procedures can be developed, whether they are expressed in land-use development plans, social development programmes or separate plans prepared in specialized departments. This framework can be provided by a "local authority policy plan". The need for local authority policy plans and planning would barely exist if local authorities were really a collection of separate services drawn together by accident. The problem arises because the changes that are taking place, particularly in the urban areas, are forcing us to be aware of . . . the inter-relations between various services of local government (Stewart, 1969a).

There is evidence therefore, for the existence of holistic images of society in the minds of planners and administrators, and for centralized forms of decision-making based on them. The counter-arguments about the lack of empirical relevance of such images and the dangers of such centralizing tendencies are much more forcefully put by Americans than by Britons.[6] One of the most prominent critics attesting American planning's lack of empirical relevance of its underlying holistic image of society is Banfield (1961): "American cities . . . seldom make and never carry out comprehensive plans. Plan-making is with us an idle exercise, for we neither agree upon the content of a 'public interest' that ought to override private ones nor permit the concentration of authority needed to carry a plan into effect

---

[5]Naturally, the American system with its much stronger executive in the form of the President shows the same tendency in the form of various advisory councils. Recently, Germany followed suit with introducing an advisory staff for policy planning into the Federal Chancellory which is thus assuming the rôle of co-ordinator of policies (Grossner, 1971; Lompe, 1971).

[6]But there appears to be an undercurrent on similar lines against reform of British local government. The history of local government reform will no doubt fascinate many students of politics. It is easy to surmise that they will discover many such undercurrents and ways in which these have watered down the original reform proposals.

if one were made." Summarizing views such as these held by political scientists, Rabinovitz (1967) describes their image of political systems as the opposite of holistic images held by planners, that is, "as a compound of groups of political decision-makers who can coalesce for crises but whose influence is unequal to initiating or implementing solutions to long run problems . . .".

Their criticisms therefore centre round the lack of awareness of this diversity of interests, and of conflict between them, shown by the advocates of a "strong executive" type of government with its "clean, business-like" approach, and its emphasis on methods like Planning Programming Budgeting (which seem ideally suited to its style). The background to this argument is the development of American city politics. Political scientists observed the way in which successive waves of immigrants infiltrated into city politics. A definite pattern of absorption over several generations could be identified, such as that described by Dahl (1961) in the case of New Haven. Because of their electoral strength, immigrants sooner or later became represented on the council. This gave them access to services and to employment, particularly within the municipal corporation, which opened up avenues for social mobility. Absorption was anything but free from corruption. Favours were bought and sold, the allocation of jobs and contracts and services was openly partisan, illegal business and trading with votes flourished. Political entrepreneurs ("bosses") emerged with powerful organizations trading in political influence, the famous political "machines". Opposition to these machines caused the proposal for a city-manager form of government to be originated, with its basic tenet that the administration of local services should be beyond the reach of such openly partisan influence.[7]

This is where the critics of centralized decision-making and the underlying holistic images of society come in once again. The classic planning case study by Meyerson and Banfield (1955) was for instance done in Chicago which provided a famous example of a political machine. Its housing authority was one of the institutional devices created to take the

---

[7]Short of succeeding in taking all local services "out of politics", this "conservative reform movement" advocated that new services should at least be administered by non-partisan "boards". City planning was one of these. The roots of urban planning in the conservative reform movement are the subject of extensive comment in the American literature. See Part IV in the companion volume.

administration of services (in this case the provision of low-cost housing with federal help under the 1949 Housing Act) out of politics. The authors' comments on the underlying tension were that the machines gave ". . . the mass of people with their limited interest in politics . . ." the kind of government they seemed to want by providing them with petty favours and a generally approachable, though sometimes corrupt, political leadership; that they enabled illegal business to receive political privileges and thus to continue as a safety valve for the city; that they provided a ladder for upward social mobility, first for intelligent "political entrepreneurs" who were members of underprivileged groups and subsequently for these groups themselves.[8] As against this, a form of government which is geared exclusively towards the efficient discharge of well-defined functions does not provide any of these, nor does it allow for the possibility of conflicts between different groups in society, and therefore does not make adequate provision for conflict resolution. The "clean" form of government is therefore an unstable form of government:

> Naïvely to destroy the political machines and to undertake to govern the city in the way its 'best elements' think is impartial, business-like and in the public interest is to incur the risk of deepening the conflicts which already exist while at the same time discarding a social structure by which conflicts may be confined and managed (Meyerson and Banfield, 1955).

Thus, the danger is that government and its procedures may not reflect the true nature of society which, in the view of the critics of streamlined

[8]There is an interesting parallel to this argument in the discussion on local government reform in Britain. The Maud Committee proposed a form of institutional structure which was similar to that of the American council-manager form. It also proposed the reduction of the number of committees and of councillors. The Royal Commission on Local Government in England (1969) adopted this recommendation. But, though accepting the Maud Report, the Labour Government did not include this proposal in its White Paper. It is argued that, for the Labour Party, the machinery of local government serves as a reservoir of political skills. Like the political machines for ethnic minorities in the United States, local government is the most important stamping ground for Labour politicians next to the trade union movement. It is also a means of gaining status for people who would otherwise be deprived of such avenues of social mobility. The reduction of the number of councillors would therefore tend to have effects similar to those of introducing a "clean" form of city government in the United States. It would favour the middle and upper classes simply by barring more working class people from one of their few opportunities for sharing in the control of society.

administration, is that of a plurality of conflicting groups. As conflict becomes increasingly more evident in what has come to be called the "urban crisis", criticisms of this kind have also grown. They have culminated in two separate developments. One started with Davidoff's proposal that planners should engage in *advocacy planning* (Davidoff, 1965), thereby participating in social conflict (and making it more meaningful in terms of the balance of expertise available for stating alternative points of view). The other is the opposition which the most recent and most sophisticated of the procedures of comprehensive decision-making, *Planning Programming Budgeting*, meets from social scientists.

Davidoff's proposal that the planner should assume the rôle of an advocate (explicitly linked with the notion of society being *pluralist* in the title of his famous paper) is documented and commented upon in the companion volume.[9] The opposition against Planning Programming Budgeting (PPB) also reflects, as does advocacy planning, the image of society as an aggregate of groups, each pursuing its own ends. This may be inferred where Wildavsky (1970) claims that PPB reflects a spurious holistic image of society and positively enhances "strong executive" forms of government complementing such an image:

> Within the great federal organizations designed to encompass the widest ramifications of basic objectives, there would have to be a strong executive. Cutting across the sub-units of the organization . . . the program budget could only be put together by the top executive. A more useful tool for increasing his power to control decisions *vis-à-vis* his subordinates would be hard to find.

Thus, both planners and administrators aiming to enhance the effectiveness of planning, and their critics who warn against doing so, are agreed that images of society affect the mode of planning by ways of institutional structures and procedures reflecting them. These then create the tendency for planning to incline towards comprehensive or disjointed incrementalist planning (which is what the definition of a "determinant" is; see p. 129). This tendency of planning to reflect images of society is subject to constraints, and it is to these that we now turn.

[9]The gist of these comments is to re-interpret its meaning so as to relate it to a qualified holistic view of society. Thus, advocacy planning may be seen, not as an alternative, but as a complement to public planning, keeping planners on their toes and enhancing the creativity of public bureaucracies.

Scope of Images

The image held by planning agencies of their area of concern was the key determinant relative to the dimension of blueprint versus process planning. But, as regards the dimension now under discussion, it acts as a constraint. It does so not only on the comprehensiveness of planning (which is perhaps more obvious) but also on disjointed incrementalism. An image which incorporates knowledge about the interdependency of the areas of concern of two or more planning agencies (or knowledge of overlaps of their action space) must by and large result in steps being taken towards some form of co-ordination, and hence towards more comprehensiveness—atomistic images of society notwithstanding. It therefore becomes evident that one here is concerned with an aspect of the image which differs from the firmness or uncertainty with which it is held. This aspect is its *scope*, that is whether there is knowledge available for linking the actions of various planning agencies together. I shall quote examples to show that a narrow scope of the image constitutes a constraint on rational-comprehensive planning and a wide scope constrains disjointed incrementalism.

Examples of the image as a constraint on comprehensiveness are as numerous as human ignorance is great. Indeed, truly comprehensive planning would require an omniscient planning agency. Anything less than an all-embracing image therefore constitutes a constraint on rational-comprehensive planning which can frustrate well-meaning attempts to implement policies.[10]

This lack of an adequate knowledge-base for comprehensiveness is much exploited by its critics. Thus, Braybrooke and Lindblom (1963) are quick to point out that "synoptic planners" cannot be rational without understanding their problems in all their ramifications. Little such understanding is found in practice. Often, it is the very nature of the organization, rather than that of the problem, which determines the kind of action which it can take. This is amplified by Meyerson and Banfield's (1955) Chicago study. They found that the agency was precluded from investigating alternative means of achieving its ends of providing more housing for lower-income

[10]Townsend (1970) gives a revealing account of how the Labour Government's attempts to implement its social policies were frustrated amongst others by the absence of comprehensive images, the conclusion being that "success in one area of policy seems to depend much more on success in others than we had believed hitherto . . .".

people because the only way by which a housing authority would pursue this end was by *providing* public housing. The alternative of handing out cash benefits was excluded from the start. Normally, housing authorities do not even have any notion of alternative courses of action. This applies particularly to public agencies because they require specific powers which are usually defined in terms of certain types of action to be taken and not in terms of the ends to be achieved: for instance, they are constructed on the basis of an image which suggests that the provision of housing is the only means by which to remedy the housing problem. Their legal powers, their ideology and their staff are such that even alternative ways of thinking are outside the realm of what is feasible.[11]

However, what the critics of comprehensive planning fail to take account of is that, limited though the scope of available images may be, there is the possibility of extending it. Where this occurs, and where the potential for rational-comprehensive planning exists in the first instance, an improvement of the image (for instance by improving knowledge concerning linkages between the activities of various planning agencies) probably means a move towards more comprehensiveness. For instance, in the case of the reform of local government in Britain an increase in the general awareness of the existence of linkages between the areas of responsibility of individual departments followed in the wake of official reports (Stewart, 1969b): Buchanan's study on *Traffic in Towns* (Ministry of Transport, 1963) demonstrated the linkage between traffic and the environment; the Plowden Report (Central Advisory Council for Education, 1967) showed the effect of parental environment on education; the Committee on Local Authority and Allied Personal Services (1968) found close interdependence between the work of children and welfare officers (who worked in different departments until 1971) in that children under the care of a council were likely to have parents receiving other benefits and vice versa; the Sharp Report (Ministry of Transport, 1970) pleaded for integrated land-use and transport planning. The ensuing organizational changes were administrative unification which resulted in a greater potential for rational-comprehensive planning, this time occasioned by a changing image.

[11]The phenomenon of thinking being restricted by a narrow image built right into an organization, and of action being less than rational because of that, is by no means limited to public agencies, as Ackoff (1962) relates from his experience as an industrial management consultant.

The image acting as a constraint in disjointed incrementalism may have exactly the same effect as is seen in comprehensive planning and limit the extent to which planning follows its prescriptions. One example of this is the way in which the first German regional planning board was created in the Ruhr area in 1920. The area had previously been divided into many authorities each jealously guarding their independence and sometimes even counteracting each other's policies. The notion of local autonomy was firmly embedded in German constitutional thinking and the fragmentation of administrative responsibilities for an area which, both socially and economically was one complete whole, reflected an image of society as divided into local communities. But when an additional 150,000 miners and their families had to be introduced into an already congested area so that French demands for war indemnities in coal could be met, it was obvious that the area could not take the additional strain. Thus, legislation was introduced which took certain responsibilities away from local authorities and gave them to a board which is now the best known of the German regional planning agencies. What was structurally a situation for disjointed-incrementalist planning had become less so as a result of the image (Berkowitz, n.d.).

A final example for the effect which the variable scope of images has on planning is that provided by Dower (1971). He argues that one dimension of comprehensiveness, the geographical scale on which, in this case, the water supply problems of England are being tackled, varies with the image:

> Thus, in northern England, the large hill masses and large conurbations lead, essentially, to a regional water supply system. Southern England, with an even larger regional population, and low rainfall, probably needs a larger than regional solution. The south-west, with dispersed population, small cities and small river basins, needs a more localised approach.

The case for the scope of the image acting as a constraint having thus been made, we now turn to the second constraint on rational-comprehensive respectively disjointed-incrementalist planning.

Relative Autonomy

Relative autonomy refers to the range of controls exercised, that is whether or not the planning agency exercises control over factors having a bearing on its problems. Its control over any one factor need not be complete because this would mean blueprint planning. It could be a flexible framework within which the control variable could find its own level.

The difference between a single-purpose agency (for instance a Passenger Transport Authority) and a multi-purpose agency like local or central government illustrates the difference between low and high relative autonomy. The single-purpose authority may have control over some variables but it will not plan comprehensively. For any agency to be able to plan comprehensively, it must be able to influence most of the factors which have a bearing on its problems, and it must have the powers of using its resources in alternative ways, which is clearly what a single-purpose agency cannot do so that low relative autonomy acts as a constraint. Conversely where an agency does enjoy high relative autonomy, it will tend to develop more wide-ranging images covering its area of control. It would thus move away from seeing them as disconnected, as disjointed incrementalists would do. In this way, relative autonomy may act as a constraint on both modes of planning.

A RESEARCH DESIGN

As with the concepts and variables developed in the previous chapter, those discussed now may help in clarifying the meaning of rational-comprehensive planning as an ideal. Before turning to this, I shall summarize the core of this chapter in the form of a table to be read in conjunction with Table 8.1. However, this time the variables used in locating observed instances of planning along the dimension being considered deserve special attention. From our previous definitions of the rational-comprehensive and the disjointed-incrementalist mode of planning it seems that a suitable variable would be the range of alternatives considered relative to the available action space. However, it is difficult to identify the available action space (see Chapter 5). Some parts of it may be reasonably well explored, but its image will almost certainly be fuzzy at the edges. It is therefore difficult to determine its extent, and thus whether it has been covered by a range of alternative programmes or not.

In this situation one can use a proxi-variable which is the action space which is already known by virtue of it being covered by other agents operating in the environment of a planning agency. Thus, a researcher wishing to place observed instances on the dimension of comprehensive versus disjointed-incrementalist planning has to investigate *relationships between planning agencies (and other agents) with an overlapping action space* (that is working towards one or more of the same objectives and/or manipulating one or more of the same variables in the environment). For instance, if programmes devised by the housing department are the result of investigating, not only its own, but also the current and conceivable programmes of its social services counterpart; or if transport planning investigates the reduction of the use of private cars as an alternative to building more roads, then these are indications for comprehensiveness. If, on the other hand, programmes are based only on an investigation of the action space available to one planning agency, disregarding other agents with an overlapping action space, this counts as an indication for disjointed incrementalism.

TABLE 8.2

VARIABLES FOR RESEARCH INTO RATIONAL-COMPREHENSIVE
VERSUS DISJOINTED-INCREMENTALIST PLANNING

Concepts	*Variables*
Mode of planning (rational-comprehensive vs. disjointed-incrementalist)	Extent of investigation preceding formulation of programmes relative to the overlapping action space with other planning agencies
Images of society underlying (holistic or atomistic)	Centralization or decentralization of decision-making structures and procedures
Scope of images (wide or narrow)	Number of known linkages between the areas of responsibility of planning agencies
Relative autonomy (high or low)	Range of powers; flexibility in the use of resources for alternative purposes.

Again, a hypothesis can be formulated from this. The mode of planning (indicated, say, by the thoroughness with which alternatives are investigated before formulating an action programme which involves several planning agencies with an overlapping action space) will vary with the image of society underlying (as indicated by the centralization or decentralization of the structure and procedures of planning). This will be subject to the constraints of the scope of available images (as indicated by the number of known linkages between the areas of responsibility of various planning agencies) and of the relative autonomy of the planning agency (as indicated by legal powers and by flexibility in the use of resources). This is again a proposition which may be compared with empirical facts as is the corollary proposition concerning disjointed-incrementalist planning. As with the previous dimension, the concepts involved therefore provide a basis for research into planning and thus help in developing a positive theory.

RATIONAL-COMPREHENSIVE PLANNING IN MULTI-PLANNING AGENCIES

For the various reasons already outlined in Part II, I believe that rational planning is an ideal worth striving for. I thus accept comprehensiveness as its important corollary and reject the disjointed-incrementalist position of limiting the scope of investigations to the action space available to only one agent. This complements my somewhat holistic image of society (one which nevertheless incorporates a great variety of groups and individuals) to be described in the Epilogue on *The Planning Society*.

But from this present chapter it becomes evident that planning agencies cannot be expected to command either a wide enough image or enough autonomy to engage in truly rational-comprehensive planning. There must therefore be a plurality of planning agencies, operating with enough measure of independence to put forward their points of view, but also co-ordinated by decision-making structures and procedures to provide a measure of unity. In short, in order to be able to plan comprehensively, planning agencies must form clusters whose interrelation reflects this idea of unity and diversity. Such clusters will be described as multi-planning agencies (see Chapter 11). I would like to think that the subtle balance which they need to maintain between the autonomy of individual member agencies on the one hand and collective decision-making on the other reflects the image of society as balancing unity and diversity in its own membership which I hold.

REFERENCES

ACKOFF, R. *et al.* (1962) *Scientific Method: Optimizing Applied Research Decisions*, John Wiley, New York.

BANFIELD, E. C. (1961) Quoted by DYCKMAN, J. W. (1961) What makes planners plan? *Journal of the American Institute of Planners*, Vol. **27**, pp. 164–7.

BERKOWITZ, B. (n.d.) *Regional Planning in Germany's Industrial Ruhr*, Siedlungsverband Ruhrkohlenbezirk, Essen.

BRAYBROOKE, D. and LINDBLOM, C. E. (1963) *A Strategy of Decision: Policy Evaluation as a Social Process*, Free Press, New York.

CENTRAL ADVISORY COUNCIL FOR EDUCATION (1967) *Children and their Primary Schools* (Plowden Report), HMSO, London.

COMMITTEE ON LOCAL AUTHORITY AND ALLIED PERSONAL SERVICES (1968) *Report* (Seebohm Report), HMSO, London.

COMMITTEE ON THE CIVIL SERVICE (1968) *Report* (Fulton Report), HMSO, London.

DAHL, R. (1961) *Who Governs?* Yale University Press, New Haven.

*DAVIDOFF, P. (1965) Advocacy and pluralism in planning, *Journal of the American Institute of Planners*, Vol. **31**, pp. 331–8.

DONNISON, D. (1972) Ideology and policies, *Journal of Social Policy*, Vol. **1**, pp. 97–117.

DOWER, M. (1971) Planning water, *New Society*, 30 September, pp. 615–6.

DROR, Y. (1964) Muddling through—science or inertia? *Public Administration Review*, Vol. **24**, pp. 153–7.

DROR, Y. (1968) *Public Policymaking Reexamined*, Chandler, Scranton, Penn.

*ETZIONI, A. (1967) Mixed-scanning: a "third" approach to decision-making, *Public Administration Review*, Vol. **27**, pp. 385–95.

ETZIONI, A. (1968) *The Active Society*, Collier-Macmillan, London.

FAGIN, H. (1959) Organizing and carrying out planning activities in urban government, *Journal of the American Institute of Planners*, Vol. **25**, pp. 109–14.

FALUDI, A. (1973) *A Reader in Planning Theory*, Pergamon, Oxford.

GROSSNER, C. (1971) Wenn Zukunft verplant wird, *Die Zeit*, 9 April, S. 8–9.

HAWORTH, L. L. (1957) An institutional theory of the city and planning, *Journal of the American Institute of Planners*, Vol. **23**, pp. 135–43.

HYMAN, H. (1969) Planning with citizens: two styles, *Journal of the American Institute of Planners*, Vol. **35**, pp. 105–12.

*LINDBLOM, C. E. (1959) The science of muddling through, *Public Administration Review*, Vol. **19**, pp. 79–88.

LINDBLOM, C. E. (1965) *The Intelligence of Democracy*, Free Press, New York.

LOMPE, K. (1971) *Gesellschaftspolitik und Planungsprobleme politischer Planung in der sozialstaatlichen Demokratie*, Rombach, Freiburg.

MEYERSON, M. and BANFIELD, E. C. (1955) *Politics, Planning and the Public Interest*, Free Press, Glencoe.

MINISTRY OF HOUSING AND LOCAL GOVERNMENT (1967a) *Staffing of Local Government* (Mallaby Report), HMSO, London.

MINISTRY OF HOUSING AND LOCAL GOVERNMENT (1967b) *Management of Local Government* (Maud Report), HMSO, London.

MINISTRY OF TRANSPORT (1963) *Traffic in Towns* (Buchanan Report), HMSO, London.

MINISTRY OF TRANSPORT (1970) *Transport Planning: The Men For The Job* (Sharp Report), HMSO, London.

PERLOFF, H. S. (1965) New directions in social planning, *Journal of the American Institute of Planners*, Vol. **31**, pp. 130–42.

*RABINOVITZ, F. F. (1967) Personality, politics, and planning, *Public Administration Review*, Vol. 27, pp. 18–24.

ROYAL COMMISSION ON LOCAL GOVERNMENT IN ENGLAND (1969) *Report* (Redcliffe-Maud Report), HMSO, London.

ROYAL COMMISSION ON LOCAL GOVERNMENT IN GREATER LONDON (1960) *Report* (Herbert Report), HMSO, London.

ROYAL COMMISSION ON LOCAL GOVERNMENT IN SCOTLAND (1969) *Report* (Wheatley Report), HMSO, Edinburgh.

STEWART, J. D. (1969a) The administrative structure of planning: 1, *Journal of the Town Planning Institute*, Vol. 55, pp. 288–90.

STEWART, J. D. (1969b) The case for local authority policy planning, *Town and Country Planning Summer School Nottingham, 1969* (Conference Proceedings), The Town Planning Institute, London.

TOWNSEND, P. (1970) The reorganisation of social policy, *New Society*, 22 October, pp. 722–4.

WALKER, R. A. (1941) *The Planning Function in Urban Government*, 2nd ed., 1950. University of Chicago Press.

WILDAVSKY, A. (1970) The political economy of efficiency: cost-benefit analysis, systems analysis, and program budgeting, *Planning Programming Budgeting: A Systems Approach to Management* (Edited by LYDEN, F. I. and MILLER, E. G.), 3rd ed. Markham, Chicago.

*Included in FALUDI, A. (1973) *A Reader in Planning Theory*, Pergamon, Oxford.

CHAPTER 9

The Normative versus the
Functional Mode of Planning

THE issue that underlies the third and last of the dimensions is the ability
of planning agencies simultaneously to evaluate both ends and means. I
shall argue that there are specific limitations imposed by the planner's rôle
(and also as we shall see later by hierarchical organizations).

We must of necessity cover some theoretical ground before identifying
the pertinent factors affecting research into this dimension of planning.
After these factors have been described we shall draw implications from
the insights thus gained and shall consider a point which has already
surfaced briefly in the previous chapter: the importance of multi-planning
agencies.

ENDS AND MEANS IN PLANNING

This section and the next draw on the extensive writing of John Friedmann who builds on Karl Mannheim and to a lesser extent on Max Weber.[1]
The underlying problem of how planning could become coextensive with
the application of reason to all kinds of human choice (including that of the
ends of action) permeates his thinking. It has resulted in his more or less
elaborate frameworks for planning thought incorporating many forms of
planning such as the one presented in Part V of the companion volume.

Of the various distinctions which Friedmann draws between, in terms
of the ends of action, more or less inclusive forms of planning, I shall
settle for the one between normative and functional planning. This, in

---

[1] As far as I am aware, the two concepts of normative and functional planning
have been formulated by Friedmann (1966/7).

my view, reflects the underlying issues most clearly. Functional planning is a mode of planning in which ". . . the planner assumes the goals to be given in the situation and is rational with respect to the means only . . ." (Friedmann, 1966/7). It does not make much difference whether these goals are handed down to a planner by some higher authority or whether, as is often the case, he simply postulates his own set of goals. What is important is the clear distinction which is made between ends and means, holding the first constant and systematically scrutinizing only the second. Normative planning, however, extends this scrutiny to the ends pursued. In Friedmann's words: ". . . normative planning is chiefly concerned with the ends of action of a social system. The goals of normative planning are those of the system itself".

One might assert that the "ends of action" reside in the political sphere and not in planning. But the making of such choices (if they are not to be blind and thus not deliberate) requires an informed basis. Normative planning is to make choices concerning ends whilst simultaneously taking cognizance of available knowledge.

This distinction between functional and normative planning rests on the writings of two German sociologists, Max Weber and Karl Mannheim. Both were eminently concerned with the increasing *rationalism* of society. Weber's study on *The Protestant Ethic and the Spirit of Capitalism* (1965) investigated the origins of this phenomenon. He later developed the "ideal type" of *bureaucracy* as the optimal organization for the rational discharge of specified tasks (Weber, 1947). But his thinking always remained critical of the trend towards greater rationalization, and formed the basis of Friedmann's differentiation between functional and normative planning. Weber distinguished between two types of rationality. The type that expanded during the growth of industrial society he called "formal" or "purposive" rationality, the ". . . rational orientation to a system of discrete individual ends" (Weber, 1947). This he set against another type of rationality ("material" or "value" rationality) concerned with basic considerations of human purpose, which he found to be disappearing in modern society.

The same distinction was made by Karl Mannheim who also shared Weber's concern. He, too, held that industrial society promoted a very specific form of rationality which he termed functional rationality. Like Weber's purposive rationality, functional rationality is a form of thought which is rational with respect to means, not to ends. This, Mannheim contrasted with substantial rationality, which parallels Weber's value rationality (Mannheim, 1940).

His concern was that the spread of functional rationalization (for example the increasing division of labour that geared organizational sub-divisions towards the attainment of a fairly specific but narrow set of ends) rendered intelligent insight into the inter-relations of events in a given situation, as required by substantial rationality, an increasingly remote possibility. Indeed, as society becomes more and more complex, the decisions fundamentally affecting our lives become more and more inscrut-able. This produces a polarized society with only a relatively few strategi-cally placed people commanding the ability for substantial rationality. The rest occupy a "mass society" with its implicit danger of fundamental irrationality. Mannheim's writing is imbued with the notion of functional rationalization as self-defeating. This clearly reflects his recognition of the development uppermost in the minds of many of his contemporaries: the rise of Fascism in Central Europe.

The relationship of Mannheim's thinking with the concepts of functional and normative planning is that functional planning remains on the level of functional rationality. In failing to consider alternative ends, it may become substantially irrational, with all the possible consequences. Bureaucrats faithfully serving barbarian ends set by a nihilistic leadership may lead ultimately to the rational administration of the concentration camp and the gas chambers.[2] Only where both the ends and the means of action are judged rationally, that is when it is both functional and norma-tive, can planning be described as substantially rational.

ADAPTIVE, DEVELOPMENTAL, ALLOCATIVE AND INNOVATIVE PLANNING

I shall now consider two related pairs of concepts: adaptive versus developmental and allocative versus innovative planning. Their analysis will help in identifying factors on which normative and functional planning

[2]The autobiography of Hitler's architect and Minister of Armaments gives a vivid description of how single-minded experts come to serve nihilistic ends; see Speer (1969).

depend. However, I must first resolve a difficulty which these two pairs of concepts, and their relationship to functional and normative planning, pose.

Friedmann's comparison of adaptive versus developmental planning seems identical with that of functional versus normative planning. Thus, as its name suggests, adaptive planning is a weaker form of planning in which the ends pursued by a planning agency are circumscribed by outside constraints imposed by other agents. Because of these constraints, such planning agencies do not normally consider many alternative ends. Adaptive planning, therefore, like functional planning, puts more emphasis on the rational choice of means than of ends.

Developmental planning, on the other hand, is not subject to the same constraints. It is relatively more autonomous and thus able to consider alternative ends, as in normative planning. Yet Friedmann (1967) relates the other pair of concepts, allocative versus innovative planning (allocative planning assigning resource increments to competing uses with view to maintaining the system in balance; innovative planning aiming at producing major changes by ways of institution building) to functionally and sub-stantially rational thought. He thereby implies that they, and not the first pair presented in the same paper, correspond to functional and normative planning.

The solution to this difficulty seems to be that in comparing allocative versus innovative planning with the first pair of adaptive versus develop-mental planning, one notices that they refer to two different dimensions of the problem of how normative planning may be achieved. Relative auto-nomy refers to planning agencies of different kinds, for instance lower-versus higher-tier authorities. Allocative versus innovative planning refers to different ways in which planning agencies go about their business hold-ing autonomy constant.

Apart from holding autonomy constant for the purpose of comparison, one must also think of it as being reasonably high. Otherwise, with a plan-ning agency enjoying only little autonomy, it would clearly not be meaning-ful to think of it as pursuing entirely new ends. A low degree of autonomy means limitation of the ability to pursue ends freely. It follows that allo-cative and innovative planning must refer to ways in which developmental planning enjoying high relative autonomy is performed.

My interpretation is therefore that adaptive and developmental planning refer to the potential of planning agencies for normative planning, this potential depending on their autonomy. A small degree of autonomy means a limited potential, and a high degree a much greater potential. Allocative and innovative planning, on the other hand, refer to different approaches taken by planning agencies enjoying enough autonomy to engage in normative planning. Here, allocative planning is the approach which is more limited, counteracting the attainment of a normative mode. The concepts underlying the two distinctions correspond to what I described as determinants and constraints: relative autonomy is the determinant causing a planning agency to move towards one mode of planning or the other; the approach to the consideration of ends, whether allocative or innovative, may act as a constraint.

THE MODES DEFINED

In the terms used in discussing the operations of planning agencies in Chapter 5, the two modes of normative and functional planning may be defined as follows: normative planning is a mode of planning *whereby the goals and objectives defining, inter alia, the limits of the action space of a planning agency, are themselves the objects of rational choice, and whereby that choice is reviewed as and when the need arises.* Functional planning, on the other hand, is a mode of planning *whereby the goals and objectives defining, inter alia, the limits of the action space are not questioned.*

In considering the limitations of functional planning we recall that objectives were defined in Chapter 5 as describing a hypothetical situation where one problem (a source of tension at the interface between the ends of a subject and his future image) has been removed. It follows, first of all, that formulating objectives requires knowledge and is to that extent an analytical and rational activity, and secondly, that objectives must be allowed to change when future images change. A truly rational approach cannot therefore accept objectives as given. Functional planning, by excluding objectives from rational consideration, thus falls short of the ideal of rational planning.

In practical terms, functional planning cuts out a whole dimension of choice, that of the choice of alternative ends. Again in the terms introduced in Chapter 5, functional planning therefore draws the limits of the action space too narrowly. This is borne out by examples of functional planning. Friedmann quotes one which is familiar to physical planners:

A projected increase in the number of certain population groups over a given period automatically gives rise to specific quantitative 'needs': new housing, schools, transportation facilities, and the like. The trends of standards and tasks for the use of these facilities are then studied, and are applied with certain modifications reflecting changes in income and the like, to the projected population. No values which are extraneous to the system are introduced (Friedmann, 1966/7).

The situation is similar to that where, again in Friedmann's words, ". . . the planner seeks to smooth out certain 'frictions' in the performance of a system and to restore its operation to a 'normal' state". This is a reference to the analogy which is often drawn between planning and medicine: the planner is the doctor at the sick bed of his patient, society. It is a favourite model for planners, with its connotation of the high status enjoyed by the medical profession.[3] But, whereas there may be reasonable consensus about the definition of health (and even here there are problems in areas like mental health, family planning and so on), there is considerable argument about what is normal for society. Personal views reflecting class biases can enter far too easily into the cures prescribed by planners. Housing provides a familiar example: often high standards are imposed without consideration either of the life styles and the spending power of the people affected or, for that matter, of the ecology of cities. Much the same applies to many other standards invoked in planning. Community centres are provided instead of public houses, and sports fields instead of bingo halls, evidently because the first are thought to induce more healthy activities than the second. By invoking such standards, planning often achieves the opposite effect to the one intended. Evidence for this is provided by the phenomena of low-income groups being pushed out of the market instead of being housed; by the high incidences in some new housing estates of adolescent violence and adult stress and so on.

One might of course say that this results not from functional planning but simply from planning for the wrong ends, the planners' ends and not the people's. But there is no need to invoke the spectre of conspiracy on the part of "establishment" planners. More likely than not, such unintended consequences are simply the result of well-intentioned planning where the action space is conceived too narrowly. "By failing to consider planning explicitly, by concentrating only on the immediate problem in view, the

[3]See, for instance, Gutkind (1946).

planner neglects to bring the real choices into the open" (Friedmann, 1966/7).

Functional planning does not of course exist in its pure form. The decisions of any planning agency must invoke some consideration of objectives. An architect designing a house to conform even to the most stringent specifications still has a certain element of choice. By exercising his discretion and his own interpretation of housing needs he can amplify choices made by others. This also applies to normative planning, the other extreme type: nobody can simultaneously attend to all his ends. As with the two previous dimensions, the value of these two concepts is primarily analytical with empirical instances falling somewhere between the two extremes.

DETERMINANT AND CONSTRAINT

The two factors making for one or the other of the two modes of planning have already been identified. They are the relative autonomy of a planning agency, and the approach taken where a reasonably large degree of autonomy exists. This approach, as will be argued, depends on the planner's rôle-concept. Two concepts will be identified: the bureaucratic and the political. Table 9.1 summarizes the hypothesis advanced: great relative autonomy makes for normative and small autonomy for functional planning, subject to the constraints of the "bureaucratic" or "political" concept of the planner's rôle.

TABLE 9.1

DETERMINANT AND CONSTRAINT OF NORMATIVE VERSUS
FUNCTIONAL PLANNING

Normative planning		Functional planning
Determinant		
Great ◄─┼─	Relative autonomy ─┼►	Small
Constraint		
Bureaucratic ◄─┼─	The rôle of the planner ─┼►	Political

Relative Autonomy

Relative autonomy has already figured as a factor influencing planning. In Chapter 8 it was seen as a constraint, the prime determinant being the images of society underlying the structure and procedures of planning agencies. This same factor can now be seen to create a potential for normative or functional planning, and thus to be the determinant of planning along this dimension.

As relative autonomy can only be discussed in the context of several planning agencies constraining mutual freedom of manoeuvre, it will be explained by using the example of a well-known form of multi-planning agency—the hierarchical organization. The points made will also apply to other forms (for instance independent planning agencies pursuing conflicting ends in a market-type situation), but the contrast between a great and small relative autonomy is more easily made using hierarchical structures. The one which I have selected is the British system of central and local government, but a local authority and its individual departments, or an industrial corporation, would have served equally well as examples.

In a hierarchical structure, the relative autonomy of the lower-tier agency is appreciably less than that of the higher tier because the higher-tier agency gives directives to the lower one. In the example of British central government, there are various channels through which such directives flow (Fig. 9.1). These channels link central government with those local government departments holding the images; with the council and its committees as the decision-takers; and with yet other departments acting as the effectors of programmes. These channels transmit not only a plethora of technical information (standards, circulars, directives concerning the content and the form of plan documents) but also specific directives to embark on certain courses of action, or arbitration decisions in the case of disputes between, for instance, unsuccessful applicants for planning permission and the Local Planning Authority. Obviously, these directives curtail the autonomy of local authorities in more ways than one. For instance, a Local Planning Authority cannot decide to give cash incentives for industrialists to move into their area; or to subsidize private cars as an alternative to public transport; or to run an industrial enterprise and subsidize the ratepayers from its profits. It must, on the other hand, provide all kinds of services to meet central government requirements.

Thus it is limited in the choice of ends which it pursues.[4]

Limitations of the autonomy of local government reach even further into areas where central government does not exercise prescriptive control. In these areas too, the kinds of programmes operated by an agency do not depend entirely on what its planners and politicians decide is best. Central government can manipulate the context of their choice by making some programmes more attractive than others, thus influencing local authorities

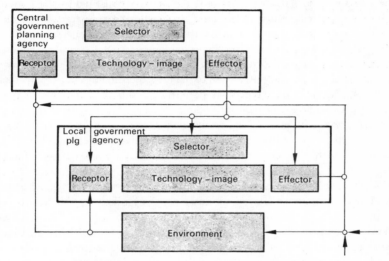

FIG. 9.1. Normative versus functional planning

[4]There are parallels in many fields where hierarchical structures occur. Thus, management science classifies decisions into three groups: policy decisions, administrative decisions and executive decisions:

> Policy decisions start with the formation of business. To begin with, there must be an idea or set of ideas . . . and someone or some group must decide that the business based on it has a good chance of success. Then decisions must be made on bye-laws and membership, on the board of directors, on key executives . . .
>
> Below this level is another series of decisions, less important but still very far-reaching in effect: the administrative decisions. If policy states for example that the company will produce a produce of a given quality, administrative decisions must then be made on the ways in which this will be achieved.
>
> Finally, there are executive decisions made at the point where work is carried out . . . (Dale, 1965).

to pursue its ends rather than their own. At one time for example it was easier for local authorities to obtain grants for high-rise development than for low-rise buildings. This was a strong enough incentive to make them build high-rise blocks irrespective of their preferences.[5]

The differential in the degree of relative autonomy enjoyed by central and local government is illustrated by disputes between the two (and by the tactics used by lower-tier agencies resisting directives from above). A well-known case is that of the famous Circular 10/65 issued by the Labour Government which instructed local authorities to prepare and submit plans for reorganizing secondary education on comprehensive lines. Six model schemes were set out, leaving considerable scope for local authorities to opt for the type of comprehensive education best suited to their own ends. What they could not do was to depart from the lines of policy which the government of the day had adopted. As a group of Ealing parents were told by the defence counsel of Ealing Borough Council in a test case: "What the plaintives . . . were really complaining about was that . . . they did not like the national policy of comprehensive education . . . . Those were . . . matters which should be determined by the ballot box" (Batley *et al.*, 1970).

Certain subversive tactics for fighting such directives are typical of the under-dog situation: delayed submissions, or mobilizing public sympathy to make it less palatable for central government to use its powers. Thus, there is a general tendency in centralized structures to push such decisions upwards and to change the framework set. This creates problems of over-load at the centre, so that centralization has a certain self-defeating element built into it.

The Rôle of the Planner

Relative autonomy determines the extent to which a planning agency

[5]This kind of "contextuating control" (see the chapter on implementation) is available to all potent planning agencies, whether they exercise legal authority or not. For instance, the Kennedy administration wanted one Californian city to embark on a planning exercise similar to that undertaken by cities on the Eastern Seabord. They offered federal subsidies to San Francisco that the city fathers felt compelled to take advantage of. Nevertheless, the city's support was only luke-warm, and the famous San Francisco Housing Model originating from this exercise was shelved as soon as federal support ended, and despite the world-wide fame which the model acquired in professional circles (Robinson, 1969).

may engage in normative planning, or be limited to functional planning. But the rôle of the planner may counteract its effects. This is more obvious in the case of an agency with some considerable potential for normative planning, that is one enjoying great autonomy. From time to time, any such agency has to review the effectiveness of its operations (or of those of its subordinate agencies). There are two ways of doing this. One is to investigate the allocation of resources to various tasks; the other is the more fundamental approach of reviewing these tasks themselves.

The first is less demanding and also less disquieting because fewer questions are raised. Also, its necessity is more obvious. To exhaust one's resources means to lose operational capability to pursue the present set of ends, or any other. Therefore, budgeting resources in cash, land, manpower and the like is the more common way of reviewing a set of activities and balancing objectives against each other.

Reason suggests that any such review should go hand in hand with that of the ends pursued with the help of these resources. But in the recent past this has certainly not been done explicitly. Even nowadays, when the effects of programmes are assessed by so-called "output" budgets (Eddison, 1973), this appears to be only a more sophisticated means for allocating resources to *existing* uses. Rarely does it amount to a really fundamental review of the set of ends pursued (Wildavsky and Hammann, 1970), for in most public bureaucracies there are forces entrenched behind every individual item in every budget. For them, every review is a threat.

But if normative planning is to realize its potential, it must be able to set new ends. To advocate innovation inevitably generates opposition, which must be overcome in the same way that battles are won on the political front, that is by winning enough support to overrule entrenched forces. A planner who perceives his rôle as political is likely to be more successful in this than the planner who sees his rôle merely as that of a bureaucrat.

But are these alternatives open to the planner? In the first instance, he seems to have precious little choice. Many people would subscribe without hesitation to Beckman's view of "The planner as a bureaucrat" (1964) with the ". . . vital but more limited rôle that our system assigns to the public employee". This rôle reflects how bureaucracies in general, and public bureaucracies in particular, are seen as instruments for the rational and impartial implementation of policies handed down to them by some higher authority. In the case of public bureaucracies, democratically elected politicians are that higher authority. This is basic to the ethos of public bureaucracies, and it is also upheld by politicians as the chairman of Darlington's Education Committee who was reported as saying: "This is democracy as we know it. . . . We decide the policy, the administrators have to put it into practice and find answers to problems . . ." (Batley *et al.*, 1970).

But, the bureaucratic concept of the planner's rôle is not the only one as can be demonstrated in the case of the American planning profession.[6] At the beginning of the sixties, the path before it seemed that of increasing absorption into public bureaucracies. Indeed, planners expected to play a leading part in an evolving system of urban government. The scene has changed. Academics and the younger American planners in particular are now engaged in a wide variety of activities outside bureaucracies (and partly counteracting their policies). Thus, American planners see themselves as adopting not only bureaucratic rôles but also the overtly political ones of advocates of minority interests, and agents for change. In short, they see themselves as standard-bearers of innovation, by which normative planning realizes its full potential.

But, it is not only outside public bureaucracies that a "political" concept of the planner's rôle gains currency. The more recent literature abounds with evidence that effective planning involves building "winning coalitions" around projects (Bauer, 1968). Thus, Bellush and Hausknecht (1966) conceive of successful urban renewal directors as public entrepreneurs; Gamberg (1966, 1969) writes of the innovatory rôle of planners in the stultified political climate of middle-sized American cities; Friedmann (1966, 1967) sees a similar rôle for planners engaged in institution-building in the not so dissimilar planning environment of developing countries; and Rabinovitz (1969) refers to the rôle of effective planners in localities lacking coherent power élites as that of a political "mobilizer". More recently, Friend and Yewlett (1971) report of decision networks being built around one town expansion scheme in Britain and speculate on the increasing importance of the highly political, "reticulist", skills invoking this concept put forward by Power (1971) in a back-up paper to theirs.

---

[6]For a more detailed discussion and documentation see Part IV of the companion volume.

There is clear evidence, therefore, for the existence of these two alternative rôle concepts which we have termed "bureaucratic" and "political" and for the innovative capacity of planning agencies depending on the political concept, whilst being constrained by the bureaucratic one. There is perhaps less evidence for the reverse being the case, that is for a political rôle-concept to counteract a tendency toward functional planning. But one may guess that a planner with a strongly political view of his rôle will at least seek to extend the limits of the autonomy of his planning agency. He will therefore move its planning further towards the normative end of the dimension and away from its original, more functional, position. Thus, figuratively speaking, he acts as a constraint on functional planning. At least, this seems to be the reasoning behind the suggestion of a "bureaucratic guerilla" rôle for radical planners (see Chapter 13).

A RESEARCH DESIGN

The concepts and variables defined in this chapter are summarized in Table 9.2 to be read in conjunction with Table 9.1.

TABLE 9.2

VARIABLES FOR RESEARCH INTO NORMATIVE VERSUS
FUNCTIONAL PLANNING

Concepts	*Variables*
Mode of planning (normative versus functional)	Range of ends taken into consideration; statements of objectives and assumptions supported by argument or not.
Relative degree of autonomy (great or small)	Range of legal powers; flexibility in the use of resources for alternative purposes.
The rôle of the planner ("political" or "bureaucratic")	Terms of reference and administrative rules; informal arrangements; occurrence of political conflict involving planners.

The hypothesis which a study into this dimension would investigate is the following: that the mode of planning (indicated by the range of ends considered and/or whether statements of objectives are supported by argument) depends on great relative autonomy of the planning agency (indicated by the range of its legal powers and by any "float" in the allocation of its resources) subject to the constraint exercised by the rôle-concept of the planner (indicated by the occurrence of political conflict involving planners). Alternatively, a reverse study could investigate functional planning as depending on small relative autonomy and so on. As with the hypotheses stated in the previous two chapters, these may be tested for their correspondence to reality.

NORMATIVE AND FUNCTIONAL PLANNING IN MULTI-PLANNING AGENCIES

To plan on the level of substantial rationality subjecting both the means *and* the ends of planning to rational consideration is an ideal which is a natural corollary of reason, which ultimately requires that whatever is susceptible to rational analysis will be analysed in this manner.[7] Thus, normative planning can be equated with the application of reason.

Functional planning plays the same rôle within the context of normative planning as blueprint planning does in process planning: it frees problem-solving capacity by hiving off whole sub-routines of the total planning process to certain planning agencies, thus facilitating normative planning by others.

Functional and blueprint planning also tend to go hand in hand. Where functional planning is practised, it tends to proceed in a blueprint mode and *vice versa,* because keeping the ends of a programme constant (that is to plan in a functional mode) facilitates the formation of a firm image. In order to be able to construct such a firm image, and to derive the benefits of (real or apparent) certainty which it affords, planners may be tempted to hold the ends of their planning constant, however wrong this may be.

There is a further parallel relating to control. Functional planning means to split control over the environment between many agencies, each exercising relatively high control over a limited number of variables. It thus plays into the hands of the blueprint planner. Therefore, the conclusion drawn about blueprint planning in Chapter 7 also applies here: in a perfect world, just as limitations on the frequency and scope of reviews demanded

[7]On the compromises and the use of planning strategies see Chapter 6.

by process planning would be unacceptable to a rational planner, so would limitations on the range of ends considered. The world being what it is, however, functional planning may be accepted, as blueprint planning is, as part of the planning strategies designed to cope with notorious limitations on information-handling capacity. It has the advantage of allowing technical experts to concentrate their efforts and to cumulate experience, just as does any division of labour. Since no one person or planning agency can command all the expertise required to engage in really comprehensive planning involving both functional and normative planning (that is, since no person can plan on the level of substantial rationality), it is sensible to let functional planners pursue their comparatively narrow investigations. But, because of the limits which functional planning puts on the consideration of alternative ends, this must occur within the framework of planning strategies deliberately chosen so as to balance the advantage of functional planning against its costs. These strategies, in particular mixed scanning, thus determine the balance of effort involved in choosing the overall framework of decision-making by planning agencies engaged in functional planning, as against that involved in functional planning itself.[8]

One may therefore conclude that normative planning in an imperfect world only becomes feasible by using planning strategies. Predefining problem situations which are the concern of functional planning agencies thus giving them a framework to operate in, rather than prescribing actual solutions to problems, is therefore the main way in which normative planning on the highest level of a multi-planning agency ought to proceed.

REFERENCES

BATLEY, R. *et al.* (1970) *Going Comprehensive: Educational Policy-making in two County Boroughs*, Routledge & Kegan Paul, London.
BAUER, R. A. (1968) The study of policy formation: an introduction, *The Study of Policy Formation* (edited by BAUER, R. A. and GERGEN, K. J.), Collier-Macmillan, London.
*BECKMAN, N. (1964) The planner as a bureaucrat, *Journal of the American Institute of Planners*, Vol. **30**, pp. 323–7.
BELLUSH, J. and HAUSKNECHT, M. (1966) Entrepreneurs and urban renewal, *Journal of the American Institute of Planners*, Vol. **32**, pp. 289–97.

[8]As a guideline for determining what could be planned functionally, Friedmann (1967) suggests that stable and general ends cannot be changed as easily as specific ones.

DALE, E. (1965) *Management: Theory and Practice*, McGraw-Hill, New York.

EDDISON, T. (1973) *Local Government: Management and Corporate Planning*, Leonard Hill Books, Aylesbury, Bucks.

FRIEDMANN, J. (1966) Planning as innovation: the Chilean case, *Journal of the American Institute of Planners*, Vol. **32**, pp. 194–204.

FRIEDMANN, J. (1966/7) Planning as a vocation, *Plan Canada*, Vol. **6**, pp. 99–124, Vol. **7**, pp. 8–26.

*FRIEDMANN, J. (1967) A conceptual model for the analysis of planning behavior, *Administrative Science Quarterly*, Vol. **12**, pp. 225–52.

FRIEND, J. K. and YEWLETT, C. J. L. (1971) Inter-agency decision processes: practice and prospect, *Beyond Local Government Reform*, Institute for Operational Research, Tavistock Institute, London.

GAMBERG, H. (1966) The professional and policy choices in middle-sized cities, *Journal of the American Institute of Planners*, Vol. **32**, pp. 174–7.

GAMBERG, H. (1969) *The Escape from Power: Politics in the American Community*, Exchange Bibliography, No. 106, Council of Planning Librarians, Monticello, Illinois.

GUTKIND, E. A. (1946) *Revolution of Environment*, Kegan Paul, Trench, Trubner & Co., Ltd., London.

MANNHEIM, K. (1940) *Man and Society in an Age of Reconstruction*, Kegan Paul, Trench, Trubner & Co., Ltd., London.

POWER, J. M. (1971) Planning: magic and technique, *Beyond Local Government Reform*, Institute for Operational Research, Tavistock Institute, London.

RABINOVITZ, F. F. (1969) *City Politics and Planning*, Atherton Press, New York.

ROBINSON, I. M. (1969) Lecture delivered at the Summer Workshop of the American Yugoslav Project at Ljubljana, Slovenia.

SPEER, A. (1969) *Erinnerungen*, Propyläen, Berlin.

WEBER, M. (1947) *The Theory of Social and Economic Organisation*, William Hodge, Edinburgh.

WEBER, M. (1965) *The Protestant Ethic and the Spirit of Capitalism*, 7th ed., Allen & Unwin, London.

WILDAVSKY, A. and HAMMANN, A. (1970) Comprehensive versus incremental budgeting in the Department of Agriculture, *Planning Programming Budgeting: A Systems Approach to Management* (Edited by LYDEN, F. J. and MILLER, E. G.), 3rd ed., Markham, Chicago.

*Included in FALUDI, A. (1973) *A Reader in Planning Theory*, Pergamon, Oxford.

CHAPTER 10

The Planning Environment and the Style of Planning

THIS final chapter of Part III summarizes those factors which have been identified as determinants of, and constraints on, planning. To a considerable extent they reflect the *planning environment*, that is the context within which a planning agency operates.

The concept of a planning environment links the ideas advanced in this book with those of others. It also promises to be of use to planning practitioners. There are certain characteristic types of planning environment requiring certain *planning styles*. But in ending this chapter, I shall raise the question of whether planning should, within a certain planning environment, automatically seek to adapt its style, or to attempt to change the environment. The question provides the link between this part and the next.

THE PLANNING ENVIRONMENT AS A UNIFYING CONCEPT

In the three previous chapters, certain factors were identified which were said to influence planning: the firmness and scope of images; the degree of control exercised, the images of society as reflected in the structure and the procedures of planning agencies, and so on. However, none of these factors is independent of the environment of a planning agency. New knowledge may change images; the pace of social change may vary, and lead to different time-lags; constitutional thinking about planning may take a new turn; images of society reflect whether conflict is prevalent or not. All these features of the environment of a planning agency (some relatively more dynamic than others) set limits within which a planning agency can operate, with these limits changing in turn as the *planning environment* changes.

Apart from improvement to the planner's understanding, there is another reason for introducing the concept. As pointed out in the previous chapters, the factors influencing planning are to some extent interdependent. For instance, a planning agency with little autonomy (that is with relatively few variables to control) tends (other things being equal) to have a firmer image than one controlling more variables. In this case, then, functional planning tends to occur jointly with blueprint planning and, conversely, normative with process planning. Such recurring combinations of several modes of planning correspond to what Friedmann, in the paper referred to below, terms a planning style. His proposition is that certain planning styles fit certain planning environments. Knowledge of the types of planning environment focuses the attention of both the researcher observing planning and the practitioner learning from examples drawn from a different context: by using this concept they are better able to attend to the *reasons* for variations in planning styles.

THE CONCEPT OF THE PLANNING ENVIRONMENT IN CROSS-NATIONAL RESEARCH

In this section I shall compare American and British planning styles based on an appreciation of their different types of planning environment. Before this I shall discuss Friedmann's earlier work on the context of planning decisions on which my thinking is based, showing why the latter represents a modest improvement on Friedmann's proposition.

Friedmann's Work on Latin America

Friedmann's paper on the institutional context of planning decisions (what he calls *decision environment*) was part of a large-scale effort to promote cross-national comparative research into, in this case, national economic planning (Friedmann, 1966). The reasoning behind this project was that economic planning had become far too complicated to be based on economic theory alone: "Any deep analysis of the economic planning process in any country would require a skillful blending of concepts from political science, organization theory, sociology, social psychology and anthropology" (Gross, 1964).

A conference brought an international group of scholars from various disciplines together, and resulted in the volume of studies *Action Under Planning* (Gross, 1966) in which Friedmann's paper dealt with "The institutional context". His argument runs as follows: there is an "environment for decision" in every country which

> refers to characteristic conditions of choice behavior such as the relative ignorance of the deciders, the extent of their uncertainty about the future, the number of relevant interests and the need for recognizing them, and the ability of the deciders to influence the decisions (and actions) of others. At an appropriate level of generality, these conditions describe the social context of decisions.

As this context is relatively stable over time, there will be a distinctive "style of national planning" corresponding to the particular context of that society. This style influences the substantive content of plans. Knowledge of this "decision environment" and of the particular style going with it therefore helps in the "design of optimal planning systems", as well as in the "design and evaluation of program proposals". This is related to Simon's concept of *bounded rationality*, taking the limiting context of rational choice into account on the strength of the argument that the ". . . 'best' decision is always a feasible decision".

On this basis Friedmann presents a preliminary model for cross-national research into the institutional forms of national planning decisions, incorporating the following three groups of major elements: criteria for classification of national systems; descriptive categories of aspects of the decision environment; aspects of the institutional form of national planning decisions.

The first set provides a broad distinction of societies according to their level of development, political organization and historical tradition. Of the many possible clusters, Friedmann selected a group of seven "traditional modern" countries with a political organization termed "reconciliation system" in the "great Latin American historical tradition". The paper characterizes their "decision environment" by a relatively large number of interests; by tolerance of political opposition and the acceptance of conflict; by a substantial degree of potential government control over a poorly developed private sector; by inadequate information systems with substantial delays occurring in reporting, analysis and dissemination of information; by weak and sometimes corrupt administration; and by great vulnerability to external conditions resulting in the outcomes of planning efforts being largely unpredictable. The ensuing style of planning is characterized by high government involvement by default in all fields of economic development; by an uneven distribution of planning capabilities with a prevalence of planning for transport, electric energy development, irrigation and housing;[1] by focused planning resulting from this uneven distribution; by an emphasis on short- as opposed to long-range planning; by a low degree of co-ordination; by a lack of coercion despite the pre-dominance of the public sector; and by vague and diffuse goals aiming more at building a broad consensus than at guiding concrete action.

An Improvement on Friedmann's Proposition

Many of the features of Friedmann's "decision environment" relate to the factors determining planning as outlined in the previous three chapters. For instance, the number of organized interests and the acceptance of political conflict relate to images of society, and predictability of change to the firmness of images held. Similarly, some of the features of the ensuing planning style relate to the dimensions of planning presented earlier, for instance the scope and comprehensiveness of planning and the degree of co-ordination to the rational-comprehensive versus disjointed-incrementalist dimension. One could therefore translate some of Friedmann's findings into the language of this book.

The relationship does not end here. Using some of the concepts developed previously helps to indicate how this idea of variable planning styles as corresponding to different planning environments could become even more intellectually satisfactory. Strictly, what Friedmann suggests is only that the two co-vary. He does not fully *explain* how the planning environment actually influences the planning style. Such an explanation could only be given by invoking laws of planning such as stated previously (albeit in hypothetical form).

Certainly, implicitly Friedmann does draw on generalizations concerning planning and he invokes those to explain why the Latin American planning

---

[1]Friedmann comments on these fields as "closely allied with architecture and engineering and consequently built on a certain tradition of physical planning", a tradition which is "overly simplistic" and "normally devoid of any but the crudest kind of financial consideration".

style shows its characteristic features. Stated as an explicit hypothesis, one generalization might for instance read like this: where the future is highly uncertain, the planning style is characterized by an emphasis on short-term over long-term planning (this leads us to one of the stated conclusions concerning planning in Latin America). As will readily be seen, this proposition is of the same nature as the hypotheses advanced in the previous three chapters. I shall therefore show in the rest of this section how the concept of the planning environment might be used to explain variations of planning styles more fully than Friedmann has done by laying bare the mechanisms by which one affects the other.[2] These mechanisms are provided by the three earlier hypotheses. Since it is not their empirical status that we are here concerned with, but rather the possibility of using them to bridge the gap between planning environment and characteristic planning styles, I shall assume that the hypotheses have acquired the status of laws of planning.

Comparing British with American Planning

What I shall offer is a tentative explanation of the difference exhibited by the planning styles of Great Britain and the United States, planning styles referring to a syndrome of various modes of planning. For each of the dimensions I shall ask the questions: Where are American and British planning to be found? How can their position be explained in terms of the differences between the planning environment in these two countries (thereby applying my hypotheses as if they were laws of planning).

Taking the dimension of *blueprint versus process planning* first, one may observe that in the American literature there is emphasis on planning as a continuous process. As against this, process planning is only just becoming a prominent concern of British planning, which is closer to the blueprint end of the dimension. This reflects different ways of thinking about what urban settlements are (that is, different images); different degrees of control exercised by planning agencies, and different time-lags. The features of the planning environment which account for these differences are the pace of change in the two countries, the relative importance of market forces and government control, different degrees of strength of the social sciences,

[2] I presented this argument before (Faludi, 1970). The terms used in the present version are slightly different, to bring them in line with the rest of this book.

and the extent to which the two planning professions open their ranks to social scientists.

In more detail, American process planning may be explained, firstly, in terms of a much more dynamic image which planners hold of "urban systems", one characterized by a greater awareness of uncertainty. Such an image is the result of the fast pace of social and economic change, resulting in shorter time-lags and hence greater pressure to revise spuriously firm images; the greater availability of social-science skills;[3] and the greater openness of the American planning profession to influences from academics in general and social scientists in particular. Secondly, the lower degree of control exercised by American planners, making for process planning, is but a reflection of the general mistrust in government which characterizes America. It compels planners to co-operate much more with market forces than their British colleagues do, and to establish a consensus between many groups who would otherwise impede the implementation of policies. Both these implications of the relatively low degree of control exercised by American planners contribute to its greater flexibility and thus to its process orientation. This is evidenced for instance by the emphasis on the "intelligence" rather than the control function of planning (Meyerson, 1956; Fagin, 1959; Webber, 1965; Peterson, 1966). Thirdly, and finally, the political process which evolves around planning proposals arouses more interest from American political scientists than it does on this side of the Atlantic. This has resulted in numerous case studies which have increased still further the planners' awareness of the complexity of urban communities.

Conversely, British blueprint planning may be explained in terms of the firmer image which British planners hold, which stems from the fact that there is less compulsion on them to change such images. Change is cushioned and regulated by a host of controls; central and local government are much more evident as the providers of services than in the United States; social-science skills are less abundant and the access of social scientists to planning much more circumscribed.[4]

[3]As early as 1961, Dyckman could report that "the young professionals show a strong pattern of majors in political science, economics, and sociology along with the traditional majors" (Dyckman, 1961). The only social scientists who have been attracted into planning in large numbers in Britain are geographers (Faludi, 1972).

[4]For a report on research into the relations between social scientists and planners see Faludi (1971).

The case concerning the second dimension of *rational-comprehensive versus disjointed-incrementalist planning* is more complex. American planning presents a clear-cut case of disjointed incrementalism coming from an atomistic image of society underlying planning agencies and their procedures. The ensuing fragmentation of planning[5] is only barely checked by efforts to act on the basis of wide-ranging images concerning interdependencies between, say, the physical fabric of cities and their social ecology. This atomistic image of society pervades the whole of the fabric of American institutions, and has its roots in the constitution of the United States and the tradition of the "frontier". To these, one must add the existence of numerous ethnic minorities and the cleavages between them which still further fragment American society.[6]

British planning is more difficult to place. One could describe it as disjointed-incrementalist by default. The constraint operating is that of a limited image with each of the many services concerning themselves with only a few environmental variables. The system of local authority planning is based "on separate parts, in each of which is gathered the individual service, with its professional departmental hierarchy led by a principal

[5]On disjointed incrementalism as but a reflection of the fragmentation of planning see Broady (1968) and Dror (1968). American authors are therefore often inclined to advocate a certain amount of *centralization* as a precondition of effective implementation of social policy: ". . . the social democracy which is a precondition to collective social planning in a political democracy depends on social gains which will be engineered, for the most part, from Washington. The achievement of economic democracy, the securing of equality in civil rights, the abolition of gross regional differences in education, and other major social gains will be forged by federal power, or not at all" (Dyckman, 1966; see also Warner, 1966, and Frieden, 1965).

[6]Allied to this image of society one finds in the United States a notion of the public interest as the sum of the interests of individuals. Kaplan (1963) refers to both as the "single comprehensive ideal: individualism", and Warner (1968) as "privatism" holding it responsible for Philadelphia's inability to meet the demands of an increasingly urbanized society. Privatism means "that the individual should seek happiness in personal independence and in the search for wealth; . . . that the individual should see his first loyalty to his immediate family, and that a community should be a union of such . . . money makers, and . . . keep the peace among individual moneymakers and, if possible, create an open and thriving setting where each citizen would have substantial opportunity to prosper." In all fairness one should remember that the almost unlimited resources of the United States in the eighteenth and nineteenth centuries did create conditions under which ". . . it was relatively easy for the common man to make his own way . . . without the benefit of a watchful, paternalistic government . . ." (Becker, 1960).

officer, and supervising it, a committee of members . . . There may be unity in the parts, but there is disunity in the whole" (Ministry of Housing and Local Government, 1967). This is an important feature of British local government and thus of the immediate environment of most British planning. But, currently, one can observe the adoption of many ideas developed under the hothouse conditions of American urban government. Although it is difficult to pinpoint, the impression is that their application tends to be more successful in Britain (Eddison, 1971). While, therefore, theoretical images are often more encompassing and more sophisticated in the United States, there is the distinct possibility of the images underlying British planning practice becoming relatively more comprehensive, especially where they are influenced by American thinking.

This may be explained in terms of a much greater *potential* for comprehensiveness resulting from an underlying image of society which is certainly more holistic than that held in the United States. Again, this does not only apply to planning but is a prominent feature of British culture and institutions. Government commands more sweeping powers and may contemplate more fundamental changes than is possible in the United States.

This is because of its tradition of trust in public authority and of the public interest taking precedence over private ones (Glass, 1959; Foley, 1960). Also, British institutions, both on the central as well as on the local level, are currently being reorganized to reflect this holistic image of society more adequately. One may therefore expect that British planning will fulfil its potential for comprehensiveness to a much greater extent in future than it now does enhancing the contrast with American disjointed incrementalism.[7]

As with the previous dimension, the case of *normative verus functional planning* is complex. Comparing like with like, planning agencies probably enjoy greater autonomy in Britain than in the United States, despite the fact that American local authorities are not subject to central government control. Autonomy does not simply mean absence of control. It means having a capacity for exercising control. Lack of power generally, and the fragmentation of American local government to a point where it is

---

[7]On possible advantages of the simpler and more stream-lined political system of Britain over that of the United States (reflecting, as it does, a more holistic view of society) see, for instance, McKay (1972).

hardly possible to talk about government as such militate against the relative autonomy of American planning agencies. But, on the other hand, certain constraints on the degree to which British planning fulfils its potential for engaging in normative planning are absent in the United States: the concept of the planner's rôle. This in turn is a reflection of the character of public employment. British planners are part of an elaborate nation-wide machinery, enjoying as public servants the job security and high esteem which their society provides. There is much less incentive for planners to break out of the limitations of a bureaucratic rôle.

The situation of the average American planner is more or less the reverse. The planning system in which he operates is not very firmly structured, nor does public service enjoy a high status in a country upholding the ideals of "rugged individualism". In the absence of the rewards of high status and of job security, the appeal of a political rôle is great. Also, professionals are often appointed in America on the basis of the policies for which they stand rather than of their competence. This practice has expanded since federal funds became available to assist communities in hiring their own planners, as Davidoff had demanded in his paper on advocacy planning (Davidoff, 1965). On balance, American planning is therefore probably more normative than British planning, the lower degree of autonomy of its planning agencies notwithstanding.

In summary, one may characterize the American planning style as process-oriented, disjointed-incrementalist and yet relatively more normative than the British one which is blueprint-oriented, potentially comprehensive but effectively functional. These styles can be explained as reflecting distinct features of the respective planning environment, in particular the more atomistic image held of society in the United States, and its roots in American history and culture, as against the more holistic image held in Britain. To bridge the conceptual gap between these features of the American and British planning style and the two types of planning environment, the three hypotheses developed in the previous chapters were invoked. This was to demonstrate what a full explanation of variations of planning styles would be like which one could obtain after research had been conducted on the lines suggested previously.

The benefits of a positive theory of planning do not end here. Armed with such a theory, one would even be able to predict changes in planning style as related to anticipated changes in the planning environment. In the paper from which I draw, I have therefore predicted that, in certain areas, British planners will be faced with problems similar to those experienced by Americans. This is based on the assumption that the cleavages in British society are becoming more prominent.

Of course, this does not mean to say that the response of British planners will be exactly the same. Instead of the American way of greater fragmentation of planning, Britain may take the course of politicizing its statutory planning procedures, making use of the greater variety provided by an increasingly "pluralist" society, and yet preserving its ability to act out preferences. This would mean moving further toward normative and process planning whilst still aiming to realize the existing potential for comprehensiveness (surely an ideal planning style).

THE PLANNING ENVIRONMENT ON THE LOCAL LEVEL

Whatever the national planning environment, there are still variations between localities in any one country. This section identifies variations between different local planning environments in the United States whose general planning environment and planning style I have described above. Some of these are so different from the broad picture presented there that the environment resembles Britain more than America. Awareness of these types of local planning environment are of more immediate help to the planner choosing his planning style than any knowledge of the planning environment on the national level.

The works which I shall discuss form part of a rich body of literature on American city politics. It is not surprising that American city politics should have attracted so much interest so much earlier than elsewhere. The variation between different forms of local government organization existing in the United States has simply invited comparison, much as the variation of political institutions in classical Greece is reputed to have done thereby promoting the development of political theory.

Within the study of city politics, there is a branch concerned with identifying the "patterns of influence" in communities. This corresponds to images held of an, albeit local, society. Once recognized, they help the planner in choosing an appropriate rôle for himself as Rabinovitz (1969) suggests. I shall therefore give a brief account of the development of the study of community decision-making, drawing on a review article by

Mann (1964)[8] and leading into an account of Rabinovitz's work with a discussion of its relationship to the dimensions of planning identified before.

Studies of Community Decision-making

The first study of community decision-making was Hunter's *Community Power Structure* (1953). Basically, he found that an élite consisting of a few businessmen made all the important decisions. This is known as the "power pyramid" model of community decision-making. An alternative model was advanced by Dahl(1961). He found a much more diffuse pattern in which a plurality of groups succeeded in bringing their influence to bear. This became known as the "Yale poly-archic power" model.

Much argument arose about which model represented decision-making in American communities more accurately. The underlying issue was that Dahl's model conformed more to people's criteria of American society: each interest group exerting influence where it had a burning desire to do so. Thus, by claiming that decision-making approximated to a widely held normative model, Dahl seemed to defend, and the Hunter-type studies (and their equivalent on the national level, Mills's *The Power Elite*, 1957) to challenge, the *status quo*.

Sidestepping this controversy, a further line of thought which tried to synthesize these two models was called the "variable pattern" hypothesis. It built on the assumption that some communities would conform more to one model and some more to the other, the majority falling somewhere between the two extremes. This hypothesis was developed further by identifying factors which would make for one or the other pattern of influence rather in the way that I have developed the arguments in this book. For instance, large metropolitan areas would be more of the dispersed type while smaller, and particularly rural, communities more monolithic. In his review article, Mann claimed that this approach held some prospect for the formulation of laws of community decision behaviour, a prospect which I view with the same caution as that of finding laws of planning.

Rabinovitz on Effective Planning Styles

But even in advance of such general laws, the concepts were put to use, fortunately in the context of a planning study. This is Rabinovitz's book

[8] For a more recent review from the British point of view see Hill (1972).

(1969) identifying the features of a local planning environment, and of suitable planning styles, for different types of communities.[9]

Rabinovitz began with a working definition of effectiveness in terms of the ability of planners to affect the outcomes of decisions. On this basis, she selected five cities in New Jersey which had effective planning, and one where it was ineffective. These six cities were all medium-sized and could be arranged along a continuum ranging from "power pyramid" to "Yale poly-archic" patterns of influence in line with the "variable pattern" hypothesis. On this continuum she identified four "major bands" which were:

The cohesive system. In the one community falling into this category (which incidentally experts had described as having the most effective planning) there was a small number of people from old established families who tended to decide policy.[10] In this community there was ". . . basic agreement on what the town should look like and where it should grow".

The executive-centred system. Here, there was at the centre an influential mayor as an elected chief executive. There were also other leaders with whom he had to compromise. The system was therefore not perfectly monolithic, though it approximated to that pattern through the efforts of the mayor to settle differences within the system itself. His ability to do this because of a fair level of consensus ultimately forced community leaders to accept his authority.

The competitive system. The competitive system was closer to Dahl's model than the first two: there were several leadership cliques. Open conflict was the rule; decision-making was seen as a "zero sum game", where a gain made by one party represented a loss by the others.

The fragmented system. Farthest away from the cohesive system was one where no visible leadership group existed. This category therefore approximated most closely to ideas of a pluralist society, where interests and the powers commanded by various groups balance each other.

[9]See also Rabinovitz (1967).
[10]In that these families were benevolent and influential but normally inactive and invisible, they reminded Rabinovitz of the "British ruling class".

For each of these categories, Rabinovitz spells out the style of effective planning. Her findings, couched in terms of rôle concepts for planners, can be easily translated into terms of normative versus functional planning. Thus she holds that, in a cohesive system, the appropriate rôle for the planner is that of a *technician*. In this guise, he gains a foothold in decision-making and exercises his influence, but only while his programmes do not violate the established ethos, which is *functional planning* for the attainment of a stable set of ends. The rôle of the planner is a bureaucratic one, to use the term introduced in the previous chapter.

The set-up also showed very clearly the disadvantage of functional planning which could not cope with problems which one might term social involving the reorientation of policy to serve new ends. The cohesive community was, for instance, under pressure to allow for higher densities, to revise the school and housing conditions of the negro population, and decrease the cost of services to accommodate newer and younger residents, moves which were resisted so that, in future, ". . . the technician planner in this cohesive system might find his ability to solve this series of problems severely limited".

In the case of the executive-centred system, the planner's rôle was only slightly different. By being co-opted by an elected chief executive, he became identified with him. He thus lost some of the air of objectivity which surrounds the planner in the cohesive system. But he was still working towards ends set for him. It was only in the competitive system that the planner became active at this level. Because the competitive community had at least two leadership groups, the planner was forced to assume a broker rôle, and find mutually acceptable solutions. This active involvement of the planner had to be greater still in a fragmented system where the planner was ". . . forced to go beyond the broker rôle and to mobilize those who *might* have interests across a broad spectrum and then co-ordinate these". The planner therefore became a participant in the political process exercising choice over which issues to address himself to and what to do to get his way, which could include rallying political support. He had to assess his programme in terms of their ends, thereby engaging in *normative* planning.

In a passing comment, Rabinovitz drew another interesting conclusion concerning rational-comprehensive versus disjointed-incrementalist planning, and the alleged conservatism of the latter. The cohesive system reflected what I described as the holistic image of society and the fragmented system the atomistic one, with the others falling in between. One should therefore expect the first type to show greater propensity towards rational-comprehensive and the second towards disjointed-incrementalist planning, which she confirmed. Of the cohesive system she said that, subject to limitations outlined above, it showed ". . . a marked capability . . . to solve those difficulties accepted as problems".[11] But of the fragmented system she observed that it showed resistance against innovation. She therefore countered the disjointed incrementalists' claim that the fragmented decision-making system was preferable because it had built-in safeguards against interests being overlooked saying that ". . . it does not necessarily follow that the best policy for planning always emerges from this process".

To summarize, Rabinovitz described different types of local planning environment. Her concern was mainly to identify the conditions of the planner's effectiveness in terms of his rôle, rather than with the features of the planning style exhibited in a certain environment. But it is possible to use her findings to show that the local planning environment makes for a certain planning style, as Friedmann has shown for the national level. This style can be described in terms of the various modes of planning.

The concept that a local planning environment makes for certain planning styles is of great practical use. Knowledge of its types, and how they influence planning, enables the planner to gauge what is possible in any particular situation. Though communities are like individuals each requiring unique responses, to create typologies of communities assists the planner involved with them to find a more appropriate approach (just as the typologies which one creates of individuals do in one's dealings with confederates).

ADAPTATION OR CHANGE?

Knowledge of the planning environment may be a precondition of finding an appropriate planning style. But what precisely should it be? Should the planner always adapt to the planning environment?

Taking the last question first, one must conclude from Rabinovitz's

---

[11]For other research confirming this finding see Bolan (1969).

description of the political mobilizer rôle that it is quite conceivable for the planner to change the planning environment. By building a coalition around an issue, he introduces an element of cohesion. Though success of this kind, enabling action even in a fragmented community, may be difficult to achieve, it is nevertheless possible, as case studies show. The planner may therefore have a lasting effect on the planning environment.

It is even possible to think in terms of conscious strategies designed to improve the less desirable features of the planning environment. Friedmann describes strategies for a "search for greater rationality" which are aimed mainly at improvements to the decision-making environment itself— improving information processes and administrative structure, increasing the independence of the economy from external changes and so forth— thus demonstrating how the concept of a "decision environment" may be used in the "design of optimal planning systems".

This may seem to assume altogether too much influence for the planner. He is only one of many actors in a very complex process. But like any other participant, he *may* have an effect. Certainly, if one looks at planners not individually but as a group, they have no justification for defeatism. Collectively, planners certainly affect how planning agencies and their procedures develop: planners develop new ways of thinking concerning planning; they man the committees and working parties concerned with evolving patterns, draft proposals for legislative and procedural change and advise politicians on which course to take. Thus, as a group, planners may very well have *a policy towards planning*, including a policy towards the planning environment. Indeed, their posture has always been that they expect this policy to be taken account of, as evidenced for instance by the representations of the Royal Town Planning Institute in the reorganization of British local government.

Given, therefore, that planners may have a policy towards planning and the planning environment, what should its aims be? This question is one which goes beyond the scope of this part concerned with planning as it is, not as it ought to be, though it is one which planning theory must attempt to answer. But, as against the positive theory of planning which this part is concerned with, to answer this question requires a normative theory of planning, one which says how planning agencies and their procedures ought to be in order to serve the end of better planning. It is to *The Politics of Rational Planning* based on this normative theory that I now turn.

REFERENCES

BECKER, C. L. (1960) *Freedom and Responsibility in the American Way of Life*, Vintage Books, New York.

*BOLAN, R. (1969) Community decision behavior: the culture of planning, *Journal of the American Institute of Planners*, Vol. 35, pp. 301–10.

BROADY, M. (1968) From planning techniques to a theory of planning, *Salzburg Congress of Urban Planning and Development (SCUPAD) Bulletin*, No. 4, pp. 74–80.

DAHL, R. (1961) *Who Governs?* Yale University Press, New Haven.

*DAVIDOFF, P. (1965) Advocacy and pluralism in planning, *Journal of the American Institute of Planners*, Vol. 32, pp. 331–8.

DROR, Y. (1968) *Public Policymaking Reexamined*, Chandler, Scranton, Penn.

*DYCKMAN, J. W. (1961) What makes planners plan? *Journal of the American Institute of Planners*, Vol. 27, pp. 164–7.

DYCKMAN, J. W. (1966) Social planning, social planners and planned society, *Journal of the American Institute of Planners*, Vol. 32, pp. 66–76.

EDDISON, T. (1971) Lecture delivered at a conference on "The Future of Planning Education: Challenge and Response" held at the Department of Town Planning, Oxford Polytechnic, Oxford.

FAGIN, H. (1959) Organizing and carrying out planning activities in urban government, *Journal of the American Institute of Planners*, Vol. 25, pp. 109–14.

FALUDI, A. (1970) The planning environment and the meaning of "planning", *Regional Studies*, Vol. 4, pp. 1–9.

FALUDI, A. (1971) The experiences of sociologists in their collaboration with planners, *Uses of Social Sciences in Urban Planning*, Seminar Proceedings, Planning & Transport Research & Computation Co. Ltd., London.

FALUDI, A. (1972) The specialist versus generalist conflict, *Oxford Working Papers in Planning Education and Research*, No. 12, Department of Town Planning, Oxford Polytechnic, Oxford.

*FOLEY, D. L. (1960) British town planning: one ideology or three? *British Journal of Sociology*, Vol. 11, pp. 211–31.

FRIEDEN, B. J. (1965) Toward equality of urban opportunity, *Journal of the American Institute of Planners*, Vol. 31, pp. 320–30.

FRIEDMANN, J. (1966) The institutional context, *Action under Planning* (edited by GROSS, B. M.), McGraw Hill, New York.

*GLASS, R. (1959) The evaluation of planning: some sociological considerations, *International Social Science Journal*, Vol. 11, pp. 393–409.

GROSS, B. (1964) National planning: some fundamental questions *The American Behavioral Scientist*, Vol. 8, pp. 7–15.

GROSS, B. (1966) *Action under Planning*, McGraw-Hill, New York.

HILL, M. J. (1972) *The Sociology of Public Administration*, Weidenfeld & Nicholson, London.

HUNTER, F. (1953) *Community Power Structure*, University of North Carolina Press, Chapel Hill.

KAPLAN, A. (1963) *American Ethics and Public Policy*, Oxford University Press, New York.

MANN, L. D. (1964) Studies in community decision-making, *Journal of the American Institute of Planners*, Vol. 30, pp. 58–65.

McKay, D. H. (1972) The ghetto dwellers, *New Society*, 16 March, pp. 537–40.

*Meyerson, M. (1956) Building the middle-range bridge for comprehensive planning, *Journal of the American Institute of Planners*, Vol. 22, pp. 58–64.

Mills, C. W. (1957) *The Power Elite*, Oxford University Press, New York.

Ministry of Housing and Local Government (1967) *Management of Local Government* (Maud Report), HMSO, London.

Peterson, W. (1966) On some meanings of 'planning', *Journal of the American Institute of Planners*, Vol. 32, pp. 130–42.

*Rabinovitz, F. F. (1967) Politics, personality, and planning, *Public Administration Review*, Vol. 27, pp. 18–24.

Rabinovitz, F. F. (1969) *City Politics and Planning*, Atherton Press, New York.

Warner, S. B., jr. (1966) (Editor) *Planning for a Nation of Cities*, MIT Press, Cambridge, Mass.

Warner, S. B., jr. (1968) *The Private City: Philadelphia in three Periods of its Growth*, University of Pennsylvania Press, Philadelphia.

Webber, M. M. (1965) The role of intelligence systems in urban systems planning, *Journal of the American Institute of Planners*, Vol. 31, pp. 289–96.

*Included in Faludi, A. (1973) *A Reader in Planning Theory*, Pergamon, Oxford.

PART IV

THE POLITICS OF RATIONAL PLANNING

TOWARDS the end of the previous chapter, I suggested that planners should have collective policies of promoting rational planning. This part indicates what their policies should be, assuming that the rationale of planning as promoting human growth is accepted. It therefore presents a normative theory of planning, drawing on the conceptual framework of planning thought developed in Part II, its amendments made while working *Towards a Positive Theory of Planning* in Part III, as well as research findings which seemed relevant.

The areas which appear the most obvious targets of the politics of rational planning are: those multi-planning agencies which alone can engage in a desirable planning style, in particular in a rational-comprehensive mode of planning; respective rôles of politicians and planners in decision-making; preferred organizational forms for planning departments; procedures used during the planning process to make the kinds of proposals aimed at the previous two items feasible; and the way programmes are implemented. Each of these areas forms the subject of one of the next five chapters, each one ending with a statement of aims to be pursued by the politics of rational planning.

Planning is viewed with some considerable apprehension by people who care about the advancement of democratic values. They see planning as potentially contributing to the domination of man over man, because they think it is a willing instrument of those who hold the reins.[1] In this book, and notably in Part IV, I give several reasons why this apprehension is

[1] People fear the same about science; see Kaplan (1964) and Willer (1967).

exaggerated. Planning, rather than being an obliging instrument, enhances democracy when it operates from a proper understanding of its own inevitable limitations. Thus, it is argued that planning agencies must not impose themselves forcibly on their environment, because this would rob them of their chance to learn; that they must be capable of relaxing the rigidity of their procedures so that they can engage in creative planning; that they must carry out an open form of decision-making to maximize the chances of relevant information being brought to bear; and that they must build wide-ranging networks of communication from which they can learn the unintended consequences of programmes. Lastly, it will be shown that programmes are best implemented if the people concerned have been involved in their formulation from the start, and if control is minimized.

Also planning has a critical potential that may serve to enhance justice simply by laying bare the reasons for problems occurring. For instance, Ball (1972) reports of the effect of efforts of rendering social work more effective by creating so-called area teams:

> But with all those in need—children, the elderly, the homeless, the physically and the mentally handicapped, the deprived and the socially inadequate— calling at the "one door", a common factor is being recognized. In most cases there is a basic shortage of money . . . . Through the area teams, a "generic" problem has emerged.

These are all grounds for planning to proceed in a manner which conforms to democratic ideals, and why rational approaches (such as having area teams) lead to the identification of real obstacles in their way. However, in the first instance, the perspective was not that of advancing these ideals; it was that of improving upon the way planning is performed. This shows that planning, far from being in fundamental opposition to democracy, requires a democratic form of government for its proper conduct.

This should not surprise us. The ideas of both planning and democracy are based on a view of man as endowed with reason and capable of deliberate choice. It is therefore quite natural that the two should exist together, and indeed, that they should enhance, and be dependent on each other.

REFERENCES

BALL, D. (1972) Teams at work, *New Society*, 9 March, pp. 496–7.
KAPLAN, A. (1964) *The Conduct of Inquiry*, Chandler, Scranton, Penn.
WILLER, D. E. (1967) *Scientific Sociology*, Prentice-Hall, Englewood Cliffs, N.J.

CHAPTER 11

Multi-planning Agencies

AN ideal planning style would respond to new situations as process planning does. It would proceed in a rational-comprehensive manner, and would extend the scope of planning to the ends of action, just as normative planning does. *Alas*, none of these modes is fully feasible in practice. In Chapters 7 to 9 I therefore described the compromises which one must accept for the sake of progress in any one of these directions. I also suggested that such compromises would lead to the formation of multi-planning agencies. This chapter develops this concept.

The simple truth on which the need for multi-planning agencies rests is the limitation of information-handling capacity experienced by all problem-solvers. No individual planning agency engages in truly rational planning, because none can span the total available action space and, simultaneously, have the detailed knowledge required for formulating and implementing programmes. Much as individuals band together to increase their effectiveness, so do planning agencies: they form multi-planning agencies. Within such an agency, each one specializes in solving one particular class of problem. Such specialization has untold benefits in terms of the accuracy with which the environment is perceived, of the fund of accumulated knowledge brought to bear in formulating programmes and of the skills used in implementing them, including a close acquaintance with other agents operating in and on the environment. Benefits such as these arise in the same way as specialization in particular trades and professions increases the effectiveness of problem-solving. Unfortunately, there are also costs accruing. Multi-planning agencies attempt to balance the benefits of specialization against its costs.

Not every group of planning agencies operating next to each other forms a multi-planning agency. By a multi-planning agency I mean any number of planning agencies with an *overlapping action space* attempting to continuously co-ordinate what they are doing with a cumulative rationalizing effect so that one may see "comprehensive planning as a process" (Friedmann, 1965). Such planning agencies therefore form certain patterns of communication and control. This chapter will examine what these patterns should be. The argument will be that the patterns themselves must be subject to rational consideration by strategic planning agencies setting the framework within which other planning agencies operate. These strategic planning agencies are the central allocators of resources and tasks. The argument applies whether one is looking at groups of independent agencies growing together, or at larger planning agencies differentiating internally. Ultimately, one has to conceive of all institutions of planning as nested multi-planning agencies.

THE UNFOLDING OF MULTI-PLANNING AGENCIES

In this section, I shall explore the way in which multi-planning agencies unfold. The choice of this word is deliberate. It describes how a multi-planning agency may develop, even from modest beginnings of introducing planning, simply because rational procedures tend to project themselves sideways and upwards into other agencies, in line with Ashworth's aphorism: "Planning is like pregnancy, you can't have just a little" (Ashworth, 1969).

The unfolding of multi-planning agencies goes through a number of stages. Thus, its "natural history" begins with *specialization* and the subsequent growth of awareness of *linkages* between the operations of various specialized agencies. Then comes a stage when *networks* of communication are formed until, finally, a fully fledged multi-planning agency emerges with a *strategic planning agency* making decisions affecting the operations of several planning agencies.

Such multi-planning agencies are dynamic. At any time, one may observe them at various stages of their development: differentiating; searching for linkages; for methods of co-ordination; or in a fairly mature stage. Also, there are always multi-planning agencies whose development has reached a ceiling beyond which they cannot improve their ability to plan rationally because of institutional and other constraints. The existence of agencies whose development has been arrested does not invalidate the argument that the search for rational planning creates a tendency for the development of fully fledged multi-planning agencies.

Specialization

The prehistory of this unfolding of multi-planning agencies begins with agencies who specialize in various aspects of problems. This is a response to planning's most obvious limitation: of knowledge of the way the environment will react to the control variables being manipulated in ways prescribed by a programme. In Chapter 5, this limitation was expressed in terms of unknown variables exerting their influence, or of Friend and Jessop's (1969) "uncertainty in knowledge of environment" (UE).

The bane of specialization is that it isolates agents dealing with different aspects of the same problem and thereby results in disjointed attempts at its solution. Planning agencies responding to limited knowledge by spawning new individual units can thereby produce a plethora of specialized planning agencies, each one in danger of becoming at cross-purposes with others working on related aspects of the same problem. This situation is characterized by Friend and Jessop as "uncertainty as to intentions in related fields of choice" (UR). Multi-planning agencies are groups of planning agencies taking action to overcome their isolation and the ensuing disjointedness of their efforts.

Such action is necessary wherever the areas of concern of two or more planning agencies are interdependent. In the terms of Chapter 5 their action space is *overlapping* so that their programmes may affect each other. The action space of a planning agency may overlap not only with that of others within the same organization, but also outside. In both cases, there will be pressure for *co-ordinating* their programmes.

Co-ordination

There are two forms which co-ordination may take which Scharpf (1971) describes as negative and positive.[1] The first is an attempt to find out what the intentions of other agencies with an overlapping action space are, so

[1] Stewart (1969) refers to these as the negative and the positive concept of general management.

that these can enter as constraints into the formulation of programmes. The second involves all agencies in a joint exploration of their common action space.

Negative co-ordination is the most obvious response to the demand for co-ordination. Where agencies form part of a larger organization (for instance the education, social services and housing departments of local government), this leads to the establishment of some form of communication network such as a working party.[2] Over this network agencies become informed of each other's intentions and can take them into account. But negative co-ordination is an unstable form of co-ordination for two reasons. Firstly, it leads to confrontation of agencies with each other's procedures. In time, this results in a tendency of methods converging and agencies introducing the most rational of available techniques. This is a sideways projection of rational procedures. It generates pressure to extend the scope of the application of rational approaches to a wider field implying in the first instance joint exploration of the common action space. Secondly, the same pressure for *positive co-ordination* arises where two or more agencies are in conflict over irreconcilable issues. The intention to build housing on the last remaining site in a neighbourhood excludes that of building a school. Should this conflict not be resolved purely by the relative power of the contending agencies, then there must be joint exploration of their common action space in order to find a solution which is in the best overall interest of their client groups. Only this positive co-ordination avoids the danger pointed out by Banfield (1959) that "a developing course of action may be chosen arbitrarily and capriciously and a programmed course of action based upon it may then be selected with elaborate consideration of alternatives and consequences: in such a case there is 'functional rationality' but 'substantive irrationality' ".

Strategic Planning

Joint exploration of the action space, or positive co-ordination, has its problems. Specialized agencies are created because available images have become too unwieldy for any one planning agency to handle. There is little

[2]Tony Eddison once referred to local government as going through the "age of the working party" (Eddison, 1968).

chance, therefore, of subsequently piecing the images of such specialized agencies together again. The result must be far too complex for simultaneous exploration. Strategic planning must therefore walk the tightrope between many limited plans, each one liable to being cancelled out by uncontrolled variables, and the overextended, total plan which is equally wasteful and even disastrous (Seeley, 1962).[3] The situation calls for limiting strategic planning to embrace only key areas, or for the application of planning strategies such as introduced in Chapter 6, and notably the imposition of patterns on the vast amount of information received. These patterns reduce variety by expending with detail.

The decision to take either of these lines is of strategic importance. Because each agency is concerned with their impact on its own freedom to manoeuvre, such decisions cannot easily be made jointly by the groups of planning agencies concerned, and require the formation of a separate agency primarily concerned with interdependencies and their common interest. Since such an agency makes decisions of strategic importance, it seems apposite to call it a *strategic planning agency.*

So, positive co-ordination results in strategic planning on a level above that of the original agencies (Fig. 11.1). This directs and synthesizes their efforts by allocating tasks and resources to them. Obviously, strategic planning attempts to use rational methods (albeit ones that have been

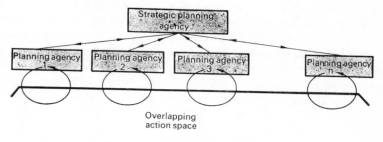

Fig. 11.1. A multi-planning agency

---

[3]In one of the earliest papers suggesting that there should be strategic planning aiming at formulating a "policies plan", Fagin (1959) showed similar awareness of the danger of overload by arguing for a high degree of selectivity in choosing the problems to be tackled.

adapted to the problems it is dealing with) much as lower-order agencies do. In effect, rational methods are being projected upwards. Once strategic planning is established, this further induces compatibility of procedures in lower-tier agencies, adding to a tendency for the sideways projection of rational methods referred to above. The two directions in which rational methods are being projected add up to the unfolding process.

APPROACHES TO STRATEGIC PLANNING

In this section, I shall amplify the two approaches which a strategic planning agency may take: to employ planning strategies or to focus attention and resources on key-problem areas and neglect others. Before doing so I shall argue that in either case a strategic planning agency needs to be given some powers to control others.

By necessity, the frameworks established in strategic planning must fail to consider a great amount of detail (which only specialized agencies can hold). For this reason, and also because agencies see their interests threatened, they often resist decisions as being subjectively harmful. This also applies to focusing: the concentration of attention on any one problem, or set of related problems, and the ensuing channelling of resources pose challenges which make the planning agency concerned, or other agencies (or both categories) resist the technique. Nevertheless, for strategic planning to be successful, it must employ these approaches, and strategic planning agencies must sometimes be free to use them, if necessary *against* the resistance of other agencies. There is little point in attempting positive co-ordination unless individual planning agencies surrender part of their autonomy and vest it in the strategic planning agency, thus giving it a measure of, albeit partial, control. The subtle relationship between strategic control and the autonomy of individual agencies may be elucidated further by discussing the way planning strategies are used.

Planning Strategies in Multi-planning Agencies

A strategic planning agency employing planning strategies (the most sophisticated being mixed scanning) proceeds by setting a general framework within which other agencies operate. This framework may consist of the goals which they ought to pursue and a specification of constraints in terms of powers of control and of resources. The point to be emphasized is that decisions concerning this framework are made relatively independently from decisions on the next-lower level. The strategic planning agency does certainly not take into account in its decisions all the implications for the agencies operating within the framework set. This is left to the lower-order agencies themselves to work out. The latter are therefore not merely executing orders received from above; they are amplifying the guide-lines set for them. It follows that, in the event of finding that the guide-lines cannot be implemented, they must be able to turn back on the strategic planning agency and ask for these guide-lines, and with them the whole framework, to be modified. This is a vital element of mixed scanning and implies that planning agencies must not be completely subservient to the higher strategic agency but share in the formulation of the framework. In particular, they must be allowed to instigate a review of that framework. Therefore, a multi-planning agency is not a simple hierarchical organization with uninterrupted flows of command from top to bottom. Each level has its own status, because each has an indispensible part to play in the overall process of planning.

Such an arrangement, allowing for breaks in the continuous flow of command, is fairly common. The differentiation of the institutions of government into two, three or more tiers is a case in point. Where such breaks do not exist, as in highly centralized systems of government, efforts to decentralize are at least under way because a concentration of decision-making at the top results in serious problems of information overload and, *de facto*, in disjointed incrementalism. Examples are the issues of regionalization in Great Britain, and even more so in France and Italy, concerned with the introduction of additional tiers of government which it is argued would improve overall effectiveness. Even countries committed to central planning, like the Soviet Union, where, in theory, at some stage up to 90 million "norms" were issued centrally (Bićanić, 1967), have had to devolve some of this fantastic load and strengthen their lower tiers so that the centre can use planning strategies instead of attempting the impossible.

The principle of devolution of control is being applied widely, sometimes with great success. Reputedly very flexible and proficient armies set their brigades broad strategic tasks only which are pursued autonomously drawing on their own support systems. The newly developed British system of structure and local plans under the 1968 Town and Country Planning Act replaces the old-style development plan, which determined broad policies and details of land use in one clumsy document (the equivalent of the hierarchical type of organization), by a differentiated system of strategic and operational plans. One may therefore conclude that, to increase efficiency, organizations differentiate their structure in such a way that each level successively refines the decisions of the next-higher level. Cybernetics (the science of guidance and control processes in all fields, technical as well as social) describes this process as *amplification*. Using cybernetic terminology, relatively small amounts of "energy" (the publication of a ministerial circular for instance) suffice to control large forces (such as the development of patterns of land use) by tapping the resources of energy of an amplifier (in this particular case the skills of local authorities in drawing up plans conforming to government policies). This is not a substantially different process from the way large and complex machinery is controlled by the puny forces of one man.

In such multi-planning agencies, there is the tendency to duplicate (or triplicate and so on) the components of a planning agency on each level. Parliament has its counterpart in local councils. In most systems, the Prime Minister finds his equivalent in the chief executive, and the government in some form of managing board. In British local government where these equivalents are absent the Maud Committee on management of local government has recommended the introduction of both into a reformed structure. Concern about the absence of one of these components does not only apply to the executive function. Where the legislative function is absent or weak, as in British regional economic planning, in American metropolitan planning or in some German regional planning organizations, this is even more detrimental to operations on that particular level. Often, the lack of political legitimation dooms this type of planning to irrelevance. Its agencies are renowned for technically elegant reports which languish in planning libraries. Thoughts about regional planning therefore tend to go in the direction of creating an equivalent to parliament or local authority councils, thereby giving regional planning decisions the requisite amount of political support.

There is a widespread evidence, therefore, for the emergence of multi-planning agencies of the kind described before, partly resulting from recognition of the need to employ planning strategies which include the devolution of detailed control and the adoption of framework controls as in mixed scanning. We shall return to this in the chapter on implementation.

Focusing in Multi-planning Agencies

The second approach to strategic planning is by focusing attention and resources of which there are two ways. One is to concentrate on geographical clusters of problems, the other to concentrate on certain substantive problems, or sets of such problems, as they apply across the board.

Overall, the linkages between education, housing and employment may be relatively weak, especially when mobility increases, but may be extremely important in areas suffering from "multiple deprivation". As regards Britain, Healey (1972) reports on a document issued by the voluntary organization Shelter, *Reprieve for Slums:*

> . . . every community of more than 50 000 people is likely to have an area of multiple deprivation. These areas, already suffering from bad housing, tend to have the worst of everything else. They have poor services, bad education, high unemployment and delinquency rates, ill health and bad communications with local and central government.

However, local authority services "were never designed to serve areas in dire need; they operate to norms, not to exceptions . . .". Also, the structure of local authorities "allows scant co-ordination between departments and means that only isolated problems are dealt with". So, it may be necessary to pull together all the planning agencies concerned with different aspects of poverty and let them focus jointly on how the specific problems of such areas may be solved.

This amounts to a reorientation of responsibilities in multi-planning agencies to match a striking interdependence between problems existing in a geographically defined part of the environment. Focusing on special areas is an approach which physical planners, social workers and educators have come to advocate in concepts like "action area plans"," area teams" (Foren and Brown, 1971) and "Educational Priority Areas" respectively. In each case the idea is that strong efforts should be made to deal with local concentrations of multiple problems. Strategic planning agencies may use this approach by directing all relevant planning agencies to collaborate with each other. The situation would then be that a team of various people with different backgrounds and from different agencies identifies itself with a locality, but at the same time is competent to interpret constraints on action imposed upon it to its clients and to feed information back to planning agencies.

Obviously, there are advantages in social workers, teachers, planners (those engaged in designing physical plant as well as in development control), and quite possibly also representatives of agencies from outside the local authority, using the same local base. They would be given a set of constraints and/or resources: the development control officer would know the policies incorporated in the development plan for the area of the local authority as a whole and would be aware of precedences and general policies. He would also become aware of problems of his area as seen through the eyes of colleagues with different backgrounds. Similarly, the educationalist could interpret the policy of his committee, but would also realize the effects of physical development on the educational programme in the locality.

Since 1971, social workers are already practising this approach on a smaller scale, administering the various social services jointly in area teams, so that they are "obliged to see the interlocking problems of their communities as a whole". The corollary is some measure of autonomy for area teams "to meet, and to budget for, the special needs of their own areas" (Ball, 1972).

These area teams are hence models for the way one could see a collection of heterogeneous services operate in future. They might very well be supplemented by citizen "task forces" (Nash and Durden, 1964) consisting of local residents who have special contributions to make to decision-making which would be a promising and realistic variant of citizen involvement in planning.

On higher levels, the components of this bundle of programmes could still be separated. Educationalists would simultaneously consider general educational policy for all local communities of a similar type; social workers would compare the problems of the homeless and compile general reports of the situation as it exists throughout the area of their authority; physical planners would exchange views and criticisms on local projects and the application of development control policies. Thus, the advantages of division of labour would be retained.

Not all efforts would go into focusing. Some problems do not occur in localized bundles, and some localities cannot accurately be designated as a community. This is as well because, as Friend and Jessop (1969) report of redevelopment projects in the centre of Coventry, the effort of co-ordinating development work put a heavy strain on decision-making bodies so that there were doubts whether such efforts should be extended to development taking place in outlying areas. Focusing on areas of highest interdependence, and abstaining from co-ordinating others, facilitates the problems of planning to a degree where many planning agencies may carry on as they do presently: running a school may be treated as a relatively self-contained problem in which neither the social worker nor the planner nor the general practitioner nor anybody else needs to be permanently involved unless a syndrome of problems such as the one which one now describes as "multiple deprivation" exists. Nor, for that matter, is physical planning always that closely related to social problems. Tens of thousands of planning applications concern isolated developments with no ramifications other than those which the development control officer normally considers. The same is true of many local authority development projects and programmes which concern changes to the physical fabric with little significance outside the realm of physical planning. It is therefore perfectly sensible to plan them in isolation. Focused planning is costly in every respect, and it is as well to use it sparingly.

The second method of focusing attention on certain sets of substantive problems to the exclusion of others is now being practised as an alternative to comprehensive approaches like Planning Programming Budgeting. For instance, British central government practises an approach called *Policy Analysis and Review.* It consists of the examination in depth of important areas of policy one after the other, but not simultaneously, thus implying that, at any point in time, vast areas are being planned in a functional and maybe even in a blueprint mode, as suggested in Chapter 9. The problem seems to be that choices of the policy areas to be reviewed, and the order of their investigation, are not made systematically but arise from expedience and inter-departmental politics. Systematic methods of "problem-structuring", that is of choosing sets of problems by drawing on rational procedures (Scharpf, 1971; Institute for Operational Research, 1972) have not yet been applied in practice.

Decisions to formulate programmes in isolation or to bundle them by localities (or in any other way) are of the essence of strategic planning. Its agencies operate to a very large extent not by affecting the environment, but by reshuffling other planning agencies, by allocating tasks and resources to them, and by monitoring their performance. A multi-planning agency incorporating focused efforts is shown in Fig. 11.2. It incorporates features

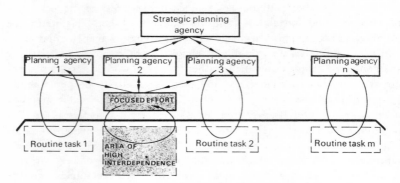

Fig. 11.2. Focusing in multi-planning agencies

of traditional hierarchical organizations, as well as of those "matrix organizations" which are credited with being flexible allowing for a "proliferation of centres" (Schon, 1971; Department of the Environment, 1972).

ALLOCATIVE AND INNOVATIVE PLANNING IN STRATEGIC PLANNING AGENCIES

A strategic planning agency may set its sights on two levels: it may simply co-ordinate the programmes of lower-order planning agencies by ensuring that they keep within the limits imposed by available resources. This was described as allocative planning in Chapter 9. Alternatively, it may initiate new types of programmes in response to newly perceived problems in the environment, thus realizing its potential for normative planning. This is what we have called innovative planning.

Allocative planning is a very important function of any strategic planning agency. To exhaust vital resources such as land, man-power or finance[4] impairs the ability of planning agencies to solve problems. However, the need to engage in allocative planning arises primarily from administrative convenience. For instance, there may be plenty of land available outside a town or city, but the local authority may still wish to promote development within its administrative boundaries to increase the rateable value. It will thus create a shortage of land, a shortage which is not absolute but relative to the needs and intentions of the *authority*. For this reason, resource budgets have less to do with the environment of a planning agency than with its intentions and aspirations. People in the environment of a planning agency usually care little about the total budget of a local authority, its man-power resources, and how much land reserves are available; they care about the services which they expect and about the houses which they wish to purchase. It is nevertheless entirely sensible for an authority to keep a record of these resources and to plan their use.

To present the various resources budgets on which a strategic planning agency draws, one must introduce an additional dimension to the diagram representing a multi-planning agency (Fig. 11.3). It signifies that overall guidance over the programmes of lower-order planning agencies is exercised by paying regard to the effects which they have on this series of budgets.

These budgets are abstract representations of internal states of the multi-planning agency. They have three important characteristics. Firstly, they deal with *finite* resources. Because of that, they are, secondly, *exhaustive* in the sense of reflecting *all* the activities of the multi-planning agency, including those in which it will engage in the foreseeable future, and all the anticipated effects of developments occurring outside its boundaries. Thirdly, they are *one-dimensional*: each resource budget reflects the internal state of a multi-planning agency only in so far as it impinges on one resource.

---

[4]Stewart (1969) and the Bains Report (Department of the Environment, 1972) refer to these as the resources on which, for instance, local authorities draw. Friend and Jessop (1969) identify a fourth "resource planning activity", developmental planning, though they do not identify the resource to be allocated. Perhaps, this could be described as "connectiveness". Banfield (1959) also lists "legal and other authority, information, time, executive skill" to which Stewart makes only circumstantial references under organizational resources. The Bains Report refers to this not as a resource but as a continuous "performance review" to be undertaken by a sub-committee of the central "Policy and Resources Committee" which is on *a par* with the three resource committees. I shall describe organizational as planning resources (see below).

These characteristics are complementary. It is because these budgets deal with finite resources that they need to be exhaustive, and it is only because they are one-dimensional that they can be exhaustive. The art of strategic planning is to make decisions based on as comprehensive an image of their anticipated effects as one can obtain from piecing together several one-dimensional images.

In addition to balancing out all these resource budgets, a strategic planning agency may also initiate new programmes. This is what in Chapter 9 was called *innovative planning* (*vide* Friedmann). By engaging in innova-

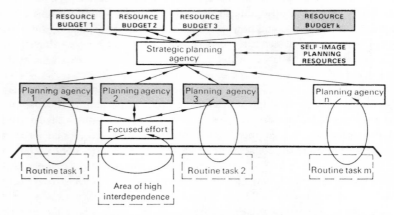

Fig. 11.3. Resource budgets in strategic planning

tive planning, multi-planning agencies are constantly evolving, responding to a changing environment by adding new agencies. Their make-up is becoming more and more complex, and the division of labour between different planning agencies more sophisticated.

One impetus for innovative planning arises from the perception of new challenges coming from the environment such as leisure and recreation constitute for existing British local government (Stewart, 1969). These new challenges are put into the context of running concerns implying review of existing agencies and procedures. Knowledge of these what one might call *planning resources* is, then, the second source for the impetus for engaging in innovative planning.

The number of resources on which a strategic planning agency draws therefore includes not only land, man-power and financial assets, but also planning resources, with innovative planning trying to make up for any perceived deficiencies in the latter. As with other resource budgets, the relevant planning resource budget is an abstract representation of the internal state of a multi-planning agency. Unlike them, it is, firstly, a knowledge resource and thus not finite[5] and secondly, not one-dimensional but incorporating all the others. It also includes images of the structure and the processes of the whole multi-planning agency, at least to the extent that they affect its capacity for successful planning. Simply, this resource budget is the highest-order feedback loop in a multi-planning agency, its self-image, or its seat of consciousness.

But I do not mean "seat" in a metaphorical sense. As Dror (1971) insists, multi-planning agencies (identical to what he terms comprehensive planning bodies)

> . . . need special units in charge of self-analysis, staff development, feedback processing, etc. Comprehensive planning units also have to program carefully their own activities, realizing that planning must be planned, with special attention, *inter alia*, to delimiting the preferable scope and detailedness of planning, to selecting suitable nominal output forms, and to utilizing the best existing tools and techniques.

In other words, multi-planning agencies will have special units devoted to the study, and the application of, planning theory! Only such multi-planning agencies which incorporate such units would be able to avoid the danger pointed out by Glass (1959): ". . . unless an administrative system is set up from the start so as to be 'self-conscious' in its operations, it will resist subsequent sporadic attempts to introduce analytical devices".

Planning theory therefore supplies general models of planning agencies and procedures, these to be fitted to the particular circumstances prevailing in a specific multi-planning agency. This can be equated with geographers supplying general models for the land resource budget, except that planning resources directly related to multi-planning agencies are more central to their operations than are other resources. Planning theory ought therefore to be more important to them than any substantive theory.

[5]Firstly, knowledge does not diminish as it is disseminated (Webber, 1968/9) because it is not subject to the conservation laws of matter and energy (Deutsch, 1966); secondly, whereas ". . . commodities constituting wealth are generally consumed in use, . . . skills grow with exercise . . ." (Davidoff and Reiner, 1962).

Policy Aims

The aims of the politics of rational planning should then embrace that of facilitating the unfolding of multi-planning agencies, including the emergence of strategic planning; the use of proper approaches to strategic planning, such as the application of planning strategies and focusing; the maintenance of a balance between allocative and innovative planning as performed by strategic planning agencies; and the advancement of planning theory as a source of general models for drawing up planning resource budgets.

REFERENCES

ASHWORTH, G. (1969) The administrative structure of planning: 2, *Journal of the Town Planning Institute*, Vol. 55, pp. 290–1.
BALL, D. (1972) Teams at work, *New Society*, 9 March, 496–7.
*BANFIELD, E. C. (1959) Ends and means in planning, *International Social Science Journal*, Vol. 11, pp. 361–8.
BIĆANIĆ, R. (1967) *Problems of Planning—East and West*, Mouton, The Hague.
*DAVIDOFF, P. and REINER, T. A. (1962) A choice theory of planning, *Journal of the American Institute of Planners*, Vol. 28, pp. 103–15.
DEPARTMENT OF THE ENVIRONMENT (1972) *The New Local Authorities: Management and Structure* (Bains Report), HMSO, London.
DEUTSCH, K. W. (1966) *The Nerves of Government*, 2nd ed. Macmillan, New York–London.
DROR, Y. (1971) *Ventures in Policy Sciences*, Elsevier, Amsterdam.
EDDISON, T. (1968) The wider role of the development plan, *Journal of the Town Planning Institute*, Vol. 54, pp. 465–7.
FAGIN, H. (1959) Organizing and carrying out planning activities within urban government, *Journal of the American Institute of Planners*, Vol. 25, pp. 109–14.
FOREN, R. and BROWN, M. J. (1971) *Planning for Service*, Charles Knight, London.
*FRIEDMANN, J. (1965) A reply to Altshuler: comprehensive planning as a process, *Journal of the American Institute of Planners*, Vol. 31, pp. 195–7.
FRIEND, J. K. and JESSOP, W. N. (1969) *Local Government and Strategic Choice*, Tavistock Publications, London.
*GLASS, R. (1959) The evaluation of planning: some sociological considerations, *International Social Science Journal*, Vol. 11, pp. 393–409.
HEALEY, P. (1972) Bangladesh-type emergency aid urged by Shelter for people in rotting inner city areas, *The Times*, 15 September, p. 3.
INSTITUTE FOR OPERATIONAL RESEARCH (1972) *Problem Structuring: A Methodological Approach to Organisation for Positive Coordination in Planning*, London and Coventry.
NASH, P. H. and DURDEN, D. (1964) A task-force approach to replace the planning board, *Journal of the American Institute of Planners*, Vol. 30, pp. 10–22.

SCHARPF, F. W. (1971) *Komplexität als Schranke der politischen Planung*, Paper presented to the AGM of the German Political Science Association, Mannheim.

SCHON, D. (1971) *Beyond the Stable State*, Temple Smith, London.

SEELEY, J. R. (1962) What is planning? Definition and strategy, *Journal of the American Institute of Planners*, Vol. **28**, pp. 91–7.

STEWART, J. D. (1969) The case for local authority policy planning, *Town and Country Planning Summer School Nottingham*, 1969 (Conference Proceedings), The Town Planning Institute, London.

WEBBER, M. (1968/9) Planning in an environment of change: Beyond the industrial age, Permissive planning, *The Town Planning Review*, Vol. **39**, pp. 179–95; Vol. **39**, pp. 277–95.

*Included in FALUDI, A. (1973) *A Reader in Planning Theory*, Pergamon, Oxford.

CHAPTER 12

Decision-making in Planning Agencies

THERE are three ways of making decisions: by authoritative choice based on commitment alone, by calculation based on firm images, and by a mixture of both. Planning is about making decisions by a mixture of authoritative and calculative choice (Häusler, 1969) (though it may employ purely the latter as part of planning strategies).

This chapter is concerned with the question of how planning agencies ought to make decisions based on a blend of commitment and analysis leading to authoritative and calculative choices respectively. The ideal model to which they should approximate is a mature person making a choice based on knowledge, including self-knowledge, and on commitment to certain causes. Such a decision based on evidence and on genuine commitment has integrity. We shall examine, therefore, the problem of how planning agencies ensure that their decisions have integrity.[1]

The root-cause of the problem is that, obviously, planning agencies are *not* individuals. On the contrary, they cast individuals into *different* rôles. The distinction between these may have divisive effects, or, on the other hand, may be more conducive to integrity of decision. It is this difference between concepts of the relation of politicians and planners in decision-making, leading to different degrees of approximation of the ideal of integrity, that I am concerned with. I shall argue that the existing concept that portrays them as masters and servants is divisive. From a

[1]This use of the concept of integrity is based on Deutsch (1966). According to him, it means "the unimpaired functioning of the *facilities* that carry the process of self-determination". In these terms this chapter is concerned with the "unimpaired functioning" of planners and politicians in carrying out their tasks in planning leading to self-determination.

discussion of its short-comings, it is possible to derive a more organic division between their tasks that complements diversities while still promoting integrity.[2]This division revolves around Friend and Jessop's distinction between *decision-taking* and *decision-making* (Friend and Jessop, 1969).

EXISTING RÔLE CONCEPTS FOR POLITICIANS AND PLANNERS: MASTERS AND SERVANTS

In terms of the components of planning agencies, planners manning their knowledge-units provide images and work out alternative programmes. Politicians are the selectors, who commit planning agencies to certain courses of action.

The basis of a view which portrays planners as the servants of their politician masters can be traced to the development of bureaucracies. The implication of this view in terms of decision-making is that politicians decide on ends, and that planners indicate the means for their attainment.

The instrumental view of planning, which is what the master-servant concept amounts to, is very widespread and rests on the traditional view of the rôle of experts in public administration which we termed "bureaucratic" in Chapter 9. Any discussion of it must begin with Max Weber's study of bureaucracy (a term which he used without its derogatory connotations in everyday language). In his work on *The Theory of Social and Economic Organisation* (1947) he conveys how, during the period of absolutism, a new system of public administration emerged. One of its key features was that officials did not derive direct benefits from its transactions (such as tax-collection) but were salaried and thus dependent on the sovereign. This resulted in a sort of instrumental ethos coupled with a tremendous increase in efficiency.

---

[2]The argument is analogous to that which has developed over Lord Rothschild's report on "The organisation and management of government research and development" (Civil Service Department, 1971), proposing the customer/contractor principle: "The customer says what he wants; the contractor does it (if he can); and the customer pays." The British Society for the Social Responsibility of Science, amongst others, has objected to this pointing out the need for a "critical science" and a "more organic relationship between the scientist and the community" (Tucker, 1972).

With the advent of officialdom in all modern systems of government the executive power was split into two—the political executive (politicians) and the career executive (salaried experts). Political executives are subject to control by the legislature and, ultimately, by the people. Their tenure is comparatively short. Career executives are the assistants and advisers to political executives and, in contrast to the latter, supply continuity in a system of government which is otherwise responsive to change in popular preferences. Administration is their career, and they are normally not removable with a change of government.

The career executive is organized in what Max Weber called bureaucracies, which are extremely useful organizations for the rational, impartial, speedy solution of well-defined problems. They are thus ideal structures for decision-making of a repetitive kind, applying predetermined rules to similar cases. This type of administration not only complemented absolutism but also the doctrine of *laissez-faire* (Harnischfeger, 1969) implying a limited view of the rôle of government. This was particularly true at the level of local government, and perhaps more so in Britain than elsewhere. Here, a notion developed of local councils not as political institutions but as trustees of public funds and as administrators of technical services. For the efficient, impartial, but not intentionally creative, discharge of technical functions, the bureaucratic model seemed again appropriate. In this way the British system of strictly departmentalized, hierarchically organized local government services has developed. A professional staff under a chief officer supplies the technical information for the policy decisions of lay committees and executes them in an impartial manner.

In terms of the steps of the planning process, it is therefore often held that the division between the rôle of politicians and of planners is that of setting the ends on the one hand, and indicating the means for their achievement on the other, this culminating into a final choice of a programme for implementation. As Dimitriou (1972) writes in his critique of systems planners allegedly extending their competence backwards to gain control over goal formulation, the "traditional approach in the U.K. has been to consider goal formulation as an exclusively political activity, and planners as receiving 'briefs' on which to base their technical activity".[3]

[3] For a similar view from the United States see, for instance, Beckman's paper on "The planner as a bureaucrat" (1964).

A CRITIQUE OF THE INSTRUMENTAL VIEW OF PLANNING

One may criticize this instrumental view of planning and its implications for decision-making on a number of counts. Firstly, it is based on an idealized, hyperactive, view of politicians; secondly, the assumption by those who insist that politicians decide on ends, namely that programmes are deduced from these (and that control over statements of ends therefore gives control over the whole planning process) is false; thirdly, the theory of bureaucracy has developed into a theory of complex organizations which replaces the idea of an uninterrupted flow of command from top to bottom (as the instrumentalist view of planning implies) by the notion of qualitative breaks occurring at any of the "points of articulation" between the various "levels" of an organization. We shall deal with each of these points in turn.

An Idealized View of Politicians

By not considering possible shortcomings of politicians in decision-making, the instrumental view of planning implicitly rests on an idealized notion of their rôle. Politicians are, on the whole, not a representative cross-section of the community. They also have interests of their own leading them to overemphasize immediate concerns, as Chadwick (1971) emphasizes: "The political view is short, conditioned by the next election, by appeasing the electorate as far as possible—or appearing to do so—the goal of politicians may be simply: to stay in power . . ."; and Altshuler (1965b) confirms: ". . . the mayor who took time from the immediate problem of running his city and winning re-election to worry seriously about long-range planning would be very rare indeed".

Most importantly, for an appreciation of the politician's rôle in decision-making, the view of his setting the ends to be pursued is a hyperactive one which is far from realistic. Politicians must often restrict themselves to amplifying previous decisions made either by themselves (or by their predecessors) or by higher authorities. In the first instance, they may not have the time nor the inclination to effect fundamental changes; in the latter, they may not have the power to do so.

Consider the case of physical planning. In Britain, there exists a body of legislation requiring local authorities to draw up plans for the orderly

physical development of their areas. In the terms of Chapter 5 this
represents the *goal* of a planning agency in the field of physical planning.
This goal is nothing which councillors can change. They can only amplify
it by determining in more detail the development plan for their particular
authority, but even here they can still not decide freely. Existing central
government or regional planning policies may circumscribe their decisions,
as do current policies of their own council. Limitations on their freedom
do not end here. A development plan is a closely defined legal and technical
instrument (as indeed are many instruments of policy-making). All other
considerations apart, politicians need advice and guidance by planners on
what ends they *can* pursue with an instrument which the planners alone
can use properly. As Meyerson and Banfield (1955) wrote of the commissioners of the Chicago Housing Authority:

> Moreover, even though they might try to avoid it, they had to depend upon
> the staff for information and direction to a large extent; probably none of
> them realized just how much latitude the law allowed in selecting a course of
> action. The commissioners tended to take the Authority's existing course of
> action for granted . . . .

The freedom of politicians to determine the ends pursued by a plan is
therefore circumscribed, with planners interpreting to them the nature
and the extent of limitations only within which context may decisions be
taken.

Even then politicians are still not free to determine the ends of action.
They are further limited because the availability of means influences the
setting of ends, as Banfield (1959) and Braybrooke and Lindblom (1963)
emphasize. By this I do not only mean the legal powers referred to above,
but other resources such as land, capital, man-power and so forth. Thus,
when planners imply to their political masters that the pursuit of further
growth of employment opportunities will result in a shortage of housing,
open space, and in traffic congestion, this may lead to a reduction of the
growth target, thus modifying the end of a plan. However, presenting
such implication involves much expertise and implies a more active
part for planners, and a less active part for politicians, than does the
instrumental view of planning. It is therefore not surprising to find that
case studies confirm what Chadwick (1971) says about goal-formulation:
"The clients of planning have never given the professional in their employ

any but the vaguest kind of goals: indeed the enunciation of goals as such by planning's clients is so rare as to be virtually unknown".

For example, Meyerson and Banfield (1955) found that the housing commissioners did not have any particular ends in mind which could be formulated and handed down to their professional staff for implementation. They perceived their rôle rather as that of part-time administrators and lay-controllers of public servants, an observation that has repeatedly been made of councillors in British local government (Committee on Qualifications for Planners, 1950; Ministry of Housing and Local Government, 1967; Harrison, 1972). Similarly, Altshuler (1965a) concluded from three case studies: "No legislature or committee or interest group leader can rationally evaluate a statement of general goals. . . . In practice, this means that they will rarely commit themselves to let . . . goal statements guide their considerations . . ." and Thorburn (1971) reported about the Notts/Derbys Study: "An attempt was made to sound out elected members' views on these objectives but they were unwilling to commit themselves until they understood the consequences of doing so. Only after seeing the strategy did they formally adopt the objectives, or agree to their publication."

Even where some of the pressures under which politicians have to make up their mind appear to be absent, statements of ends fail to materialize. Thus, the Social Science Research Council claims: "Few, if any, government departments at present have a structure which helps them to formulate problems which social science research can help to illuminate" (SSRC, 1972); Ackoff (1962) similarly relates how rare it is for management consultants to be given a clear brief by their clients, and Bauer (1968) questions even whether individuals can identify their interests.

The crux of the matter is that one does not think of ends *per se*, as the instrumental view suggests politicians ought to do. Realistic thinking in terms of ends only occurs in concrete choice situations where reasons must be found for justifying the selection of one alternative in preference to others. For what they are worth, approaches to the formulation of objectives should therefore follow Ackoff's proposals which very well reflect the collaborative nature of the exercise: "One effective technique for uncovering these objectives consists of confronting the decision-maker with each of the possible solutions to a problem and asking him whether he would follow that course of action. . . . Where he says, 'No,' further probing will usually reveal objectives which are not served by the course of action."

This relates to the second criticism levelled against the instrumental view of planning: the misapprehension of the rational planning process on which it is based.

False Assumptions Concerning the Rational Planning Process

The apprehension concerning who determines the ends of action stems from a view of planning as deducing means from ends. Control over statements of ends must then give control over the outcomes of planning which is why Dimitriou (1972) reacts so strongly to systems planning allegedly arrogating goal formulation for the professional. This rests on two false assumptions:

Firstly, planning does not *proceed* deductively, but is cyclical. Better still, it is a process of iteratively approximating a formal statement in which all parties agree on one programme in preference to others. This statement is couched in a deductive form, because this is the superior way in which to convey reasons (see Chapter 3). However, the order in which arguments are stated has nothing whatsoever to do with the order in which they are actually formulated. For instance, as suggested above, arguments concerning the ends to be pursued are more likely to arise only *after* choices become apparent, and not before.

Secondly, even in the reconstructed form of the planning "process", end-statements are not equivalent to laws from which to deduce programmes. As has been argued in Chapter 5, ends enter the formulation of programmes as statements of objectives taking the place of initial conditions. However, stating objectives cannot be the exclusive domain of the politician. Objectives describe a possible state of the environment in which one specific source of tension has been removed (see p. 87) thus implying much analytical and predictive skill for their proper formulation. For instance, to formulate the following objectives based on the goal of a "mobile" society; to reduce congestion by fifteen per cent; to double the frequency of bus services; and to reduce the average journey to work by ten minutes presupposes vast insights into the relationships between traffic and land-use, between the availability of certain modes of transport and opportunities for work, shopping and leisure. They also assume skills of measurement and the ability to influence congestion and journey to work, matters in which politicians have only limited knowledge.

Incompatibility with the Theory of Complex Organizations

Not only is the instrumental view of planning based on an idealized notion of the rôle of the politician and on false assumptions concerning the planning process; it has also not assimilated the development which has occurred in organization theory. Max Weber's study of bureaucracy has generated a whole literature in this field. Many interesting arguments have evolved, especially around the merits and dysfunctions of bureaucratic organizations. A refinement of the traditional bureaucratic model of organization which is helpful in understanding the problems of decision-making and planning organization has been advanced by Talcott Parsons (1967).

Talcott Parsons has shown that what he describes as a "formal organization" ("a mechanism by which those goals somehow important to the society, or to various subsystems of it, are implemented and to some degree defined . . .") is not simply a hierarchy with uninterrupted flows of command but something which tends to differentiate into various levels. It must be observed briefly that this means that the principles underlying multi-planning agencies described earlier also apply to the *internal* organization of individual planning agencies. Looked at in a different way, they dissolve into yet more facets, a point which will be developed further in the next chapter.

Talcott Parsons introduces three distinctive layers: the "technical", the "managerial" and the "community" or "institutional" level. Translated into the terms of British local authority structure and the statutory planning process, the "institutional" or "community" level is readily identified with the community at large, the council and the planning committee. This distinction is itself the result of an ongoing process of differentiation, and the flows of legitimation and communication between them pose their own problems. Other systems have different names and different set-ups, for instance the planning commission in the United States, the indirectly elected or appointed councils in regional planning, or the full meetings of the municipal electorate to vote on planning proposals in some Swiss Cantons. For the purpose of this discussion, these are the same: they set a context within which professional planners operate; they represent the selector.

The "technical" level on which immediate action is taken corresponds to that of development control in Britain, zoning and subdivision in the United States or the operations of the "Building Police" (*Baupolizei*) in German-speaking countries. Each of these deals directly with people applying for permission to erect buildings, to change the use of land, to cut down trees, or to extract minerals and so forth. Alternatively, the technical level may be represented by the city architect or engineer engaged in erecting physical plant on the basis of a plan drawn up on a higher level, as we shall see in Chapter 15 on implementation. In any case, we are here concerned with the effector.

Sandwiched between the "institutional" or "community" level and the "technical" level is the "managerial" level. This is where programmes are prepared. In terms of British Local Planning Authorities, this is the development plan section, in terms of the model of planning agencies the technology-image.

Compared with the idea of a hierarchy which merely executes the directives from some higher authority, the concept of levels emphasizes the existence of *qualitative breaks* in the lines of command. This means that each level of operations supplements the directives set by the next-higher level by adding its own decisions, derived from its detailed knowledge. This differentiation is superior to a hierarchical organization. It protects the higher level from exessive involvement in detail (overloading at the top is the chronic malaise of hierarchical organizations and centralized governments) and gives guide-lines to the lower level which legitimize its actions but do not narrowly confine them.

The crucial points in this model of organization are the breaks in the flow of command at the "points of articulation" between two levels, where the higher level gives guide-lines and support to the lower level and receives in turn advice and feedback. This already indicates the nature of the process occurring at these points: there is a *two-way* exchange which is in contrast to the conventional view of the lower level receiving orders.[4]

[4]Friend and Jessop (1969) demonstrate, for instance, that (a) where the flows of information between politicians and planners are inadequate "painful mutual adjustments" have to be made at advanced stages of the planning process and (b) where politicians have frequent contacts with officers, they are likely to have a particularly good overview.

Both sides can hamper the process by withholding their contributions. For effective decision-making both sides must hence co-operate and consequently share responsibility. However, this is opposed to the instrumental view of politicians deciding on ends and planners devising the programmes to attain them. This is appropriate only for routine tasks fulfilled in the pursuit of stable and agreed-upon ends drawing on well-established images. For this a bureaucratic form of organization is ideal. For all other tasks, a different concept of the relation between politicians and planners is needed.

DECISION-MAKING AND DECISION-TAKING

In terms of the ideal model of a planning agency as approximating the integrity with which a mature person makes decisions, the instrumental view is divisive. It erects a barrier between those who provide the knowledge on which decisions are based and those who take decisions and provide the commitment required for their implementation. This barrier prevents planners and politicians from communicating as often and as frankly as true integration of knowledge and commitment requires. Most importantly, it prevents planners from criticizing politicians: the servant does not question the motives and the wisdom of his master. It thus casts planners into an inferior rôle. They frequently compensate by emphasizing privately their superiority as the providers of the knowledge-base and denouncing the whims and the pettiness of politicians (thus satisfying their psychological needs); and by using subversive tactics to get their way, even against the will of their political masters (thus making the politician even more suspicious and insistent on his prerogatives). The result is the lack of mutual respect and of trust which appears to characterize the relationship between planners and politicians (Friend and Jessop, 1969).[5]

Even so, reality far from conforms to what the instrumental view of planning would lead one to expect. Most proposals do not generate in the council or committee at all, but in the department, and there is usually only *one* proposal which the department head favours as his policy. It is

---

[5]Beckman (1964) gives the same diagnosis. Only, his cure is to suggest that the planner should accept his inferior rôle.

for this proposal that he seeks approval, which implies a much more active orientation than does the concept of a mere adviser. Indeed, as things are, he is probably the key figure in the planning process, a view which will concern us in the next chapter.

There are parallels to this central position which administrators hold in the process of decision-making. Students of government the world over are concerned that the initiative in drawing up legislation has shifted away from the legislature. More specifically in Britain, a whole class of statutes can be described as "Civil Service" legislation, originating in the ranks of the Civil Service (Brown, 1970) whose members then become *Statemen in Disguise* (Fry, 1969). Similarly, Chamberlain (1965) writes about national planning in France that parliament had neither the time nor the expertise to produce an alternative to the one put before it by the planning commission. Parliament thus in effect had to renounce its part in decision-making. Shonfield (1965) describes this phenomenon as a "reversal of the separation of powers", where the executive arm assumes some legislative as well as judicial functions. Concern about this apparent decline of legislatures is reflected in proposals to increase their armoury by providing their members with expert services, as in the American Congress and in the parliament of the Federal Republic of Germany (Harnischfeger, 1969). This again illustrates our central point about the increasing importance of expertise in decision-making on all levels.

A more satisfactory view of the relationship between politicians and planners which takes account of this growing importance of expertise is that based on the distinction made by Friend and Jessop (1969) between decision-taking and decision-making:

> Sooner or later, the formulation and comparison of possible actions leads to choice of one particular course of action; a formal commitment is then generated through an assignment of resources or a public statement of intent, and the stage of intervention in the community system begins. This is the stage of decision-*taking* as opposed to the wider process of decision-*making* which can be said to embrace all stages . . .

Decision-taking is unquestionably the prerogative of politicians. Only they can formally commit a planning agency to pursue a programme, thereby spending public resources and sometimes sharing out differential costs and benefits to various groups in the community. But this must never mean that politicians dominate the entire process of decision-making.

In the preparation of formally binding decisions, planners and politicians should interact freely as equal partners and responsible agents. They participate in a collaborative exercise to which they both have different, but equally decisive and complementary, contributions to make. Except for the stage of formal choice, this applies to all the phases of the planning process.

Based on the distinction between decision-taking and decision-making, we now turn to a further exploration of the separate rôles of politicians and planners.

The Rôle of the Politician: Acceptance of Risks

When criticizing the instrumental view of planning I emphasized the weakness of the rôle of the politician relative to an inflated assessment of his freedom of manoeuvre and power of insight. But, of course, the politician does have an important and active part to play, much more so than appears feasible under current arrangements, where their work is unpaid and part-time, for their rôle is to supply the commitment necessary for accepting risks.

In every phase of the planning process, there are assumptions to be made. Never can conclusions be arrived at by analytical means *alone*, either in problem definition, or in the formulation of programmes. To start with, goals (such as that of an orderly development of the physical environment set for Local Planning Authorities) must be amplified. The law, for instance, cannot identify all the sources of tension which exist at the interface between the ends of a local community and the image of its physical environment. Nor can these ends simply be deduced from the goal of an orderly physical development as embodied in the planning acts. There are a great number of assumptions to be made before a series of objectives can be drawn up to amplify the goal of physical planning in any particular instance: assumptions concerning the local community's perception of the physical environment, the way it is affected by it, and so forth. This involves the interests of diverse groups and their preferences for certain ways of life. The same applies to assumptions needed in generating alternatives and during their evaluation leading up to the final choice of one programme.

Politicians are in a better position than planners to supply assumptions. Firstly, though by no means fully representative of their constituencies, they are more representative than planners. Planners are professionals and public servants and thus members of the middle class, with its perceptions and its world outlook. Furthermore, their pattern of promotion is such that, usually, they come from elsewhere, spend a relatively short spell in an area, and then move on to their next appointment. Thus they have less intimate knowledge of the particular context of their work than local politicians do.[6] Secondly, the political process has, by and large, a built-in self-correcting element against gross misconception of the views of the local community which gives politicians an incentive to develop the means and the sensitivity for acquiring an intimate knowledge of their constituencies.

This is as well, because it is the politician who must "carry the can" for assumptions entering the formulation of any programme. His prerogative is therefore not so much that of setting the ends of action towards which planners work as their loyal and unquestioning servants (which is not really feasible, anyway), but more of choosing deliberately to accept the risks of pursuing one course of action in preference to others, including the assumptions on which this course of action is based. This is no small matter. It is an essential element of decision-making in planning, bringing it closer to the ideal model of a mature person as a free and responsible agent choosing to accept risks in the pursuit of a cause he thinks worthwhile. Politicians have been elected precisely because they have shown this strength of conviction. It is the essence of *their* rôle to act on this basis and it is therefore inconceivable to take away from them their true prerogative— the *taking* of decisions and the acceptance of risks involved, based on their commitment.

The Rôle of the Planner: Analysis of Risks

The complementary rôle of the planner is that of an analyst of the risks involved in the politicians' decisions. This is not limited to the final choice but applies to every phase, and the assumptions made therein,

[6]On the other hand, skilful high-ranking planners may develop a more intimate knowledge of their situation than local politicians, especially where they operate in the same area over long periods of time and where they find it necessary to play a quasi-political rôle to hold their own against their political masters.

which is why close collaboration between planners and politicians is so vital throughout the planning process.

But the analyst proceeds in a different manner from the politician who may be held accountable for a decision. In the absence of reliable information, the exploration of courses of action based on assumptions should be a normal way of proceeding. Even his failures show to him something about the environment in which he operates. The planner therefore only stands to gain from assumptions, even from erroneous ones, and from criticisms concerning their efficacy, except that in experimenting he draws on public resources and affects people's lives, so his assumptions must be legitimized.

Legitimation can only be given by accountable politicians. Professional experts cannot provide it because, if they had to, that is if they were to be held accountable for the assumptions made in formulating a programme, then they would only make the most conservative assumptions and planning would become stultified.

This may seem as if it is only the planner who gains from collaboration with the politician. After all, he gains legitimation. But in withholding legitimation the politician would have a bargaining counter, even in a free-wheeling situation where the planner was not formally subservient to him. He could require planners to clarify the risks involved in any one assumption, and in taking decisions based on it. He would thus seek to minimize his risk, or at least be fully aware of its extent. The politician therefore also stands to gain from collaboration. With the help of the planner, he can weigh risks more accurately and operate more consciously in a field in which only he may operate: that of taking decisions which commit public resources and affect people's lives.

Rules for their Collaboration

From the rôle-concepts described above, one may deduce two rules which should govern the way in which politicians and planners collaborate. The first is that, in contradistinction to present arrangements, where planners are subservient to politicians, the importance of their contribution should be recognized by giving them equal status in decision-making. The second is that they should feel bound by decisions formally taken by politicians after due consideration of the risks involved, decisions which would have to occur much more frequently and much earlier on in the planning process than at present.

The first rule simply means to acknowledge what has been said before about decision-making. It means that until a decision has been taken, planners may go public with all their findings and their proposals and thus exert pressure on politicians to face up to the risks and implications. A few examples will elucidate this point:

As, for instance, the fate of the British National Economic Development Council shows, politicians are often inclined to forsake long-term benefits for short-term gain. Here, an immediate improvement in the economic situation was sought and all expert staff thrown into this work without considering their advice about long-term problems of economic development. Now, whilst there is nothing inherently wrong in either position, both need to be balanced against each other. Had the National Economic Development Council and its professional staff not been constructed as master and servant, a more successful balance could have been struck (Shonfield, 1965).

Seers (1972) quotes changes in an educational syllabus, like those attempted in Cuba and Tanzania, and also population policy and finally reforms of land tenure, like those in Chile, as other examples of policies which "will only achieve their full impact over a period of 20 to 30 years". Jackson (1972) shows that the same applies to physical development on a sub-regional scale. Seer's comment is that short-term plans "have their place, of course, but only if they are seen as steps towards long-period goals".

Neglect of implications of current policies is not limited to those which are long-term. It has equally been argued that politicians prefer middle-of-the road policies and disregard inarticulate groups. For instance, Minns (1970) suggested concerning the homeless in London that "publicly accountable, electorally based social service organizations" would narrowly limit the focus and aim of mandatory research (as it was then under discussion) to assess housing need. His answer was to free such research from narrow, local control by creating a "free-ranging central authority with powers of inquiry which could assess the ideological constraints and social injustices in boroughs". Planners and researchers in local government who are not completely subservient to their political masters as at present would have at least some of the effects which Minns expects this central authority to have: "By the dissemination of information, minority groups could be made more aware of the varying possibilities for change if they wanted to exert pressure . . . ".

The need for independent groups of experts has therefore been widely recognized. The President of the United States has his Council of Economic Advisers, the French their *Commissariat Général du Plan*, but nowhere is this institution better developed than in Britain, with its Royal Commissions. These are, indeed, superb devices for bringing all available expert opinion to bear on decision-making. Admittedly, on the local level it would not be feasible to have such completely independent institutions. But if the local community is to get the best advice from the expert teams it employs, these must be given some measure of those rights which Royal Commissions enjoy. They may be given their terms of reference, but they ought to be left to fulfil them as they see fit. They must be free to receive communications, and they must be able to *publish* their reports in full.[7]

Publicity is a tremendous stimulus for the political process. The Swedes have thrown all their records open to the public with untold benefit to the quality of public debate (Shonfield, 1965).[8] Public debates, as they arise when Royal Commissions ask for evidence or publish their reports, are like mock battles. The real participants in the game show their strength without seriously hurting each other, rather like tribal warfare used to be— a lot of noise and minimum bloodshed. The government can sit back and watch, and then make a better decision than would otherwise have been possible. This is, however, exactly what would be achieved by letting planners air their proposals. Politicians could take political decisions in a political way, that is with the maximum knowledge of alternatives and implications and before the forum of an informed public (Teschner, 1969). In this sense one might even claim that to let planners go public will improve not only the rationality of planning decisions but also, in the course of time, the political process: ". . . by publicly exposing

[7]This relative independence of planners from close supervision by their political masters seems to be implied in proposals made for the organization of the planning function such as Meyerson's (1956) and Friedmann's (1965).

[8]In his submission to the Franks Committee on the Official Secrets Act, Professor H. W. Wade proposed that similar rules should be introduced in Great Britain "making it a crime for a public servant to withhold information except under six headings" (Wade, 1971).

probable social consequences of legislative actions, legislators are less likely to respond insensibly and less likely to retreat from political responsibility . . ." (Webber, 1963).

This leaves the second rule unaffected. Decisions taken formally by politicians in their capacity as members of the legislature and its committees are binding. It has therefore never been my aim to suggest that experts should *take* the decisions in planning, but merely that there is a need for them to take a much more prominent part not only in the technical process of preparing and implementing programmes, but also in the political debate concerning what these alternatives ought to try and achieve; not as the deciders but as contributors of vital elements to the argument. Without this element, no deliberate choices can be made at all. With it, planning may draw closer to the ideal of a mature person making decisions. The unity required for approximating this ideal model would be provided by the strict adherence to the rules of the game making it imperative that decisions, once taken, are acted upon.[9] The integrity of these decisions is safeguarded by a clear understanding of the difference between the rôles of planners and politicians as the providers of analytical skills and of the willingness to take risky decisions respectively; and by an arrangement which helps both participants to fulfil their particular rôles.

Policy Aims

The aims of the politics of rational planning to be derived from this chapter are then simply to construct planning agencies in such a way that planners and politicians may better fulfil their respective rôles than they seem to be able to do at present, when their relationship is misconstrued as that of servant and master. This implies adherence to the two rules spelled out above that planners and politicians are equals in decision-making, but that it is the politicians' prerogative to take binding decisions.

[9]This does of course not mean that they should never be changed after their results become known.

REFERENCES

ACKOFF, R. L. (1962) *Scientific Method: Optimizing Applied Research Decisions*, John Wiley, New York.

*ALTSHULER, A. A. (1965a) The goals of comprehensive planning, *Journal of the American Institute of Planners*, Vol. 31, pp. 186–95.

ALTSHULER, A. A. (1965b) *The City Planning Process*, Cornell University Press, Ithaca.

*BANFIELD, E. C. (1959) Ends and means in planning, *International Social Science Journal*, Vol. 11, pp. 361–8.

BAUER, R. A. (1968) The study of policy formation: an introduction, *The Study of Policy Formation* (edited by BAUER, R. A. and GERGEN, K. J.), Collier-Macmillan, London.

*BECKMAN, N. (1964) The planner as a bureaucrat, *Journal of the American Institute of Planners*, Vol. 30, pp. 323–7.

BRAYBROOKE, D. and LINDBLOM, C. E. (1963) *A Strategy of Decision-Policy Evaluation as a Social Process*, Free Press, New York.

BROWN, R. G. S. (1970) *The Administrative Process in Britain*, Methuen, London.

CHADWICK, G. (1971) *A Systems View of Planning*, Pergamon, Oxford.

CHAMBERLAIN, N. W. (1965) *Private and Public Planning*, McGraw-Hill, New York.

CIVIL SERVICE DEPARTMENT (1971) *A Framework for Government Research and Development* (Green Paper), HMSO, London.

COMMITTEE ON QUALIFICATIONS FOR PLANNERS (1950) *Report* (Schuster Report), HMSO, London.

DEUTSCH, K. W. (1966) *The Nerves of Government*, 2nd ed. Macmillan, London.

DIMITRIOU, B. (1972) The interpretation of politics and planning, *The Systems View of Planning* (DIMITRIOU, B. *et al.*), Oxford Working Papers in Planning Education and Research, No. 9. Department of Town Planning, Oxford Polytechnic, Oxford.

*FRIEDMANN, J. (1965) A reply to Altshuler: comprehensive planning as a process, *Journal of the American Institute of Planners*, Vol. 31, pp. 195–7.

FRIEND, J. K. and JESSOP, W. N. (1969) *Local Government and Strategic Choice*, Tavistock Publications, London.

FRY, G. K. (1969) *Statesmen in Disguise*, Macmillan, London.

HARNISCHFEGER, H. (1969) *Planung in der sozialstaatlichen Demokratie*, Luchterhand, Neuwied.

HARRISON, M. L. (1972) Development Control: the influence of political, legal and ideological factors, *Town Planning Review*, Vol. 43, pp. 254–74.

HÄUSLER, J. (1969) *Planung als Zukunftsgestaltung*, Gabler, Wiesbaden.

JACKSON, J. N. (1972) *The Urban Future*, Allen & Unwin, London.

*MEYERSON, M. (1956) Building the middle-range bridge for comprehensive planning, *Journal of the American Institute of Planners*, Vol. 22, pp. 58–64.

MEYERSON, M. and BANFIELD, E. C. (1955) *Politics, Planning and the Public Interest*, Free Press, Glencoe.

MINISTRY OF HOUSING AND LOCAL GOVERNMENT (1967) *Management of Local Government* (Maud Report), HMSO, London.

MINNS, R. C. (1970) Letter to the editor, *New Society*, 22 October, p. 745.

PARSONS, T. (1967) Some ingredients of a general theory of formal organization, *Administrative Theory in Education* (edited by HALPIN, A. W.) 2nd ed., Collier-Macmillan, London.

SEERS, D. (1972) The prevalence of pseudo-planning, *New Society*, 18 May, pp. 352–4.

SHONFIELD, A. (1965) *Modern Capitalism*, McGraw-Hill, London.

SSRC (1972) Submission to the Secretary of State for Education, printed in: Social science and the Rothschild report, *New Society*, 17 February, pp. 341–4.

TESCHNER, M. (1969) Contribution to discussion at a conference on planning education organized by the Akademie für Städtebau und Landesplanung in Munich.

THORBURN, A. (1971) Preparing a regional plan, *Journal of the Town Planning Institute*, Vol. 57, pp. 216–18.

TUCKER, A. (1972) Filling social gaps in science, *The Guardian*, 28 January, p. 5.

WADE, H. W. R. (1971) Quoted after *The Guardian*, 11 December, p. 7 ("Professor wants anti-secrets act").

*WEBBER, M. (1963) Comprehensive planning and social responsibility, *Journal of the American Institute of Planners*, Vol. 29, pp. 232–41.

WEBER, M. (1947) *The Theory of Social and Economic Organisation*, William Hodge, Edinburgh.

*Included in FALUDI, A. (1973) *A Reader in Planning Theory*, Pergamon, Oxford.

CHAPTER 13

The Organization of Planning Departments

UNDERLYING this chapter is the problem that the ends which planners themselves think ought to be pursued colour the advice which they give. This is not because planners are wicked, but because they are human and their perception is subject to limitations. In Chapter 4 these limitations are represented by two filters built into an individual's perceptual apparatus which determine what he sees (Fig. 4.4). Experts are no exception to the rule of selective perception.

This affects the advice which politicians receive, which currently is only from chief advisers: it is coloured by personal views. To increase the importance of the rôle of experts, as suggested in the previous chapter, without simultaneously ensuring that politicians and the public receive the views of more than one planner, would therefore simply mean increasing the extent to which a handful of non-elected people exert their influence. It would not substantially improve the quality of public debate. It follows that the right to participate in public debate must be extended to other planners besides chief officers. This chapter is about a form of organization which is oriented towards the attainment of this aim.

This form of organization has not only built-in safeguards against biased advice, it also creates the manifold links between planning agencies and the outside world which creative planning needs. The argument is that if rank and file planners were encouraged to establish links amongst each other and with the outside world, this informal network would provide the channels for more "divergent thinking" in planning agencies (see Chapter 6).

The following propositions will, frankly, be as controversial as the ones made in the previous chapter. No local government planning department incorporates these principles, although one suspects that some of the more successful show similar features in the informal pattern of interaction that supplements any formal organization (and makes it workable). The principles that are advanced run counter to one basic assumption of public administration which is that all executive organs of government should have unity of command and clear lines of authority. It is this principle which is under attack. However, removing it will no doubt create problems of how to "get on with the job". I shall therefore emphasize the rôle of agreed procedures as providing that element of unity which presently is provided by the control exercised by chief planning officers. The next chapter will illustrate the working of these procedures.

THE INFLUENCE WIELDED BY CHIEF OFFICERS

In the previous chapter we saw how, even in the existing set-up, planners sometimes succeed in exerting their influence in the formulation of programmes. We shall amplify this by seeing that it is the *chief officer* in particular who wields the power to impress his particular views on planning policies.

The reality of the process of "articulation" is that it is a collaborative one involving members of the planning committee and their chief officer. During this process the chief planning officer is in an exclusive position. He is the only member at the "managerial" level who regularly attends the meetings of the planning committee. Friend and Jessop (1969) therefore observe in their study of the planning process in Coventry that the chief officer tended to be exposed more fully to the views of elected members than were most of his departmental subordinates, and thereby tended to develop an implicit understanding of the issues on which his committee expected to be consulted and the extent to which they were prepared to let him act on his own authority.

There is further evidence of the strong and relatively uncontrolled position of chief officers where Friend and Jessop relate how officers exercise their judgement ". . . to a point where they could put forward either a single recommendation, or at most a limited set of alternatives with some clear guidance as to the factors which they believe should determine the committee's choice between them". In controlling the flow of information to committee, chief officers could also sometimes withhold information; time the information largely according to their own convenience; give (or withhold) advance information privately to the chairman; give (or withhold) advance information to committee members; and emphasize particular aspects of a problem and neglect others. This array of alternative strategies throws some light on the power which a chief officer wields not only over his staff but also over his political "master". Implicitly, Thorburn (1971) confirms this in his revealing account of the way in which he has gained acceptance for the Notts/Derbys Study team's proposals:

> From the outset the study was conditioned by a number of decisions made by myself which, for tactical reasons, have never been made public. The most important decision was that the principal study recommendations must be agreed with the chief planning officers and other relevant chief officers of the four authorities sponsoring our work before they were presented to elected members and the public. Without such agreement there would be no hope of the plan's being accepted by all four authorities. . . .

There are parallels to the dominant position of chief officers in local government in the higher ranks of the Civil Service. The National Executive Council of the Labour Party submitted in its evidence to the Committee on the Civil Service (1968) that the Civil Service withheld information from ministers "in efforts to persuade them to adopt particular policies". This statement is different only in tone from what Laski (1938) says on the rôle of officers as advisers: "An officer has to hint, to persuade, to learn by trial and error the delicate art of letting facts speak for themselves. He has to learn to press advice without arousing antagonism and to invent policy without seeming to be its author. . . ."

One can perfectly understand how the position of chief officers developed out of certain assumptions built into the very structure of British (and also other types of) local government. The administration of services was originally left to lay committees. They were subsequently required to employ professional advisers, but initially these were local practitioners working part-time. Only gradually did the technical services develop into full-scale organizations aiding the chief officer, who retained his central rôle of adviser to his committee.[1] Such a position of authority is evidently

---

[1] It is, for example, common practice in local government that every communication, not only of a highly official but also of a very routine kind, as well as professional work by staff like reports, should bear the name of the chief officer.

very useful where departments are merely implementing programmes because it affords clear lines of responsibility. If it was still possible for a lay committee to make decisions without depending fundamentally on the initiative taken by their chief officer, this arrangement would continue to be satisfactory. But as far as the formulation of programmes is concerned this is not the case. Planners are not merely implementing policies. They initiate lines of action which the planning committee very often only sanctions or vetoes.

SHORTCOMINGS OF PRESENT ARRANGEMENT

The shortcomings of the present arrangement are that most "articulation", that is the exchange between the planning committee and the planning department, is filtered through the mind of one person, namely the chief planning officer (Fig. 13.1). This is problematic because planning

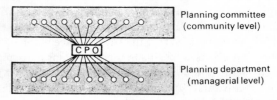

Planning committee
(community level)

Planning department
(managerial level)

FIG. 13.1. The Chief Planning Officer as a filter

decisions almost invariably advance some causes to the neglect of others. One example (out of many) is the implementation of the 1968 Caravan Sites Act. The siting of gipsy-caravan camps is regarded as a threat to amenities and property values by most neighbourhoods. The law requires local authorities to designate sites for gipsies, which invariably hurts some other section of the community—if only subjectively. Such planning decisions are therefore fraught with uncertainties concerning "who gets what, when, and how" (Beckman, 1964) and for what ends.[2] It is inevitable that, as communications are filtered through the mind of the chief officer, these decisions are also influenced by his personal

[2]Friend and Jessop (1969) describe this as uncertainty concerning values (UV).

outlook. This not only gives one person more weight in decision-making than our democratic ideals may tolerate; it is also detrimental to the quality of planning decisions, with their high discretionary content. What are absent are social control and accountability, because the chief officer is neither required to lay his judgement open, nor is he answerable for his views to the community. He is appointed as an expert and not elected as a representative. Indeed, public servants value this position highly and show a tendency to remain in the background, shielded by accountable politicians and building support for their judgement as professionals (Rabinovitz, 1967).

Of course, neither high-ranking civil servants nor chief officers wield unlimited power. The discretion of a chief officer is subject to his perception of the need to maintain a relationship of trust among his chairman, the committee and himself. As evidence by Friend and Jessop suggests, officers handle their relationship with the committee with great care in respect to information released to them, on the strength of the argument that "committees could be so capricious and unpredictable in their behaviour". The consequence in their case-study was that ". . . it was comparatively rarely that a committee seemed able to address itself successfully to the task of making a balanced selection between alternatives" so that the formulation of programmes tended to become largely concentrated within departments, much as legislation has been shown to generate in ministries (see Chapter 12).

This is not to say that there is something wrong. Indeed, if one observes organizations, one realizes how widespread this phenomenon is: it applies for instance to corporate management, or school administration. In most organizations there is a middle level of men who have a job to do and who supply continuity of operations and managerial capability. The next-higher level supports them by securing their means and shielding them from undue pressure. This latter level (for instance the board of governors in a school) cannot mingle in management, lest it should become ineffective by being open to constant interference. In the abstract language of organization theory this means that the higher level has the function of "focusing legitimation and community support" (Parsons, 1967). It is an arrangement which is eminently sensible because it gives the "managerial" level freedom of action whilst maintaining its responsiveness to the basic needs of the "community" level. What is disquieting is the absence of a meaningful choice between alternatives made by committees. Often, it is the personal policies of the chief planning officer (or the headmaster) which are followed, whether he pursues them consciously or not. The example of London's notorious motorway box illustrates that these are not always characterized by great foresight. When its planning began, some planners suggested doing local research: "The suggestions were all very vague, but within three days a directive came from the top of the department which said: 'Don't touch this, it's politically hot'" (Dix, 1972). One may at least surmise that, had there been such local research, the Greater London Council would have anticipated the trouble over its proposals.

PLURALISM IN THE PLANNING PROCESS

The key problem of existing planning organizations can be summarized as follows: there is an absence of discussions and confrontations of different views in the organization itself. This can be interpreted as the absence of *pluralism*, and results from the dominant position which the chief planning officer holds in "his" department, and the underlying assumption about the technical nature of local government services (Committee on Qualifications for Planners, 1950).

In the remainder of this chapter I shall identify organizational principles which would ameliorate this situation. These are the same on which chief officer teams engaged in corporate or local authority policy planning are based. I wish to see them extended to all departments or sections engaged in the formulation (as against the implementation) of programmes.

As regards safeguarding pluralism, the first principle which springs to mind is participation by the public, which has now been introduced. This will indeed provide for additional links between the planning department and the outside world. On the face of it, public participation may thus be seen as a step towards more pluralist planning. But, these additional channels will still be subject to the control of the chief planning officer. He will have authority over information released by the planning authority, and considerable power to influence the kind of information that is received from the community simply by authorizing links established by junior personnel. The following excerpt from an internal memorandum of a planning department illustrates that it is indeed the intention to control these links:

> The key to this whole issue is a responsible attitude. To the public, an officer is a representative of the Council . . .
> Attendance at meetings of social workers should be by responsible staff able to represent the division authorised by Divisional Head . . .
> Memberships of organisations in the Borough and even attendance at meetings (i.e. meetings concerning subjects related to the department's work) in a private capacity must be discouraged. If the Department is to maintain its reputation for objective advice, then its private interests must not be seen to be synonymous with its public work . . .
> Before ANY meeting a clear outline of objectives and aspects to be covered must be established. It should also be clearly understood by all, what policy issues should be avoided and to what decisions the Council is already committed . . .
> Group Leaders must specifically authorise attendance at any meeting with established representative bodies or their committees. The Divisional Head must be kept informed by the Group Leaders of all such meetings. This is essential in case Council members raise points. . . .

Participation in the sense of an exchange of information, however comprehensive, cannot ensure meaningful choice while the planning authority attempts to represent a unified policy and to enter into a dialogue with the public as from one totally coherent body to another. So long as this is the case, the temptation will always be to use participation as what some suspect already it has been introduced for: a strategy for forestalling awkward protest by vociferous civic groups.

Relating this back to the discussion of creative planning in Chapter 6, a chief planning officer directing all operations has the effect of the planning department only being engaged in a, figuratively speaking, more "convergent" form of thinking. By way of contrast, more channels linking the planning department to the world outside could create a network enabling a much more "divergent" form of thinking to take place,[3] thus giving it a greater creative potential.

For instance, Fig. 13.2 illustrates how the one channel between the planning committee and the department through the chief planning officer's mind would be supplemented by a whole network of links (not

---

[3]To be precise, this network exists anyway simply because, as explained in Chapter 6, every member of a planning department fulfils more than one rôle and has many links outside. To remove restrictions imposed by the chief officer exercising control simply means to activate and add teeth to this network.

necessarily limited to those established at formal meetings) on which the planning committee could then draw in making its choices. This network would be strengthened by yet further links not represented in Fig. 13.2 between the planning department and the outside world enabling planners to draw on a wider range of views when presenting alternatives.

What is therefore required for pluralism is the *participation of the planners*, which means more than one planner heading a unified body of other planners. With the planning authority having privileged access to planning resources (such as technical know-how and managerial capability) there is no better way of making the dialogue between it, the higher-order institutional structure and the public meaningful than to extend decision-making *into the organizational structure of planning offices*. Only this gives

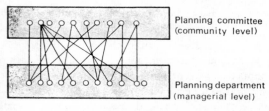

FIG. 13.2. The effect of opening up communication

a fair chance that alternative programmes (including those which pursue alternative ends) are given sufficient consideration from a technical point of view, and that a really political choice between them is made based on full awareness of their implications.

This is tantamount to saying that departments formulating programmes, instead of being hierarchically structured, ought to be of a collegiate, self-directing type. In simpler terms such organizations should work as *teams* in the real sense of the word. Before rejecting this as unfeasible, one ought to consider that institutions for the purpose of making decisions under conditions of uncertainty (in particular concerning values) are of exactly this collegiate type. Witness the structure of parliament (Grauhan, 1973), academic institutions, supreme courts, Royal Commissions, the *Commissions de Modernisation* with their 3000 members thrashing out French plans, and the European Commission, a collegiate body administering the Common Market (Shonfield, 1965), as well as the Central

Policy Review Staff introduced into the British Cabinet Office in 1971 (Cabinet Office, 1970; New Society, 1970, 1971).[4]

There is also evidence to suggest that, on a more mundane level and for certain tasks, collegiate organizations are superior to hierarchical structures. This seems to be so in research institutions and architectural practices. Even the average time of convalescence after the appendectomy can be shown to vary with the type of hospital management: less authoritarian structures release patients significantly earlier than more hierarchical ones (Broady, 1968).

Apart from facilitating discussions of alternative programmes, including those which pursue alternative sets of ends, a collegiate form of organization has the added advantage that it aids collaboration with people from outside disciplines. Specialists are always needed in planning work, and even more so in the present situation, where the badly needed social-science skills are exceedingly rare. However, my own research findings suggest that collaboration with town planners is very difficult for social scientists, be they on the staff of authorities or employed as outside consultants.[5] Not the least barrier to successful collaboration appears to be that a hierarchical form of organization of departments makes communication with the planners on the job difficult. As an illustration one may quote how one consultant sociologist described his collaboration with a planning team, this time a consultancy firm:

> There was something of a different view on the part of Firm X. . . . They had team meetings . . . in which there were two grades of people, the partners and the consultants, who were allowed to speak, and the staff who were not

---

[4]The Central Policy Review Staff provides a particularly interesting example of a "collective organization for policy-making" being set up to help another collective body, the cabinet, better to discharge its responsibilities, the argument being that the CPRS would reduce dependence of the cabinet on the necessarily partial views emanating from established departments. There is, as Galbraith (1967) suggests, a general tendency for private and public organizations to change from hierarchical to collegiate types when faced with complex problems. The examples quoted may thus be seen as evidence for the increasing complexity of the problems which planning agencies face.

[5]This is a project on sociology in planning education. As part of this, I interviewed social scientists with experience in collaboration with planners. For a preliminary report on my findings see Faludi (1971).

allowed to speak but were spoken to. . . . There was much less real interaction with the boys who were doing the work. What it meant to me was that I was in a somewhat unreal situation. . . .

This is not necessarily typical of planning consultants, where the impression is that they are much less rigidly structured than local authorities. One is therefore led to assume that collaboration for social scientists should be easier with consultancies than with statutory authorites. This was indeed substantiated by the findings of this research and supports the contention that collegiate forms of organization would improve collaboration with experts from outside.

The same point can of course be made of collaboration with people from other sections within the same authority. Instead of the very formal approach to inter-departmental co-ordination in strictly hierarchical organizations where all the information is channelled through the top, such a collegiate form of organization would enable the use of many informal links between sections to involve people with the requisite expertise for solving particular problems. This also applies to those who have to implement programmes. Indeed, their collaboration should be sought as a matter of course so as to make sure that there is an adequate level of feedback from implementation to the formulation of programmes (Grauhan, 1973).

A TEAM OF PLANNERS

Starting from the collegiate character of the organization as a basic principle, there are four particular areas that need looking into: rights and obligations of members of planning teams; recruitment; tenure and reward; procedures. The last will include some consideration of the rôle of chief planning officers as informal leaders of their teams.

The rights and obligations of team members could be, in a way, similar to those of legislative bodies. They would have to give an undertaking that they would work for the good of the community. Subject to agreed procedures, they will enjoy the rights to express their views, to form factions, and to present counter-arguments against other factions. The "bureaucratic guerilla" rôle of planners "working for local government where their aims are different from and in conflict with those of their employers" (Dix, 1972) would thus become a standard rôle, with the only modification that it would now be seen as a contribution towards attaining the aim of good planning. "Advocacy planning" by freelance planners (Davidoff, 1965) would then cease to be the *only* way in which professionals could plead the case of interest groups: "Advocates would provide a broad general basis for understanding social costs and benefits, and public agency planners would be responsible for improving the precision of definitions, analyzing alternatives, and providing advocates with the technical studies they need" (Skjei, 1972) thus removing some of the problems which advocacy planning seems to face at present.

One may of course argue that, in all this, an essential ingredient of parliamentary institutions is absent—the accountability of members to the electorate. But this is missing the point. The planning team would not be a decision-taking body, but a body to prepare the decisions by another body, which is in turn accountable to the community. For this reason, the rights of team members would also include the right of presenting alternatives to the planning committee or its equivalent, thus giving it a wider variety of alternatives to choose from (though, obviously, one would have to think carefully about the procedure of doing so to prevent planning committees being immobilized by having to consider too many alternatives or by dissenting planners using Filibuster tactics).

As to recruitment, elections seem to be rather far-fetched, although they are known in Germany and America. In the initial stages, planners would probably be appointed with a measure of self-recruitment supplementing this mode at later stages. The exact mix is certainly open to experimentation, the principle being that the interest of neither party—the local authority representing the community and the planning team—should be overlooked. Mixed interviewing boards seem to be one solution. In addition, some form of delegation ought to be possible by which local groups, opposition parties and other government agencies send planners of their choice into a planning team to represent their interests. For reasons of equity one might even consider the introduction of "Planning Aid" so that lack of resources would not prevent a group from being represented. The Americans have pioneered this with federal funds to help grass-roots organizations to hire their own experts. The then President of the Royal Town Planning Institute suggested this for Britain (Amos, 1971). Other proposals were made by grass-roots organizations (Blackledge, 1972) and a limited planning aid service is provided by the Town and Country Planning Association (*The Times*, 1973).[6]

The tenure and pay of public servants combines long-term security with the intrinsic rewards of job-satisfaction and status esteem in exchange for comparatively modest salaries. However, to what degree the one offset the other is a matter for discussion. The British Civil Service finds it difficult to recruit enough entrants and has been ten per cent understaffed in certain classes for some time (Brown, 1970). Even a High Court Judge is known to have resigned and taken up a post in the City. This indicates how values are changing and that the reward system ought to be flexible. In exchange, modification of the tenure system could be contemplated. What is necessary is to strike a balance between the need of the members of prospective planning teams for protection against undue pressure and the need of the community for a measure of control over its public servants. With the greater personal independence which members of prospective planning teams would have, this control might need some strengthening. Certain technical and administrative experts in Germany have a term of office of only six years, after which they come up for re-election by the councils of their "constituencies" for a further term of twelve years. This shows that some arrangement is certainly feasible.

Differential salaries would not be incompatible with the collegiate character of teams. In the Urbanistic Bureaux of Yugoslav Republics where the principle of self-governance of semi-independent planning agencies is in operation (as in all enterprises in Yugoslavia), salaries still vary. A differentiated pay-scale would indeed enable teams to have diverse membership which is a great asset.

How, the practical man will ask, is such a collegiate body going to work? How will the allocation of work take place? However, these problems are not insurmountable. After all, parliament and local councils, even though

---

[6]The possibility of delegation, together with that of planners inside teams advocating special interests, is vital to the meaningfulness of the planning process as a preparation of political choices. Planning techniques become very complex, especially with the advent of computers. Even for professional planners it becomes difficult to understand the theoretical concepts underlying simulation models developed by a new breed of "urban analysts", and there is evidence for bias creeping into these. Even quite innocent looking "information systems" have their political undertones, as Hoos (1972) shows.

collegiate bodies, do set their own procedures enabling them to discharge their functions, as do Royal Commissions and citizen-jurors passing judgement whilst being protected against their own fallibility by judicial procedures. What is envisaged, therefore, is a set of agreed procedures which would govern the day-to-day interaction of team-members, these procedures being developed on the basis of a thorough study of the planning process itself. They would give the team its operational efficacy whilst maintaining a requisite variety in the organization simply because it could be built right into these rules (just as it is written into the standing orders of councils).[7] As with pluralistic decision-making in general, it is expected that a maximum of available expertise from all walks of life will come forward to inform choices. However, rather than the free-wheeling position which Lindblom advocates, I envisage agreed procedures to provide an element of unity: they may weld the plurality of views together into coalitions, albeit temporary ones. In this way, the inertia which is the bane of disjointed incrementalism may be overcome.

Continuous reflection on procedures would form part of the team's efforts to build a clear self-image. One assumes that forming such an image would be part of the ongoing activities of the planning team and in particular its leaders. This brings us back to the position of chief planning officers. There are a number of permutations: he could be a chairman elected by team-members, he could be appointed. Leadership could be a permanent position, or could rotate (a principle which the Yugoslavs adopt in most of their institutions). Any of these would be acceptable as long as the fundamental principle is not discredited: that the chief officer ought *not* to exercise rigid control over information flows to, from or within the planning team.

This is of course not to say that he would have no rôle to play. But his influence, whether appointed or elected, would depend on his informal leadership and on his awareness of the rules and the laws governing the interaction of team members, much in the same way as does that of a committee chairman. The advantage would be that leadership would have

[7]This concept of a procedural accord providing an element of unity to an otherwise diverse body of people complements the very general, "qualified unitary" view of the public interest which will be advanced in the Epilogue. It is also one which the main proponent of "advocacy planning", Davidoff (1965), would endorse. In his seminal paper, he draws the analogy between planning and the due process of the law.

a built-in self-correcting element in that, if exercised without care and sensitivity, it would rapidly be lost. Leadership has its value, but one feels concern about its inflexible and often repressive character where no such self-correcting element exists.

OBJECTIONS

Possible objections against the proposed collegiate organization for planning departments are: that this is already the way in which a good planning team works; that the creation of teams similar to legislative bodies would merely duplicate these and thus be wasteful; that it would be impossible to have, for instance, the several thousand odd planners in Britain work in "self-governing teams"; that the absence of tangible controls over the members of planning teams would make them un-workable; that such planning teams, though giving "democracy to the planners" (Palmer, 1971) would do nothing for democracy outside the confines of planning departments.

As to the first objection, it is hopefully true that the informal patterns of communication in planning departments often show some of the features of a collegiate body. A sensible chief planning officer allows at least his senior personnel scope for autonomous decisions. In particular he sees to it that they are in touch at the "community" level by having them deputise for him at meetings of the planning committee and encouraging them to speak to the chairman and to members of the planning committee at less formal occasions. The main point of contention is therefore whether to formalize this pattern and to extend it to more junior officers. This ought to be the case because there seems to be more than one plan-ning authority that does not show any of these features, not even infor-mally; and because there are signs of frustration among practising plan-ners which can clearly be traced to the hierarchical pattern of their organization (Faludi, 1971).[8] Such "constitutional" changes, whilst they do not by themselves guarantee success, may still create its preconditions.

[8]On the frustrations of graduates working at a relatively low level yet being "only too able to identify and articulate their feelings", and on the results of such frustrations, see Dix (1972). The same article gives another perspective to this: the misgivings about the performance of young graduates voiced by London's Chief Strategic Planner, David Eversley, on leaving the Greater London Council.

Concerning duplication, the example of multi-planning agencies quote d earlier becomes relevant. There is this tendency for duplication of simila r institutions on different operational levels. British local government is, in theory and in practice, to a large extent compelled to execute central government policies. Nevertheless, few people would argue seriously that local councils are wasteful, and that the execution of central government directives could safely be left to appointed officials. By the same token, the duplication of collegiate bodies in planning agencies is not wasteful but rather of the essence of good planning.

As regards numbers, certainly, not all planners in local government could be taken out of their jobs and thrown into this kind of exercise. It will be remembered that this argument was only concerned with the formulation of programmes; planning authorities are also concerned with the time-consuming task of development control and other ways of implementing programmes. Actually, it is very difficult to determine what proportion of planners does one or the other. One may at least surmise that the actual formulation of programmes involves a minority. An indication as to the future need for planners in a new local government structure comes from a report on the manpower needs of transport planning (Ministry of Transport, 1970). Outside Greater London the figure would be in the order of 400 to 450. This is not excessive, even if one trebles the number for structure plan teams to cover land-use and transport. On these assumptions, the largest teams would have thirty to forty members, the smallest twelve to fifteen, not counting any members who might be delegated into teams from other departments or from interest groups. The problem of organizing collegiate teams of such size may be formidable, but not prohibitive.

The fourth point concerns the sheer workability of collegiate teams. How will the collaboration of all members be secured, if virtually no controls of a tangible kind are available? If no one is charged with the personal responsibility of seeing to it that all members of the organization pull their weight? Perhaps this is a pessimistic view of human nature which puts too much weight on threats and rewards. More optimistic people would hold that the influence exercised by colleagues would suffice most of the time. To support this argument, one only has to refer to academic institutions. Department heads do not only rely on disciplinary measures to induce the members of their faculty to cooperate. The same will be the case in planning teams. The main inducement of members will be their sense of commitment, which will be furthered by the influence exerted by their peers.

The advantage of this is that it does not alienate as strict discipline does.[9] This relates to the final point, which is a vision underlying this proposition of collegiate bodies replacing existing hierarchical planning organizations. One of the ultimate justifications for planning is that it has the potential to increase self-direction in society and to lead to human growth. Such a self-directing or planning society might be a better society than the existing one,[10] a belief which is obviously based on certain assumptions about human nature and human purpose. An organization that frustrates its own members by not allowing them to exercise self-direction, that reduces them to cogs in a machine, cannot adequately serve the purpose of increasing self-direction in society.[11] To put it differently, a future planning team, set up on the basis of the propositions advanced here would create, within reasonable limits, a paradigm of that kind of future world which would hopefully result from the dissemination of planning ways of thought and of action.

But, would the creation of a self-directing body of planners make any difference at all for the achievement of self-direction in society? Some people would probably deny this. Perhaps though, the analogy with an institution which is based on principles similar to those proposed in this chapter is an instructive one: the British Royal Commission. Hanser (1965) in a rare study of this unique institution, suggests that the Royal Commission makes "one of the most effective contributions" to the solution of the problem of "how to increase efficient participation in decision-making without succumbing to the least informed". It does this by "the initial

---

[9] On normative versus coercive powers in implementing programmes see Chapter 15.

[10] On the planning society see the Epilogue.

[11] Michels (1949) argues similarly about political parties that an organization which has *external* democracy as its goal should have an *internal* democratic structure. Etzioni's objections to this argument, namely that political parties cannot tolerate internal conflict lest they should become ineffective as organizations (Etzioni, 1960), does not apply to the teams envisaged. This is because the teams would not be what Etzioni calls "segmental organizations" (like parties are) but organizations serving the whole community, not by suppressing conflict, but by bringing it into the open and making it more informed.

enlistment of Commissioners from all walks of life . . ., the secondary enlistment, as witnesses or researchers, of many more citizens . . ., and the provision of a deliberation forum, open to the public, itself instigating other citizens in the press, the universities, the professions, and in other areas, to add their contributions." With the exception of the enlistments of members "from all walks of life", collegiate planning teams would operate similar principles. They could thus have effects very similar to those ascribed to Royal Commissions: to stimulate, and better to inform, the democratic process itself which, I believe, answers this final objection.

Policy Aims

As far as the organization of planning departments is concerned, the aims of the politics of rational planning should therefore be to devolve the power of control wielded by chief officers and to create a more collegiate form of organization than exists at present so as to increase the chances of alternative programmes being considered (including programmes aiming at attaining alternative ends).

REFERENCES

AMOS, F. J. C. (1971) Presidential address, *Journal of the Royal Town Planning Institute*, Vol. 57, pp. 397–9.
*BECKMAN, N. (1964) The planner as a bureaucrat, *Journal of the American Institute of Planners*, Vol. 30, pp. 323–7.
BLACKLEDGE, M. (1972) *Environment on Trial: A Case for Legal Aid*, published by the Bedford Society, Bedford.
BROADY, M. (1968) *Planning for People*, The Bedford Square Press, London.
BROWN, R. G. S. (1970) *The Administrative Process in Britain*, Methuen, London.
CABINET OFFICE (1970) *The Reorganisation of Central Government* (White Paper), HMSO, London.
COMMITTEE ON QUALIFICATIONS FOR PLANNERS (1950) *Report* (Schuster Report), HMSO, London.
COMMITTEE ON THE CIVIL SERVICE (1968) *Report* (Fulton Report), HMSO, London.
*DAVIDOFF, P. (1965) Advocacy and pluralism in planning, *Journal of the American Institute of Planners*, Vol. 31, pp. 331–8.
DIX, C. (1972) Some planners working for local government are finding that their aims are in conflict with those of their employers, *The Guardian*, 7 June, p. 12.
ETZIONI, A. (1960) Two approaches to organizational analysis: a critique and a suggestion, *Administrative Science Quarterly*, Vol. 5, pp. 257–78.
FALUDI, A. (1971) The experiences of sociologists in their collaboration with planners, *Uses of Social Sciences in Urban Planning*, Seminar Proceedings, Planning & Transport Research & Computation Co. Ltd., London.

FRIEND, J. K. and JESSOP, W. N. (1969) *Local Government and Strategic Choice*, Tavistock Publications, London.

GALBRAITH, J. K. (1967) *The New Industrial State*, Houghton Mifflin, Boston.

*GRAUHAN, R. R. (1973) Notes on the structure of planning administration, *A Reader in Planning Theory* (edited by FALUDI, A.), Pergamon, Oxford.

HANSER, C. (1965) *Guide to Decision: The Royal Commission*, The Bedminster Press, Totowa, N.J.

HOOS, I. R. (1972) Sozialplanung und die kontrollierte Gesellschaft, *Stadtbauwelt*, No. 35, S. 221–8.

LASKI, H. (1938) Quoted after BROWN, R. G. S. (1970) *The Administrative Process in Britain*, Methuen, London.

MICHELS, R. (1949) Quoted after ETZIONI, A. (1960) Two approaches to organizational analysis: a critique and a suggestion, *Administrative Science Quarterly*, Vol. 5, pp. 251–78.

MINISTRY OF TRANSPORT (1970) *Transport Planning: The Men For The Job* (Sharp Report), HMSO, London.

NEW SOCIETY (1970) Efficiency and accountability (Leader), 22 October, p. 715.

NEW SOCIETY (1971) Ross reviews, 11 February, p. 223.

PALMER, J. (1971) Contribution to discussions during a seminar series "Bold Conjecture: New Directions in Planning Thought and Practice" held at the Department of Town Planning of the Polytechnic of Central London.

PARSONS, T. (1967) Some ingredients of a general theory of formal organization, *Administrative Theory in Education* (edited by HALPIN, A. W.), 2nd ed., Collier-Macmillan, London.

*RABINOVITZ, F. F. (1967) Politics, personality and planning, *Public Administration Review*, Vol. 27, pp. 18–24.

SHONFIELD, A. (1965) *Modern Capitalism*, McGraw-Hill, London.

SKJEI, S. S. (1972) Urban systems advocacy, *Journal of the American Institute of Planners*, Vol. 38, pp. 11–24.

THE TIMES (1973) Planning aid service to advise objectors, 5 February, p. 3.

THORBURN, A. (1971) Preparing a regional plan, *Journal of the Town Planning Institute*, Vol. 57, pp. 216–18.

CHAPTER 14

The Planning Process: An Experiment

THE previous two chapters proposed that planners should not be sub-servient to politicians but should participate openly in public debate, thus increasing its relevance and the depth to which alternatives are investi-gated in terms of their present and future consequences for various interest groups in the community. They also showed that the freedom to participate in public debate should not be limited to the top brass of planning hierarchies, but that planners should rather operate in teams with each one having the right to air his views. These planning teams would then approximate to the diversity of viewpoints required for truly creative responses to complex and highly political planning problems, with the requisite element of unity provided by agreed procedures for making decisions.

This present chapter is about a set of procedures which might be used by a planning team in formulating rational programmes. The proposed procedure reflects ideas incorporated in Chapter 5, in particular those relating to solving ill-defined problems, and my views concerning planning strategies needed to cope with limitations of information-handling capacity. Though, in practice, procedures may vary, I assume that, as regards these two points, effective planning will proceed in ways similar to those de-scribed below.

THE CONTEXT OF THE EXPERIMENT

The experiences on which this chapter is based were made during "laboratory" experiments in planning education.[1] The situation approxi-

---

[1] For a short report on the project see Faludi (1972).

mated to "real life" planning because the groups of students engaging in this exercise had problems to solve for which there were no ready-made answers. Indeed, the experiences were real enough in the sense of troubling us at the time, and of requiring creative foresight in dealing with an, albeit hypothetical, problem.

My views on project work reflect my thinking on planning, as I try to introduce into projects an element of self-guidance which, as argued previously, should exist in any planning team. This team I see as engaging in a dialogue with a community over a set of alternative plans. For the dialogue to become realistic it must not be construed as a dialogue between two coherent bodies. The "community" consists of various groups engaged in a complicated game of co-operation and conflict, mostly within procedural limits. The argument has been put in the previous chapter for allowing a similarly complex game to be played *within* planning teams. This chapter is about how this could be done. Beyond this, I assume in project work that the exercise forms part of an ongoing process performed by a larger multi-planning agency. This means that the terms of reference and other guidelines received by the study group are deemed to have resulted from the deliberations of a strategic planning agency and that these instructions define the task and resources (a segment of the total action space available to the multi-planning agency as a whole) for a planning team. No claims are therefore made for this exercise to be comprehensive in the sense of investigating all alternative courses of action, simply because no one planning agency can engage in such comprehensive planning (Chapter 8). The only claim is that it represents an attempt at rational planning made by a planning team which itself operates in the context of rational-comprehensive planning performed by a multi-planning agency.[2]

My third view about project work concerns the difficulty of linking a simulated exercise to its social and political context. Standard solutions, for instance what planning educators term life projects, may not really be the answer. Therefore, the study group *simulated* the political process

---

[2]Of course, this does not mean that this context itself is immutable, and that the terms of reference and guidelines must be adhered to at all cost. As argued in Chapter 11, every multi-planning agency should have facilities for feedback and review so that information concerning the feasibility of finding a programme within a given context may be received by the strategic planning agency setting this context.

which would develop around a set of proposals using a voting procedure. I propose in this chapter that a similar approach could be used by a planning team engaged in solving real-life problems. This would be to the advantage of the community, which would in participating learn a great deal about itself and its options for the future. The following, therefore, is a slightly idealized account of the two projects on which these experiences are based, and how these may be relevant to planning in the outside world. Advantage will be taken of many helpful suggestions which members of the two groups have made.

UNDERLYING ASSUMPTIONS

The problem which the project addressed itself to was a very conventional physical planning task: to find the best way of expanding a small town in an area of great population pressure. Not only was the problem conventional, but so was the format which the solution took: a document called a town map, of which many have been produced in Great Britain. The assumption was that a slice of the action space (in this case the physical structure of the town and the powers conferred upon a Local Planning Authority) had been preselected by a strategic planning agency rationally evaluating alternative ways of allocating such segments to planning agencies on the next-lower level. In this way we assumed the problem had been predefined and that we were engaged in amplifying general policies by filling in a framework with more concrete proposals.

There were, of course, the problems of whether the physical environment should be planned in isolation from other variables in the total environment. In the language of this book, the problem is that of whether the technology-image underlying a conventional town map is an adequate one; whether it provides a rational basis for decision-making. As in the project, I suggest this question be ignored on the strength of the argument that some selection of a relevant technology-image has to take place anyway. What we shall be concerned with is how planning teams ought to proceed on the basis of *any* given technology-image, not the substantive content of this technology-image itself. Planning procedures are similar, no matter what the technology-image is like.[3]

[3]This must be qualified to the extent that a firm image results in different procedures than an uncertain image (see Chapter 7) and a wide one in different procedures than a narrow one (see Chapter 8).

This does not mean that technology-images should not be criticized, but that this criticism must be brought to bear on higher levels where controls and procedures are devised. Experiences of failure to solve a problem on the basis of a given technology-image prescribed by a strategic planning agency is an important piece of information which ought to be fed back to that higher level as a basis of criticism.

The problem which we set ourselves was an anticipated expansion by almost a hundred per cent over fifteen years. The assumption was that the decision to expand had been made on the higher level of the county development plan. If there had been opposition to growth, or to the amount of expansion, then that would have been brought to bear during its pre-paration. So it was deemed that this conflict had been resolved and an overall programme arrived at which now provided the framework within which plans for any one of the many towns concerned were to be prepared.

Again, this does not mean that there should not be criticisms of assump-tions underlying a development plan and in particular of target figures set. But assuming that there had been a proper planning process fully inte-grated with the political process on the county-wide level, then this criticism can only be fruitful if new facts come to light or if political constellations change. In the absence of such changes, such issues may well be regarded as temporarily solved.

Concepts of the Planning Process

These assumptions reflect views concerning the setting of ends to be pursued in planning which were expressed in Chapter 12 above. I argued there that politicians do not in any sense "set" the ends which planners subsequently try to achieve. Firstly, institutions and their procedures already have a great number of assumptions concerning ends built into them (the goals of orderly physical development, of education for all children in certain age brackets, of medical care for those in need and so forth) around which agencies in the fields of physical, educational and health planning evolve. In amplifying the goals set, these agencies must consider general policies first and attend to detail after that. We therefore assumed that we had a set of general goals (as embodied in the very notion of town and country planning) and more specific targets for the growth of

our town. Within this framework clearly still more specific objectives had
to be met.

Even here, we thought it unrealistic to expect the "institutional" or
"community" level (politicians and "the people") to produce an exact
description of a realistic physical structure of their town as it would be in
the future after sources of tension had been removed (which is what a set
of properly formulated objectives is). An objective is more than a statement of what is desirable; it incorporates awareness of what exists and of
what may change which rests to a large extent on images which planners
hold. We did not therefore distinguish between the setting of ends and
their translation into programmes as two distinct steps performed by
politicians and planners respectively. Rather, we thought of these as in
collaboration so that the planners' technical expertise and the politicians'
interests and their "feel" for the needs and aspirations of the local community would rub off on each other.

Beyond this we took it for granted that the planning process aimed at
formulating a rational programme. But we could not plan in a fully rational
manner. Though it had been predefined for us in the ways outlined above,
the problem was still too complex. We could not therefore simply select
the optimal programme out of the total number of programmes filling the
available action space because, in the first instance, we could not enumerate all programmes. So we had to explore that action space from the centre
towards its limits. As suggested in Chapter 5, such an exploration best
proceeds in the same manner as the identification of an optimal programme
out of the set of conceivable programmes does: that is by formulating and
evaluating alternatives in as explicit a manner as possible. Explicitness in
the way in which alternatives are formulated and evaluated is of prime
importance because it alone enables, on the one hand, continuous improvements to the assumptions made, these improvements resulting from criticisms, and the exercise of truly deliberate political choices on the other.
It is therefore only through explicitness that the planning process may
become what I think it ought to be: a joint learning process for planners,
politicians and the public.

In deciding on the actual approach to be taken, we paid regard to
limitations of our information-handling capacity. From considerations
similar to those in Chapter 6 on rational planning and its limitations,
we rapidly became aware of the fact that we would be unable to generate,

let alone to evaluate, all alternative ways in which even the limited problem of physically expanding a small town could be approached. The solution to which we turned was mixed scanning, a planning strategy outlined in Chapter 6. This underlies not only the structure and the procedures of multi-planning agencies, but is a feasible approach for any planning agency to take on its own.[4] We therefore differentiated between a "strategic" and a "detailed" level of programme formulation. As in the idea of structure and local plans, this allowed us to concentrate on broad policies first, and to focus on specific problems afterwards, leaving us the option of returning to the strategic level as and when required.

To talk about a "strategic level" in the case of a town map for a small country town seems grandiose. But all but the most insignificant problem could be differentiated into a strategic and detailed level with some advantage. Even in simple situations a large number of alternatives exist. Only by cutting out every possible detail may one be able to define a relatively small but exhaustive set of strategies, each of which can potentially be developed into a number of more detailed plans. Therefore, we conceived of a two-stage procedure of generating and evaluating alternatives, the procedure allowing for interactions with the (simulated) political process. Figure 14.1 gives an overall view.

Generating Alternative Strategies

We adopted a systematic method of generating all conceivable alternative strategies. This implied that, with some imagination, the *type* of solution which we would produce was by and large known. But this is precisely what planning within a defined context means. Solutions of other types will only be investigated after recurring failure to find satisfactory solutions within the existing framework, such as mixed scanning suggests. Until such failures become evident, the risk must be borne of implementing a solution which is optimal only within a given context,

---

[4]However, where a planning agency has to solve many complex problems of a similar kind, it will tend to differentiate internally, reflecting the strategic versus detailed level of programme formulation. Thus, once again, the planning agency takes on something of the character of a multi-planning agency. Witness, for example, the formation in planning departments of special "central area development", "urban design" or "village policy" groups operating on a more detailed level within the framework set by overall policies.

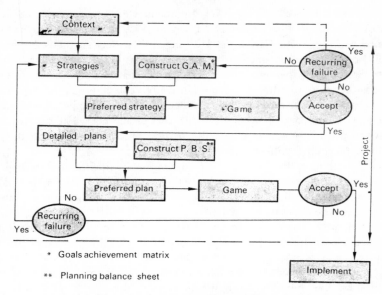

FIG. 14.1. The planning process (Source: Journal of the Royal
Town Planning Institute, March 1972)

but sub-optimal if evaluated more comprehensively. The aim of rational
planning is not that of pursuing a distant ideal of *total* rationality, but of
producing optimal results in given circumstances, which include the
limited capacities of decision-makers.

The type of solution to our problem was therefore defined as that of a
town map providing for nearly a hundred per cent population expansion
with all the necessary facilities, incorporating some other features resulting
from policies set within a wider framework (for instance a bypass). The
envelope to all conceivable solutions defined the action space available to
us. We then proceeded by opting for morphological analysis as a method of
generating all alternative strategies. This method has been developed in
engineering design. Its best publicized application is the generating of all
conceivable forms of jet engines (Bayliss, 1968). It is widely referred to
in the literature on planning and design (for instance Chadwick, 1971).
In its logic, it is similar to another method advocated by the Institute for

Operational Research, Analysis of Interconnected Decision Areas, or AIDA (Luckman, 1967; Friend and Jessop, 1969; Centre for Environmental Studies, 1970; Carter and Hickling, 1971). Both methods break a problem down into parameters (or decision areas), investigate alternative states which these parameters can take (or alternative decisions made in specific decision areas) and arrive at all conceivable alternatives through permutation. All the solutions are excluded which are incompatible (where the state of one parameter conflicts with that of another). The difference between the two methods is mainly in their presentation, and in their initial application to different sets of problems.

Following morphological analysis, we began by identifying strategic parameters of every town map showing the required features of additional housing, shopping area, road improvements and so on. These parameters determined the structure of our action space.

At the outset, there was obviously uncertainty as to what constituted a strategic parameter. We had to ask ourselves, in each case, whether some feature of our plan would fundamentally affect the final outcome or not. The answer was sometimes straightforward, but sometimes it had to wait until later. The important thing was to keep the options open for as long as possible revising the set of strategic parameters as one proceeded.

The question of how many "parametric states" should be defined was equally problematic. Some parameters could be described qualitatively such as the bypass which could go either north or south. In some others an almost infinite number of variable parametric states was conceivable. This clearly constituted a problem, since, with any additional parametric state, the number of permutations increases steeply. The answer was to identify such parametric states that were broadly representative for a number of others, and to remember throughout that these represented general policies and not detailed solutions.

The method could be improved by making the various assumptions in each solution explicit. One such improvement was suggested during the project. It concerned the exclusion of certain way-out "parametric states". Clearly, technical solutions existed to some of the problems which appeared unreasonable from the start, such as building a fly-over over the town centre instead of a bypass. The problem was that of uncertainty of the limits of our action space. We excluded esoteric possibilities on pragmatic grounds, but this left a nagging feeling of limiting the rationality of choice. A solution would have been to note all way-out possibilities such as fly-overs and tunnels but to attach low degrees of probability to them (these degrees expressed in numerical terms).

As a further extension of this approach, the same could be done with linkages between "parametric states" or "options". Instead of identifying incompatibilities between them leading to the introduction of one hundred per cent "option bars", this would mean to distinguish between many different shades of "incompatibility". All the probabilities would then be multiplied to give the overall probability of any one strategy being implemented. Evaluation would subsequently begin with the group of strategies with the highest probability (that is those in the centre of the perceived action space), and would proceed to groups with lower degrees only if none of these proved to be satisfactory (thereby moving towards the limits of the action space). The advantage of this would be that, if an impasse occurred such as that described in the case study of public participation on pp. 120–122, one could fall back on strategies which, at first glance, had appeared unreasonable.[5]

Another variation to this procedure of generating alternative strategies was discussed: bringing the interaction between the planning team and the (simulated) political process forward to the stage of generating alternatives. No specific methodology was developed at the time. However, it seems that the previous idea of estimating probabilities could provide a vehicle for this interaction. Estimating probabilities of a solution being acceptable is what politics is largely about. During such an exercise political choices would therefore be entirely appropriate. An extension would be to involve the community itself in the definition of parameters. A short exchange between Hall (1970) and Friend (1970) suggests that the thinking of proponents of AIDA follows similar lines. As the logic of morphological analysis parallels that of AIDA, it is evident that we may say the same about it as about AIDA: if properly organized, it should bring political choices into the open.

As things were, our judgements were the crude type of either including or excluding parameters, and we ourselves in the planning team were those

---

[5]At the time of writing, the variation of this approach to the generation of alternative programmes described above is being implemented by a group in another project at the Department of Town Planning of Oxford Polytechnic.

who made all the judgements concerning parameters and parametric states. At a later stage though, we did include the option of interest groups changing these definitions during the simulated interaction with planners. This amounted to a weaker form of public involvement during the generation of alternative plans through feedback. However, the procedure which we used resulted in eighty alternative strategies, even without any of the additional refinements discussed above. There was therefore a wide range of alternatives from which to choose. It is to the evaluation of these strategies that I turn next.

Evaluation of Strategies

These strategies indicated very general patterns. Evaluation had to be kept on a level which was equally coarse. We chose the simplest form of the goals achievement matrix (Hill, 1968). This assumes that a plan serves a multitude of ends which are sought by a multitude of interest groups and that the incidences of goal achievement as related to these interest groups carry different weights.[6]

In this simple version, evaluation is limited to determining whether goal achievement is advanced, whether it is hampered, or whether it remains unaffected by any particular strategy. A value of $+1$, 0, or -1 is inserted into the matrix and this value multiplied by the weight allocated to that particular incidence of goal achievement. The results are then aggregated to one overall score for the plan as a whole.

Practically speaking this means multiplying two matrices. One represents an assumption concerning the importance attached to specific ends by certain interest groups. (Alternatively, one might include an assessment of their political strength, or any normative assumption concerning the distribution of political influence which one cares to make.) The other matrix represents the way in which any particular plan affects all the ends pursued by various interest groups forming a community. This procedure of multiplying two matrices, one representing the technical judgement of planners, and the other a political constellation, is indicative of the way in which we saw planning and politics as interpenetrating.

---

[6]These weights form a matrix indicating the overall degree of tension which exists between the ends held by the community and its physical environment.

Examples of the kinds of end statements which we included were the fairly conventional ones pursued by physical planning such as "preservation of existing character of town centre" and "preservation of proximity of countryside". Of course, there were the usual problems of aggregating the achievement of ends like amenity and accessibility and economic viability held by preservationists, car owners and industrialists respectively. But they all, in order to achieve their ends, trade in one currency which is political influence in a wide sense. All choices are in one sense political choices; for all of them influence is expended, involving time and energy; in all cases some alternative way of spending this influence can *not* be taken.

But even if this is so, is it possible to express political influence in numerical terms? It depends on the way numbers are used. We regarded the matrix merely as a convenient shorthand for expressing assumptions concerning the intensity with which interest groups hold their aims, and their ability to get them implemented. But clearly, these had to lead to a programme which was acceptable to the community. In other words, the matrix of political weights was the planners' hypothesis concerning the interests as held by their community. There was nothing particularly paternalistic about such a hypothetical statement, as long as it was put to the test, which was an independent assessment of the highest-scoring plan by the interest groups concerned. Agreement would suggest that the hypothesis was a reasonable approximation to the way they themselves reacted to a plan; disagreement would send the planners back to reconsider their assumptions. This is where the process would really begin to become an interactive one, and a learning process for both planners and community.

Simulating the Political Process

In the absence of a community, we simulated one. I shall first describe what we did in the project, and how this led to an agreed plan and later suggest that the procedure could be applied by a real-life planning team.

The idea of simulating the political process was, in the first instance, to create somebody who would talk back to us about the way in which our plan would affect the various interest groups playing their part in the political process. For this we devised a procedure of round after round of voting by representatives of the thirteen "interest groups" which we had identified. The list included institutions of government, such as the county council and the urban district council, as well as groups which are more familiar as interest groups, such as the local chamber of trade, tenants associations, land owners and the local sports council. Each of these groups had a number of votes based on assumptions of their relative strength in the political process. Voting was punctuated by clarification of issues, by bargaining sessions and announcements of scandals in the local press.

The assumption underlying this procedure was that a planning team, on the basis of its appreciation of a situation in its political context, had produced a programme which was in effect the highest-scoring strategy emerging from the previous evaluation stage. The planning team had then analysed this programme into contentious issues and put them, together with tentative suggestions as to alternative ways of resolving them, to the community to decide. Voting was simply a way of generating its reaction within a matter of one morning.

At a later stage, improvements were introduced to this procedure so that initiatives could come from the interest groups, though not without spending some votes representing their political influence. This introduced the element of feedback concerning choice of parameters and parametric states referred to above.

There were remarkable insights to be gained into the nature of the political process, even from such a limited exercise. Skilful bargaining, ruthless cheating and Filibuster tactics were used, and we learned to appreciate the importance of agendas when the lunch drew closer! Also, during the period devoted to questioning representatives of the planning team, remarkable new pieces of information came to light from the other members of our group in their new capacity as representatives of an interest group. In this way, the plan was subjected to scrutiny by planners, but from many different sectional points of view. This was in contrast to the detached manner in which the team had proceeded before.

As it happened, the highest-scoring strategy withstood all these assaults. But we felt in any case that we had learned enough to warrant a complete re-evaluation of all strategies using now a refined scale of measurement ranging from -3 to $+3$ instead of -1 to $+1$. Had the plan been rejected we would in addition have had to amend our assumptions concerning the distribution of political influence, repeated the evaluation procedure (possibly also some parts of our "technical" assessment of the impact of the preferred strategy) and presented interest groups with another alternative. The assumption would have been that this suited their preferences better. After some time, the "best" alternative (best that is in the context of a particular political constellation) out of the number of available strategies would be found.

In a real-life situation, planners would gain additionally from this procedure considerable knowledge of the activities and intentions of politicians and interest groups in their community. Similarly, political representatives could not help making more informed decisions in terms of the facts of the situation and the implications of their choice.

Generating Detailed Plans

Before speculating on the application of this procedure in real life, a brief account will be given of how the project was completed. To generate detailed plans on the basis of a preferred strategy, instead of producing all conceivable solutions we simply formed four "consultancy groups". This departure from a wholly rational procedure was made not purely for reasons of convenience but in order to demonstrate Etzioni's point about mixed scanning: once the fundamental strategy has been determined this may be amplified by incremental or "bit" decisions. Alternatively we could also have proceeded by applying morphological analysis to the parameters on the next-lower level.

Evaluation of the four alternatives was then performed using a variation of the planning balance sheet to give their overall ranking. Again, the highest-scoring plan was broken down into contentious issues, alternative solutions were outlined to those, and the whole package submitted to the scrutiny of the simulated political process.

The point was made by members of the group that the number and relative strength of interest groups participating in the second simulation should have been varied. The county council had, for instance, less of a legitimate interest, once its overall goals of expansion and improvements to the traffic conditions on the main road had been met by the preferred strategy. The urban district council, on the other hand, could have received a larger share of the votes. These suggestions would mean an improvement in the procedures used, which would be to vary the interest groups involved in the political process during different stages of the planning process. The tendency of this improvement is towards internal differentiation of the planning process and of the team engaged in it. This means that during the course of time a new multi-planning agency will develop.

SIMULATION AND REALITY

The suggestion is that simulations similar to the one described above could usefully be introduced into real-life planning exercises. As a preliminary, let me reiterate what I said in earlier chapters concerning the position of planners in relation to the political process, and concerning the internal structure of planning teams:

> Planners should work in *self-directing teams*.
> They should be allowed and encouraged to take *sectional points of view* and to establish *links with the outside world*.
> Their debates and reports should be made *public*.
> There should be basic *agreement* amongst themselves and with other participants on *procedures* by which decisions would be made.

The simulation exercise, and all the stages leading up to it, constitute one set of conceivable procedures. In the event, the planning team might for instance agree to explore a problem as well as they could using morphological analysis or similar techniques; they would then list all interest groups affected by the range of strategies under consideration, identify what their ends would be, and then make tentative assumptions concerning the weights of interest groups and the relative importance they would attach to their achievement. This is the stage where the community comes in. Observations of the political process in the past and any normative assumptions relating to its future performance suggest the number of votes given to each interest group.

Alternatively, the experience of politicians, administrators, local newsmen and other close observers of the political scene may be collated to give a more adequate distribution of votes. For the purpose of translating opinions into numerical terms, approaches such as the Delphi technique exist which enable one to collect and summarize opinions on such intangible matters.

Parallel to this, individual members of the planning team and small groups can make detailed investigations of the life-style and preferences of those groups whose advocacy they assume for the duration of the planning exercise. In the course of time, these groups themselves may become interested and join in.

The simulation itself ought to be played in public. The media could relay it into every home; it could be stored and replayed and provide argument both inside and outside the council chamber. One can conceive of it receiving the publicity of quiz shows and public discussions. With the upsurge of local radio, and possibly even of closed-circuit television for local communities,[7] there would be quite a few opportunities for making a series of simulations of this kind into a very potent stimulant for local democracy.

There is no reason why politicians, administrators and members of the public should not join in with the planners in playing out certain rôles. This is already done in the training of managers and planners, with joint training and rôle-swapping giving particularly good results in terms of mutual understanding (Taylor, 1971). Cases are known where games have been put to practical use: in the Federal Republic of Germany, case studies involving administrators, politicians and planners were simulated using the provisions of a new bill in the field of urban renewal. This apparently resulted in some modification to those provisions (Sack, 1971). In the United States, so-called "charrettes" (ten-day symposia) are experimented with to "help the community indulge in meaningful decision-making" (Fagence, 1973). Perhaps this would become the rule rather than the exception.

The great amount of learning experience which the participants will undergo will outweigh any costs in terms of time and effort spent on apparently pointless exercises which do not lead directly to any tangible results. By actual investigation politicians find out much more about alternatives open to them which they rarely seem able to do nowadays. They could also, during simulations, enter coalitions which they would not dream of entering outside them and find out more about their political colleagues and opponents. The range of options would be much wider than at the present so that the staging of such simulations as part of the planning process seems both feasible and worthwhile. They would pro- bably be no more costly in terms of time and effort than is political

---

[7] A closed circuit television network to foster community spirit has been proposed for Columbia new town in the United States. Experiments have started at Green- wich in London (Lewis, 1972).

intrigue, but they would speed it up, bring it into the open, and make it less serious. They would certainly not be more costly than bad decisions. In this way simulations may improve the quality of that process upon which the idea of decision-making in democracies is based: public debate. As suggested in Chapter 12 before, public debate is nothing but a mock fight enabling politicians having a real stake in public decision-making to sit back and watch before they take their choice. Simulations give rules to this mock fight so that it shows results. Political representatives can still turn their thumbs down and reject the outcome, though they cannot avoid doing so with more knowledge than previously.

This idea of planning teams playing simulation "games" with the public may appear almost frivolous to some planners engaged in the deadly serious business of formulating complicated programmes. But the military engaged in the equally serious business of defence have invented this device for exactly the same purpose of investigating alternative strategies. Secondly, to introduce simulation in no way reduces the technical competence required by planners. But the questions which they investigate may become more relevant to the political process evolving around the formulation of every programme with benefits for the effectiveness of planning as well as the intelligence of political decisions. Lastly, it may be held that this procedure foreshadows what a future planning society may be like; that is one that is busily engaged in the direction of itself, drawing in all the sections of a community.

A simulation "game" of the kind proposed may therefore seem strange in today's conditions of isolated planning agencies making fairly disjointed efforts. But in a future situation, where planning may be performed on several levels simultaneously involving many facets with complicated links between them, procedures such as these may very well become an accepted part of life (such as public debate was for the Greeks). Thus, in a planning society, planning may not only be an accepted way of governing (Webber, 1968/9), but of going about public business generally, an art form, a pursuit with some intrinsic value.

Policy Aims

The aims of the politics of rational planning which derive from this case study are, then, to structure the planning process in such a way that it may achieve the maximum degree of rationality on the one hand (this involving the use of planning strategies) and maximum interpenetration between planning and the political process on the other (this involving simulation exercises).

REFERENCES

BAYLISS, D. (1968) *Recent Trends in Forecasting*, Centre for Environmental Studies, Working Paper No. 17, London.

CARTER, K. and HICKLING, A. (1971) *Problem Street: An Example of the Application of Strategic Choice to a Local Planning Problem*, IOR Internal Paper No. 631, Institute for Operational Research, Coventry.

CENTRE FOR ENVIRONMENTAL STUDIES (1970) *The LOGIMP Experiment*, Information Paper No. 25, London.

CHADWICK, G. (1971) *A Systems View of Planning*, Pergamon, Oxford.

FAGENCE, M. T. (1973) Citizen participation in the planning process: some lessons from U.S. experience, *Journal of the Royal Town Planning Institute*, Vol. 59, pp. 188–91.

FALUDI, A. (1972) Teaching the planning process, *Journal of the Royal Town Planning Institute*, Vol. 58, pp. 111–14.

FRIEND, J. K. and JESSOP, W. N. (1969) *Local Government and Strategic Choice*, Tavistock Publications, London.

FRIEND, J. K. (1970) Letter to the editor, *New Society*, 3 December, p. 1013.

HALL, P. (1970) Evaluating options, *New Society*, 26 November, pp. 952–3.

HILL, M. (1968) A goals-achievement matrix for evaluating alternative plans, *Journal of the American Institute of Planners*, Vol. 34, pp. 19–29.

LEWIS, P. (1972) Community television: a new hope, *New Society*, 9 March, pp. 490–2.

LUCKMAN, J. (1967) An approach to the management of design, *Operational Research Quarterly*, Vol. 18, pp. 345–58.

SACK, M. (1971) So wurde ein Gesetz getestet, *Die Zeit*, 9 April, S. 55.

TAYLOR, J. L. (1971) *Instructional Planning Systems*, Cambridge University Press, London.

WEBBER, M. (1968/9) Planning in an environment of change: Beyond the industrial age; Permissive planning, *The Town Planning Review*, Vol. 39, pp. 179–95, 277–95.

CHAPTER 15

The Implementation of Programmes

FOR planners, implementation is a thorny subject. Many would agree with Prime Minister Nehru who is reported to have complained about the Indian Five-Year Plan: "We are not quite so expert at implementation as at planning."[1]

Why should this be the case? To find the answers, one must first of all identify what implementing a programme involves. Successful implementation rests on the twin factors of *knowledge* and *power*. Both are always limited, and this has implications for the ability of planning agencies to implement their programmes. They must appreciate the nature and extent of their limitations and adapt their planning accordingly. This affects not only the tail-end of the planning process, but also the formulation of programmes.

Knowledge and Control in Implementation

In terms of the model of planning agencies developed in Part II, successful implementation involves some such agency to manipulate its control variables so that a previously identified source of tension disappears. In doing so, the planning agency converts resources into control in accordance with a programme. Difficulties during implementation must stem from inadequacies in the way in which that programme has been formulated (though to be sure some inadequacies are inevitable and no-one may be blamed for them). The reasons for shortcomings during programme formulation may be either one or both of the following: an imperfect image of the world outside, and misapprehension of the control process and of available resources. Efforts to improve the ability of plan-

[1] Quoted after Kahn (1969).

ning agencies to implement their programmes must therefore aim at improving their images and their knowledge of control processes, including rational ways of converting resources into control.

Account must be taken of the implications of choosing between various types of control processes for earlier stages of planning so that programmes are implemented with less delay, distortion and suffering on part of those affected as at present.[2] In this way, implementation will cease to be "an independent step taken subsequent to plan-making: *the kind of implementation mechanism adopted will itself influence the character of the plan and the way it is formulated*" (Friedmann, 1967).

THE IMPORTANCE OF FEEDBACK

The first reason why difficulties occur during implementation seems rather obvious. One must expect images to be sometimes inadequate. During the course of time, planners have indeed come to anticipate errors. In Chapter 7 an image which included the awareness of the possibility of error was described as *uncertain*. Subject to other considerations outlined there, uncertain images were said to result in a more cautious way of proceeding termed process planning.

The key feature of process planning is feedback. Feedback means that planning agencies spend some effort to gain information about the results of implementing their programmes, comparing results with anticipations held previously and amending images accordingly.

The effort to obtain feedback may be directed towards either intended or unintended consequences. Feedback about intended consequences must provide information about the extent to which the objectives of a programme have been achieved. This is best obtained by gauging relevant variables in the environment, using the same measurements as for the specification of objectives. Thus, feedback relating to the achievement of the objective "reduction of average journey to work by ten minutes" is best couched in terms of the actual reduction obtained: five minutes, seven minutes and so forth.

---

[2]Witness the effects of the American Urban Renewal Program (Glazer, 1965 and others), the threatened destruction of homes to build the London motorway box, and the effects of rehousing policies (Willmott and Young, 1962; Dennis, 1970; Davies, 1972).

Even here, it may be difficult to make sense out of the information: does it mean that small, additive changes are required, or that parts or the whole of the image must be scrapped? Techniques for tackling this problem exist only in those cases where variables are quantifiable. For instance, Beer (1966) describes how feedback may be used in determining whether the "parameters" or the "constants" of a model need changing (amounting to qualitative and additive changes to images respectively). But in most cases where the variables are defined qualitatively, and where the underlying assumptions are less precise, it is much more difficult to make such decisions. Unfortunately, there is also little that can be said generally about the way to proceed in these cases, apart from the very obvious point that explicitness in the formulation of images and a critical and open mind are of great help.

Unintended consequences are even more difficult to detect, because they result from the influence of unknown variables. If the planner had advance knowledge of the likelihood of some consequences resulting from his programme, then these could not be termed "unintended". The situation can only be met by keeping the environment under close surveillance. In recent years, efforts have been made to put this surveillance on a systematic footing. It is thought that by developing a comprehensive reporting system, using what one calls *social indicators*, up-to-date information on the state of the environment can be obtained on a continuous basis such as had been proposed by Meyerson (1956) even long before social indicators themselves had come into fashion.[3] However, there has perhaps been too much enthusiasm about the feasibility of such an approach and the expectations of various kinds of "information systems" seem to exceed their actual achievement. On the one hand, it is very difficult and costly to develop such systems even to provide access to those data which are already in the possession of various administrative agencies (Fehl, 1970, 1971). How much more difficult would it therefore be to gauge the "state of the system" with a wide range of new and sophisticated measurements! On the other hand, information systems may do more harm than good (Hoos, 1972) so that the widespread apprehension of data banks appears to have a rational base.

[3]For the impact of Meyerson's proposals on the American Community Renewal Program, and for possible ways of extending the logic of his approach, see Robinson (1965).

An alternative, which may be less costly and have fewer drawbacks, is that of "keeping one's ears to the ground". This requires keeping many channels open through which communication may be received. The pattern which these channels form must not be narrowly determined by the requirements of only one planning exercise. Public participation, when practised over time, provides the multiple links required for an informal but effective "early warning system" for unintended consequences. The possibility even exists of combining this approach with the techniques of social survey, using a random sample of the population as a sounding board (Grossner, 1971).

The importance of feedback applies generally, whether a planning agency deals with physical objects or with people. This is because all images are uncertain in principle and differences between them a matter of degree. It is easier to formulate images of the physical environment which, having proved themselves time and time again, are relatively firm (such as the laws of mechanics).[4] It is relatively more difficult to isolate certain aspects of people's behaviour. This makes the need for feedback much more imperative.

This difficulty in planning of dealing with people is compounded from the fact that they must never be seen merely as the object of planning, albeit one whose behaviour is uncertain. They themselves perceive this world much as planning agencies do; they formulate their own programmes and attempt to implement them. This has consequences for the way control is exercised which will be elaborated later.

CONTROL AND ITS RATIONALIZATION

In the first instance, controlling something means to do precisely what one does when shifting a weight by using a lever: apply force so as to effect change. If shifting weights was all that planning was about, then control would merely involve a thorough exploration of the laws of mechanics. But even where the control variables of planning are physical objects like houses and roads and airports, it must above all have regard to the way in which changes affect people. In the last analysis, therefore,

[4]What is really underlying laws such as these is the law of great numbers; the random movements of individual parts equalize each other out; see Oppenheimer (1955).

implementing programmes always involves, for better or for worse, exercising control over people. This is precisely where the problem of implementation lies.

Sometimes, people are controlled in ways similar to those applied to the physical environment: by applying force to make them engage in some form of conduct which conforms to the intentions of a previously formulated programme. This may involve physical force, as when the police remove a group of demonstrators engaged in a sit-in. Alternatively, it may be more subtle and involve the erection of physical objects to hinder certain movements, like the barriers outside school playgrounds. There are more sophisticated ways. I shall discuss how (a) the exercise of control can be made more efficient by reducing the expenditure of resources simply by threatening the use of force instead of applying it; (b) control can be made more rational by bringing its degree and scope in line with the images held by planning agencies.

Control and Communication

In the development from primitive to modern man operating in highly complex social organizations one can observe a process of growing symbolization (Etzioni, 1968). Increasingly, in place of the direct application of force, we announce, forebode, or threaten the application of force, with the effect of rationalizing its expenditure: we rely on the law rather than on our strength for our protection. The law tells us what indictable offences and their consequences are, so that very small amounts of force required to pursue and punish flagrant law breakers suffice to control the behaviour of a very large number of people. This not only reduces the expenditure of force, but makes life tolerable for the majority who can pursue their interests without relying on physical strength for their protection.

Planning agencies also have the force of law in reserve and can command other resources, as we shall see. But if planning agencies wish to avail themselves of this way of rationalizing control, they must communicate to people much as the agencies of law enforcement try to communicate with would-be offenders. In practice, the communication aspects of implementation far exceed the importance of force. For instance, fines, or the physical removal of buildings, are very rare in development control. Much more often the mere receipt of a notice refusing planning permission makes people abstain from certain actions. Despite this, however, planning documents, public notices and orders served on individuals often require specialized knowledge to interpret. This tends to exacerbate people's feeling that they are manipulated by forces which are beyond their comprehension let alone their control and is thus counterproductive.

There are of course perfectly valid reasons why planning reports use a technical language for a "target group" of other planners. Also, public notices and orders served must withstand security by administrative tribunals and the courts, and their language must be that required by law. But these requirements must be balanced against other considerations. Little expertise in interpreting technical language is available to the public. Quite legitimately, people are wary of the expence of obtaining professional advice when faced with some official document. Therefore, as with the law, plans and ensuing public notices are more effective (even as instruments of control) if they communicate well. It must therefore be recognized that conveying meaning to perhaps a highly heterogeneous target population is a distinct problem in implementing planning proposals. Already, some planning authorities seem to be aware of this. The display of glossy plans in the entrance to the town hall, reaching only a fraction of those concerned, is now supplemented by more active steps to reach even those whose English is limited by issuing leaflets in the languages of the immigrant communities (Cherry, 1970). American transport planners are even thinking in terms of introducing the specialist rôle of "communicators" into the transport planning process (Vorhees, 1972), a proposal which has also been made by Rabinovitz (1967), albeit in a wider and more political sense.

A Rational Basis for Control

There is another way in which control may be rationalized. This is by co-ordinating it with the image which a planning agency holds, and on which its programmes are based. Here, we return to the concepts developed in Part III where either degree of control or relative autonomy (measured by the scope of control and flexibility in shifting resources) figured in the discussion of every one of the three dimensions of planning. Table 15.1 summarizes this discussion as far as control is concerned.

The table shows the relation between control and the modes of planning with the addition of one not described earlier as a separate mode, because it represents an impossible combination of great relative autonomy (meaning great scope of control) and complete control. The demands of such an approach would defeat any planning agency, which is why I term it "utopian" planning. This is the caricature of rational planning taken to extremes, an image which opponents of planning are always ready to conjure up before our eyes (see p. 293). Apart from this, one finds a combination of rational-comprehensive, process and normative modes in

TABLE 15.1

CONTROL AND MODES OF PLANNING

Relative Autonomy	Degree of Control	
	Incomplete	Complete
Low	process planning disjointed-incrementalist planning functional planning	blueprint planning functional planning
Great	process planning rational-comprehensive planning normative planning	"utopian" planning

one quadrant. This, which may be identified as an ideal planning style (see p. 207), corresponds to great relative autonomy on the one hand, yet incomplete control on the other. It can be achieved only by multi-planning agencies employing planning strategies involving the acceptance of blueprint and functional planning (see pp. 145–146 and 184–185). The quadrant combining these corresponds to complete control, yet small relative autonomy.

The forms of control which these two quadrants represent correspond to Etzioni's concept of *contextuating* and *prescriptive* control (Etzioni, 1968). Contextuating control means setting a framework within which the object of control is allowed to operate; prescriptive control means determining every detail of its behaviour.

The dimension of contextuating versus prescriptive control is relevant to multi-planning agencies (see Chapter 11). Strategic planning controls other planning agencies precisely by the first type of framework control. An example is structure plans under the 1968 Town and Country Planning Act "controlling" local plans (and new-style county councils thereby controlling the new districts). Prescriptive control, on the other hand, should only be exercised on lower levels and for routine tasks for which there are relatively firm images available: for example, isolating persons with communicable diseases does not evoke much opposition because it is accepted as necessary to prevent epidemics, an end which is not likely to be questioned.

Such cases apart, there are good reasons for the sparing and careful use of prescriptive control. Etzioni (1968) lists three. Control is always relative, never absolute; it has a distorting effect on those who are subjected to it, as well as on those who experience it; and lastly, it has a self-generating effect.

Illustrating the first point, even prison authorities do not exercise complete control over prisoners, as the not infrequent riots show. In any superior–subordinate relationship, the underdogs can always defy their masters (if only temporarily) by pooling whatever assets they may have. This is exactly how trade unions asserted themselves against employers commanding economic assets. They used an alternative source of control, the solidarity of their members. This is also a way of interpreting what happened in American ghettos in recent years, and in Paris in May 1968: disenchantment was sufficiently great for slum dwellers and students to mobilize latent assets, such as their "nuisance value".

On a small scale, anyone who exercises control over people, like physical planners in Britain, is aware that "the authorities", "bureaucrats" and, most frequently, "the planners" are somewhat unpopular. There is always evidence of an undercurrent against planning *per se* because of its association with the exercise of control. Planning agencies must therefore be as careful as other wielders of power, lest those subject to their control should turn against them.

The second reason for exercising care is that control not only results in hardship for those whose aspirations are disregarded, but also reduces the chances of an inadequate image being corrected by feedback. This was discussed at length in Chapter 7 where it was argued that, subject to certain constraints, a high degree of control results in a blueprint mode of planning where no feedback is sought and where consequently images cannot be adapted. Great amounts of prescriptive control, as exercised for instance by authoritarian régimes, therefore do not necessarily lead to better planning, as a naïve observer might assume, despite the fact that some of the more obvious limitations on control exercised in democratic countries are absent. On the contrary, authoritarian planning tends to be extremely piecemeal. Considerations of sheer effectiveness therefore lead authoritarian régimes to introduce framework control. Examples are Albert Speer's reorganization of the German armaments industry during World War II (Speer, 1969) and similar reforms in countries of the Eastern Block (for instance Šik, 1969).

The third reason for exercising care in the control of people is that, once subjected to it, they may lose any sense of loyalty and political obligation. In Etzioni's words, control prevents the development of an "authentic community". However, with a diminishing obligation, the exercise of control appears even more important, and leads to yet more control. Thus a vicious circle is created of more power being exercised to combat the lack of acceptance of control, a circle which it is difficult to break.

For these reasons, prescriptive control should be as far as possible avoided and framework control preferred. This matches the type of image that was identified as underlying rational-comprehensive planning: wide-ranging, but not detailed (which is the only kind of image that man can hold of complex systems). However, this is subject to similar considerations to those made concerning planning strategies: much as one has to compromise on one's wish to engage in a desirable form of planning, so one has to accept prescriptive controls where they correspond to blueprint planning used as part of planning strategies (see pp. 145–146).

RESOURCES FOR CONVERSION INTO CONTROL

In exercising control, whether prescriptive or contextuating, planning agencies must convert resources. The array of these begins with legal powers and ends with goodwill. Etzioni (1968) classifies these resources into coercive, utilitarian and persuasive powers. Examples are the general who ultimately relies on the firing squad to get his men to engage with the enemy: the employer who offers good wages for onerous and monotonous work; and the chief planning officer whose leadership skill inspires his staff to solve problems in the community served by his planning authority.

Coercive power means to use, or threaten to use, force. This form of power is often used where it is deemed essential to control "deviants". In modern society, the state has a monopoly on the use of brute force but there are, however, many agents who command some form of coercive power (for instance parents and teachers). Drawing on one's *utilitarian* power means to be able to offer something in exchange for somebody complying with a prescription, and is used where the agent exercising control and the subject of his control both have assets which are necessary for a desired result. *Persuasive* power means the ability to convince others that they should perform as one wishes because they thereby contribute to a common goal. This form is used where there are strong bonds between the agent and the object of his control.

The least repressive form of power is obviously the last and the most painful the first. In the last case, the people who are controlled (for instance a mountain rescue team) may not even perceive themselves as being subject to control when called out and directed to help, if they have helped to set up the services. By contrast, people who are forced to join the army and fight, or prisoners in a labour camp, have no motivation to fulfil their tasks well. For certain types of jobs, only certain types of power may thus be exercised. You can force people to do unskilled, manual work, but not to do good research. You can force soldiers to advance, but not to become fighters with initiative. As a general rule, positive tasks require the exercise of persuasive power, and only negative or trivial tasks may be achieved by converting coercive powers into prescriptive control.

Each of these kinds of power is exercised in planning with similar effects. Coercive powers underly development control.[5] The development

---

[5]This is true in a negative sense: development control may prevent buildings from going up. For positive control, utilitarian powers must be used. For instance, where there is a shortage of land, a planning authority can make certain things happen by releasing land earmarked for certain purposes. Here their control over land gives them a bargaining counter. But unless a developer wishes to take up that offer, their power is useless.

of central areas, where existing inhabitants have no choice but to leave, amounts to the same type of control. Utilitarian powers are used less in British planning, although Improvement Grants are an example where a cash incentive is provided for compliance with certain standards. Sometimes a "deal" is made between a planning authority and a large developer such as in the granting of planning permission for the notorious 'Centre Point" project in London (Marriott, 1967).[6] Persuasive power is what planners try to exercise in mounting exhibitions, issuing pamphlets, talking in public meetings. They emphasize that there is a value in their proposals which people ought to see as their own.

CONTROL AND INFLUENCE: THE NEED FOR
PARTICIPATION

Persuasion may work, especially where there is a pre-established consensus, for instance that old buildings are worth preserving, or that the environment needs to be protected. But this does not always exist. Particularly when there are new challenges, people will not have made up their minds and new ideas of the desirable must be formed. During this process, even the application of persuasive power can distort. According to Etzioni, it ". . . suppresses the actor's preferences without changing them". What remains is the nagging feeling of being conned into accepting something which one did not wish to accept in the first instance. The exercise of genuine *influence*, on the other hand, ". . . entails an authentic change in the actor's preference . . .".

Such authentic changes occur during the process of building consensus (according to Etzioni the confluence between the perspectives of two or more actors). As against persuasion, this is a collaborative process. It involves seeing the objects of control as subjects in their own right, with the ability to participate in the formulation of programmes. It must not

---

[6]The masters of utilitarian power seem to be the Americans. In urban renewal, every dollar spent from public funds was matched by seven from private funds, surely an achievement (Glazer, 1965). On the other hand, the disadvantages of excercising utilitarian power show up: firstly the aims of urban renewal are distorted by the profit motive; secondly, there is no way of forcing wealthy suburbs to accept inducements offered so that they can shield themselves against federal policies such as housing integration (Frieden, 1965).

only be collaborative but also open-ended and requires skills other than those which have traditionally been recognized by planners as contributing to success but which are now propagated as essential to effective planning (Friedmann, 1967; Rabinovitz, 1967, 1969; Bolan, 1969; Institute for Operational Research, 1971). These skills of bringing planner's clients into play one can liken to the "social skills' of establishing and maintaining rapport which Argyle (1967) suggests are essential for competence in interpersonal behaviour.

Planners have in the past only dimly recognized the objects of planning as subjects. The impression is that public participation has been introduced to create a forum in which to dispense persuasive arguments more than an arena in which people could interact and form collective views (Dennis, 1972). However, this is the best (meaning the least antagonizing and threatening) way of implementing programmes: to formulate them in such a way that people regard them as their own because they have been involved in drawing them up. This has been recognized even within the context of business organizations. Le Breton and Henning (1961) thus say about business planning: "If members of the group who are to carry out the plan themselves do the planning then they will be implementing *their own* beliefs, re-structuring their own activities in accordance with the goals established in the plan."[7]

If they are formed authentically, people's beliefs must reflect their interests. True participation therefore tends to bring these to the fore. Since people's interests often conflict, the result will not be as harmonious as planners expected when pressing for the introduction of public participation.[8]

On the contrary, more participation will make existing conflicts transparent, including such fundamental antagonism as may exist, if the Marxist analysis of our society is correct. In any case, it is likely to make greater

---

[7]Research into managerial style seems to suggest a qualification. Findings are that there is a relationship between management style and technology with more sophisticated technology (automation) requiring more participation (Taylor, 1971).

[8]Low (1972) showed the clear differences which existed between the views of upper- and lower-class residents in Islington concerning one plan. In the event, participation had not been genuine, because only upper-class residents went to public meetings. Had it been genuine, the result would presumably have been conflict.

demands on the ability of democratic institutions to cope with change than anything which they have faced in the past. These demands arise out of perceived need for more effective implementation of planning programmes (yet with implications for all the stages of their formulation) which demonstrates the point made in the introduction to this part that planning enhances democracy.

Policy Aims

The politics of rational planning (which now transpires to be a politics of democracy) should then aim at instituting proper procedures of feedback and control on every level of planning. This will involve the replacement of prescriptive by framework control wherever possible and the participation of the people subjected to planning control in the formulation of those programmes from which these controls derive.

REFERENCES

ARGYLE, M. (1967) *The Psychology of Interpersonal Behaviour*, Penguin, Harmondsworth.
BEER, S. (1966) *Decision and Control*, John Wiley, New York.
*BOLAN, R. (1969) Community decision behavior: the culture of planning, *Journal of the American Institute of Planners*, Vol. 35, pp. 301–10.
CHERRY, G. (1970) *Town Planning in its Social Context*, Leonard Hill Books, London.
DAVIES, J. G. (1972) *The Evangelist Bureaucrat: A Study of a Planning Exercise in Newcastle upon Tyne*, Tavistock Publications, London.
DENNIS, N. (1970) *People and Planning*, Faber & Faber, London.
DENNIS, N. (1972) *Public Participation and Planners' Blight*, Faber & Faber, London.
ETZIONI, A. (1968) *The Active Society*, Collier-Macmillan, London.
FEHL, G. (1970) Towards a project-oriented information-support system, *Oxford Working Papers in Planning Education and Research*, No. 5, Department of Town Planning, Oxford Polytechnic, Oxford.
FEHL, G. (1971) *Informations-Systeme, Verwaltungsrationalisierung und die Stadtplaner*, Stadtbau Verlag, Bonn.
FRIEDEN, B. J. (1965) Towards equality of urban opportunity, *Journal of the American Institute of Planners*, Vol. 31, pp. 320–30.
*FRIEDMANN, J. (1967) A conceptual model for the analysis of planning behavior, *Administrative Science Quarterly*, Vol. 12, pp. 225–52.
GLAZER, N. (1965) The renewal of cities, *Scientific American*, Vol. 213, pp. 194–209.
GROSSNER, C. (1971) Wenn Zukunft verplant wird, *Die Zeit*, 9 April, S. 8–9.

Hoos, I. R. (1972) Sozialplanung und die kontrollierte Gesellschaft, *Stadtbauwelt*, No. 35, S. 221–8.

Institute for Operational Research (1971) *Beyond Local Government Reform: Some Prospects for Evolution in Public Policy Networks* (Conference Proceedings), Tavistock Institute, London.

Kahn, A. J. (1969) *Theory and Practice of Social Planning*, Russell Sage Foundation, New York.

Le Breton, P. P. and Henning, D. A. (1961) *Planning Theory*, Prentice-Hall, Englewood Cliffs, N.J.

Low, N. (1972) One mind, *Planning*, 7 December, p. 4.

Marriott, O. C. (1967) *The Property Boom*, Pan Books, London.

*Meyerson, M. (1956) Building the middle-range bridge for comprehensive planning, *Journal of the American Institute of Planners*, Vol. 22, pp. 58–64.

Oppenheimer, J. R. (1955) *Wissenschaft und allgemeines Denken*, Rowohlt, Hamburg.

*Rabinovitz, F. F. (1967) Politics, personality, and planning, *Public Administration Review*, Vol. 27, pp. 18–24.

Rabinovitz, F. F. (1969) *City Politics and Planning*, Atherton Press, New York.

*Robinson, I. M. (1965) Beyond the middle-range planning bridge, *Journal of the American Institute of Planners*, Vol. 31, pp. 304–12.

Šik, O. (1969) *Fakten der tschechoslowakischen Wirtschaft*, Molden, Vienna.

Speer, A. (1969) *Erinnerungen*, Propyläen, Berlin.

Taylor, J. C. (1971) Quoted after *New Society* (1971) High octane management, 3 June, p. 961.

Vorhees, A. M. (1972) Lecture given to the Eleventh International Study Week in Traffic Engineering and Safety held in Brussels, 18–23 September.

Willmott, P. and Young, M. D. (1962) *Family and Kinship in East London*, revised ed., Penguin, Harmondsworth.

*Included in Faludi, A. (1973) *A Reader in Planning Theory*, Pergamon, Oxford.

The Planning Society

HAVING based my rationale of planning theory on the view that planning promotes human growth, it is obvious that I attach much importance to planning. In my own mind, I hold the idea of a future *planning society*, and it is with this that I shall end.

To varying degrees, the authors quoted in the chapter on the rationale of planning theory hold similar ideas. To this range of writers on the planning society, others may be added, notably the early proponent of planning, Mannheim (1936, 1940); Olsen (1968) with his model of a "systemic society"; and Gould on *The Rational Society* (1971). The term planning society, an obvious one to express my idea, is drawn from Friedmann (1966/7). The views of these authors are diametrically opposed to the nightmarish visions of a totally planned, regulated political system *à la 1984* or *Brave New World*. The popular image of a planning society, and criticisms made by prominent opponents of overall planning, certainly apply to none of them.

But I hasten to add that an historical association does indeed exist between planning and the totalitarian régimes of the twentieth century. For instance, the arguments of some critics of planning who had left Fascist Germany, notably Hayek (1962) and Popper (1961), were directed against this *caricature* of a planning society that has overstretched itself by attempting to combine *comprehensive* with *blueprint* planning, an impossible combination which I termed utopian in the previous chapter.

The idea of a planning society takes account of criticisms of totalitarian planning, in particular the one that the centralization of all decision-making in one supreme planning agency is impossible. The planning society therefore leaves maximum reign to individuals and groups, amongst others to reduce the volume of central planning. Like strategic planning

agencies were said to proceed best by setting a framework for the operations of other parts of multi-planning agencies, so with central agencies in
a planning society: their aim would mainly be to set the *framework* within
which other actors in society plan.

The idea of a planning society therefore incorporates awareness of the
limitations of human knowledge and information-handling capacity.
Because of this, a planning society would tolerate widely divergent views,
indeed regard them as a source for potential creativity in unexpected
situations. Central agencies would furthermore concern themselves
prominently with maintaining the greatest variety possible. Their main
preoccupation would not even be substantive policy issues but the rules
governing planning and decision-making. In this way, the supreme planning
agency would act as the guardian of the rationality of processes by which
variety is articulated and choices are made.

But could the cause of variety not suffer from the imposition even of
such limited frameworks as would be imposed in a planning society?
Would it be better not to stifle expressions of opinion and interests by the
rules and procedures representing this framework? This question takes us
back to images of society underlying different modes of planning (see
Chapter 8).

The position which says that not even a limited framework should be imposed seems to be consistent with an *atomistic* image of society (one seeing
society as a collection of individuals) and thus with disjointed incrementalism in planning. But, as the model of the market on which it is based,
disjointed incrementalism is only meaningful if most decision-makers
adhere to certain rules. Even *laissez-faire* retains the rôle of the state as
that of maintaining law and order. "Disjointed" incrementalism is therefore disjointed only to a point. Beyond this all the various agents on whose
wit its alleged superiority relies must have something in common: a
language, certain assumptions and rules. Similarly, the view of society
as consisting of a collection of individuals is accurate only to a point beyond
which it is meaningful to attend to what individuals have in common:
a set of norms forming the framework for their actions.

The existence of a framework within which individuals operate surely
qualifies the atomistic image of society. But, if the rules making this
framework were like natural-science laws, little would have changed.
We could add these to the laws of nature which constrain individual

choice, but retain the basic tenet of the atomistic image of viewing the individual as the only meaningful unit of action. However, as indicated in Chapter 3, men can, within limits, resolve to *change* the norms governing their actions. In this way they can manipulate the framework of individual decisions which now becomes an object of planning.

The existence of this malleable framework gives the *holistic* image of society portraying society as having some standing of its own its appeal. But to avoid the impression of adhering to a totally holistic view of society, seeing it as nothing but a huge organization with a coherent set of ends (which is a spurious view sometimes held by administrators and planners), I describe mine as *qualified holistic*. This signifies my awareness of the existence of divergent views and interests without going to the extreme of saying that only these divergencies in society are significant and that its coherence does not count.

With this qualified holistic view of society goes a similarly complex position on the question of the *public interest*. Holders of an atomistic image of society have a concept of the public interest as the sum of individual interests (its *individualistic* conception); holders of holistic images adhere to the view that there exists a set of ends relating to all individuals in society, even without their explicit consent (its *unitary* conception, see Meyerson and Banfield, 1955). Personally, I think it meaningful to hold a view of the public interest which may be termed *qualified unitary* (as Meyerson and Banfield term a pluralist concept qualified individualistic). In a planning society built on this concept of the public interest, reference to it will only be made infrequently. For most of the time conflict and bargaining over substantive issues will continue, that is decision-making processes which complement a more individualistic view of the public interest and an atomistic image of society. But they will be made within an overall accord on procedures.

Of course, this accord on procedures will itself change as the planning society develops, bringing me to my final point. In Chapter 3 I stressed the importance of planning theory as a basis for meta-planning. This view was amplified in Chapter 11 by showing that it supplied models for multi-planning agencies building their self-images (the planning resource budget). If we were to assume, as is implied in the idea of a planning society, that planning would become much more widespread, and that there would be supreme planning agencies concerned mainly with this evolving framework of planning by other agents, then planning theory would provide the basis for most important decisions. It would, indeed, be the most fundamental normative theory of all, indicating how decisions in society ought to be made.

REFERENCES

FRIEDMANN, J. (1966/7) Planning as a vocation, *Plan Canada*, Vol. **6**, pp. 99–124; Vol. **7**, pp. 8–26.

GOULD, S. J. (1971) *The Rational Society* (August Comte Memorial Lecture), Athlone Press, London.

HAYEK, F. A. (1962) *The Road to Serfdom*, 2nd ed., Routledge & Kegan Paul, London.

MANNHEIM, K. (1936) *Ideology and Utopia*, Kegan Paul, Trench, Trubner & Co. Ltd., London.

MANNHEIM, K. (1940) *Man and Society in an Age of Reconstruction*, Kegan Paul, Trench, Trubner & Co., Ltd., London.

MEYERSON, M. and BANFIELD, E. C. (1955) *Politics, Planning and the Public Interest*, Free Press, Glencoe.

OLSEN, M. E. (1968) *The Process of Social Organization*, Holt, Rinehart & Winston, London–New York.

POPPER, K. R. (1961) *The Poverty of Historicism*, revised ed. Routledge & Kegan Paul, London.

Index

297

THE URBAN AND REGIONAL PLANNING SERIES

Other Books in the Series

CHADWICK, G. F.
A Systems View of Planning: Towards a Theory of the Urban and Regional Planning Process (Volume 1)

BLUNDEN, W. R.
The Land Use/Transport System: Analysis and Synthesis (Volume 2)

GOODALL, B.
The Economics of Urban Areas (Volume 3)

LEE, C.
Models in Planning: An Introduction to the Use of Quantitative Models in Planning (Volume 4)

FALUDI, A.
A Reader in Planning Theory (Volume 5)

COWLING, T. M. and STEELEY, G. C.
Sub-Regional Planning Studies: An Evaluation (Volume 6)

SOLESBURY, W.
Policy in Urban Planning: Structure plans, programmes and local plans (Volume 8)

MOSELEY, M. J.
Growth Centres in Spatial Planning (Volume 9)

LICHFIELD, N., et al.
Evaluation in the Planning Process (Volume 10)

SANT, M. E. C.
Industrial Movement and Regional Development: The British Case (Volume 11)

HART, D.
Strategic Planning in London: The Rise and Fall of the Primary Road Network (Volume 12)

STARKIE, D. N. M.
Transportation Planning, Policy and Analysis (Volume 13)

Other Titles of Interest

CLOUT, H. D.
Rural Geography

JOHNSON, J. H.
Urban Geography, 2nd Edition

The terms of our inspection copy service apply to all the above books. A complete catalogue of all books in the Pergamon International Library is available on request. The Publisher will be pleased to consider suggestions for revised editions and new titles.